# A RECOGNITION

## RECON...TING NATIVE WOMANHOOD

WOMEN'S ISSUES PUBLISHING PROGRAM

FEB-2020 - N1º

$15.72

# A RECOGNITION

# OF BEING

### RECONSTRUCTING
### NATIVE WOMANHOOD

❖

*Kim Anderson*

SUMACH
PRESS

## WOMEN'S ISSUES PUBLISHING PROGRAM

Series Editor: Beth McAuley

NATIONAL LIBRARY OF CANADA CATALOGUING IN PUBLICATION DATA
Anderson, Kim, 1964-
A recognition of being: reconstructing native womanhood

Includes bibliographical references and index.
ISBN 1-894549-12-0

1. Indian women — Canada — Ethnic identity. 2. Race discrimination —
Canada. 3. Sex discrimination against women — Canada. I. Title.
E98.W8A52 2001     305.48'897071     C2001-902020-1

Copyright © 2000 Kim Anderson
Fourth printing August 2006

Cover image by Bev Koski (Ojibway)
*The cover image was created by applying photo transfers onto handmade papers.*
*The papers were made from kozo fibre with dyes including blueberries*
*and a special paper made out of pine needles.*

Edited by Beth McAuley
Copyedited by Olive Koyama
Indexed by Jin Tan

All royalties from the sale of this book will be donated to
the Native Women's Resource Centre of Toronto.

Printed in Canada

Published by
SUMACH PRESS
*1415 Bathurst Street, Suite 202*
*Toronto, Ontario*
*M5R 3H8*

*www.sumachpress.com*

*To all the Aboriginal baby girls*
*being born this minute, this book is for you.*
*With recognition and thanks*
*for the tremendous work of your grandmothers,*
*who have so lovingly provided the way.*

# CONTENTS

*Preface 9*
*Acknowledgements 11*
*Introduction 13*

## I SETTING OUT

*Chapter 1:* Story of the Storyteller *23*
*Chapter 2:* Working with Notions of Tradition and Culture *34*
*Chapter 3:* Literary and Oral Resources *40*

## II LOOKING BACK:
### THE COLONIZATION OF NATIVE WOMANHOOD

*Chapter 4:* The Dismantling of Gender Equity *57*
*Chapter 5:* Marriage, Divorce and Family Life *79*
*Chapter 6:* The Construction of a Negative Identity *99*

## III RESIST

*Chapter 7:* Foundations of Resistance *116*
*Chapter 8:* Acts of Resistance *137*
*Chapter 9:* Attitudes of Resistance *150*

## IV RECLAIM

*Chapter 10:* Our Human Relations *158*
*Chapter 11:* Relating to Creation *180*

## V CONSTRUCT

*Chapter 12:* The Individual  *194*
*Chapter 13:* Family  *205*
*Chapter 14:* Community and Nation  *213*
*Chapter 15:* Creation  *223*


## VI ACT

*Chapter 16:* Nurturing Self  *230*
*Chapter 17:* Nurturing the Future  *235*


## VII PAUSE / REFLECT

*253*


## CONCLUDING DIALOGUE
*Kim Anderson and Bonita Lawrence  261*


*Reference List and Participant Biographies  278*
*Endnotes  288*
*Bibliography  305*
*Index  312*

# PREFACE

The phrase for the title of this book, "A Recognition of Being," comes out of my interview with Elder Shawani Campbell Star. I asked her about "the role of Native women" and her reply included this phrase that kept coming back to me as I was writing the book:

> The role of women? I would have difficulty with the word role, actually. More and more as I get older, I see this sort of *recognition of being* as being more important than role.

Campbell Star's response made an impression on me because it named a process of identity formation that I was trying to interpret. She clarified that Native womanhood is not about simply playing certain roles, or adopting a pre-set identity; rather that it is an ongoing exercise that involves mental, physical, spiritual and emotional elements of our being.

Many Native women have told me that underneath all of the oppression and confusion, there has always been a part of them that knew the strength and vitality of being a Native woman. Uncovering this part is an act of recognition, a physical, spiritual and emotional remembering that can link us back to our ancestors and to a time when Native women were uniformly honoured and respected. We recognize what we once were and what we still carry through the generations. At the same time, we need to recognize this being, to re-think and re-construct it so that it works with our realities today. Thus, we draw on our spiritual, emotional and physical resources as we make conscious decisions about who we are today and who we will be in the future.

This is our recognition of being. Thanks to Shawani and all the other women who have helped me to name it so.

# ACKNOWLEDGEMENTS

This book owes its beginnings to a woman who told me her story of abuse during interviews I was doing for Native Child and Family Services of Toronto in 1996. Sharing her story, she triggered a desire in me to know more about Native female identity. I wanted to learn and write about a magnificent Native womanhood, with the hopes that my writing might help tear down the type of abuse and disrespect that woman had endured. I offer thanks to her and all Native women who are brave enough to speak the truth and motivate change.

The vision presented in this book is born of the strength, power and beauty of the forty women who agreed to be interviewed for it. To these trailblazer sisters, aunties and grannies I offer thanks, both as a researcher and as a Native woman seeking answers about her own identity. You have inspired me greatly.

There are many people who led me to the interview participants, particularly when I began searching for interview participants in provinces other than Ontario. Thanks to all of you for trusting me with your contacts and for being so enthusiastic about my work. A special thanks to Marie Pierre Roy for helping me with the French transcription, and to Sylvia Maracle for reviewing the final manuscript.

My parents have also assisted greatly in the production of this book. They gave me life and raised me in a healthy way; they are the preliminary support behind all of my accomplishments. I give thanks for a mom who modelled self-determination and critical thinking, and for a dad who always protected, provided and nurtured. As grandparents, my mom and dad have been invaluable, caring for my babies so I can feel freer to take on other work.

None of my work would be accomplished without the support of my partner Dave, a helper in the truest sense. His support, both financial and emotional, his interest in my research, his encouragement of my growth as a person and a writer, and his shouldering of the greater part of our shared (domestic) work during the preparation of this book have made it possible. Thanks to Rajan and Denia for being patient with mommy while she worked on weekends, and to

Dave for his unconditional and loving care of the children at those times.

This work began as a master's thesis under the supervision of Dr. Sherene Razack. I wish to thank her for all that she taught me, and especially for giving me the courage to see myself as a writer. To Bonita Lawrence, thanks for the many discussions that helped me to move ahead on the work, for the friendship, for being both a sister and a colleague.

I am grateful to my publisher Sumach Press, whose staff are so supportive and open. Thanks especially to Beth McAuley for the many hours she has spent on this manuscript; for sharing with me all of the detailed work that needed to be done to make it a finished product! Thanks to Bev Koski for her work on the front cover, to Diane Pugen for helping me find Bev, to Thomas King for his work on the author photo, and to Liz Martin for involving me in decisions around the cover design. I greatly appreciate the skill and generosity of Pat Elliott who proofread this reprint edition.

Finally, the Ontario Arts Council and the Canada Council for the Arts deserve a thanks for providing financial assistance while I was writing the book.

# INTRODUCTION

❖

*The situation that we are in today is such that our women and children aren't respected as they used to be. It is not the fault of the men. It is because of the layers and layers of influence we have had from another culture. We are in a state of confusion and we are trying to work our way out of it. People are calling it healing. Well, whatever it is, we are trying to find our balance, and when we find the balance, we will know it because the women won't be lost. They will be respected and taken care of and so will the children.*

— Catherine Martin (Mi'kmaw)

THIS BOOK HAS GROWN out of my need to help the balance come home to our communities. It is about creating a vision of a society where every member has a place, a sense of value, a gift to bring. It is about recreating the circle in a way that suits our modern lives. My entry point into that circle is through the reconstruction of Native womanhood.

I began working on *A Recognition of Being* after having done some research for Native Child and Family Services of Toronto in 1996. I had been interviewing a number of women about the services of the agency, and, although it was not called for, many of them related their life experiences to me. The more I listened, the more distressed I felt about the abuses they had endured. I felt particularly disturbed by the indifferent tone which one woman used to describe an act of sexual abuse that her husband had inflicted on her in the presence of their children a few days prior to our interview. To me, it was a wake-up call about the indifference with which we treat abuses against women and children in general. It made me think about the loss of balance we have experienced in our families, communities and nations, and how this is linked to our gender relations. We have become accustomed to male dominance, and this provides the soil for social ills like family violence, incest, sexual abuse and child neglect. I see these problems as a sickness that is the legacy of colonization and something we must address as we stand at the brink of decolonization. We can talk about self-government, sovereignty, cultural recovery and the healing path, but we will never achieve any of these things until we take a serious look at the disrespect that characterizes the lives of so many Native women. We must have a vision for something better, because our future depends on it.

Although I take my cue from the violence and confusion, the focus of this book is the strength, power and beauty of Native womanhood. My way of dealing with the sickness that comes from the confusion is to share a vision of health. After listening to the stories of distress, I felt a pressing need to seek out those aunties and grannies who could nurture my sense of hope for Native women. *A Recognition of Being* represents my findings about the power of the women I encountered in my search. I hope that these aunties and grannies will inspire others as much as they have inspired me.

This book is based on existing literature as well as interviews that I conducted with forty Native women across Canada. Endnote references are to literary sources. Interview quotes and insights are not referenced, but a list of the participants' biographies and the date and place of the interviews can be found in the Reference List/Participant Biographies at the back of the book.

There are many terms to describe the Indigenous peoples of North America, among them Aboriginal, First Nations, Native, Indian. In this book, I have mostly used "Native," simply because it is the term most often heard in the Native community that I am a part of. I have also used the word "Aboriginal" in places because it makes the text less repetitive. I sometimes use the term "Indigenous" to indicate that I am talking in a more general or global sense about land-based peoples, philosophies and values.

I have approached this book as a personal journey: that of a Native woman (me!) seeking information about her identity. For this reason, Section I, "Setting Out," contains information about my personal background and my approach to writing on the subject of Native womanhood. I return to the personal in the final section, where I offer some insights related to what I have learned, and in the epilogue, where I have reproduced a conversation between me and my friend Bonita Lawrence.

In Section II, "The Colonization of Native Womanhood," I look at how Native women were understood and positioned in various traditional Aboriginal cultures, and briefly trace the changes that happened as a result of contact with Europeans. I then examine how Native femininity has been negatively constructed, and how that impacts on the lives of Native women today.

With this background I move into the central questions of the book: How do Aboriginal women maintain their power, in spite of all the oppression? What do they construct as an alternative? I present a theory of identity formation, similar to one that has been applied by other oppressed peoples, but with a distinctly Aboriginal approach. For example, in *Black Feminist Thought: Knowledge, Consciousness and the Politics of Empowerment*, Patricia Hill Collins talks about the damage that is caused by negative images of Black women,[1] and contends that Black women must *resist*, and *construct* a different knowledge of the self as a matter of survival.[2]

I propose that Native women engage in a process of self-definition that includes four steps: *resist, reclaim, construct* and *act*. I have traced this process through the lives and insights of the forty Aboriginal women I interviewed while researching this book, and have devoted a section to each step of the process.

Very simply, the identity formation process that I have documented involves:

- resisting negative definitions of being;
- reclaiming Aboriginal tradition;
- constructing a positive identity by translating tradition into the contemporary context; and
- acting on that identity in a way that nourishes the overall well-being of our communities.

What is distinctly Aboriginal is the way in which past, present and future are understood to be inextricably connected. We often hear our people say, "You have to know where you come from to know where you are going." In other words, our definition and self-determination as individuals and as nations involves calling on the past to define the future. I like the way Sylvia Maracle has articulated this, as it offers some questions that have helped me to structure the book. She says:

> In trying to walk the traditional path there are four lifelong questions we ask ourselves: Who am I? In order to answer that I have to know: Where have I come from? And once I know where I have come from, I have to know: Where am I going? And once I know where I am going, I need to know: What is my responsibility? We ask ourselves these questions and every time we think we know that answer to one, it changes all the others.[3]

I have written about the reconstruction of Native womanhood by walking through Maracle's questions and matching them up to the process of resist, reclaim, construct and act.

### DIAGRAM 1: WHO AM I?

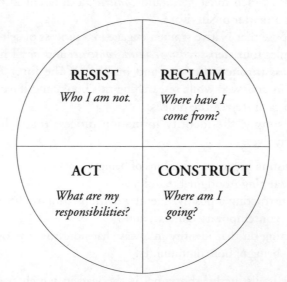

If we translate these questions from the personal to the plural, we feel the pulse of a social movement. We can hear, *Who are we?* or *What is an Aboriginal woman?* We can think about the questions *Where are we going?* and *What are our responsibilities?*

When I interviewed Sto:lo/Métis writer Lee Maracle, she talked about an "Indigenous feminist sociology":

> Anybody that knows anything about the roles of Native women in the past has got to get together. We have got to flesh out some kind of a picture that is acceptable to us, and then start creating whatever educational processes we need to pass that on.

I hope to contribute to the future by sharing the information imparted to me about the sacredness, the power and the beauty of womanhood as it is understood through various Native cultures. Perhaps my work can help to dispel the suffering endured by the women who told me their stories of abuse. Perhaps it can contribute to the dialogue that Lee Maracle is proposing. Whatever its course, I hope it will advance the decolonization of our womanhood, and in so doing, create a healthier future for all Native peoples.

This book is primarily a gift to Native women, children and men. It will also add to an evolving scholarly and popular body of work that is naming the poisons that have infiltrated Native womanhood, documenting Native female paths of resistance and defining a positive Native female identity.

LIBRARY

LIBRARY

# I

# SETTING OUT

❖

# SETTING OUT

❖

*As I have come to understand it from listening to the Elders and tra-*
*ditional teachers, the only person I can speak about is myself. That is*
*how the Creator made all of us ... All I have to share with you is*
*myself, my experience, and how I have come to understand that*
*experience.*

— Patricia Monture-Angus (Mohawk)[1]

I HAVE CHOSEN TO START this book by talking about myself because I
want to practise an Aboriginal method of contextualizing knowledge.
I could have written without mention of myself; I could have talked
all about Native women ("them") and their development, and many
readers would have been comfortable with the authoritative tone of
such a text. Professor Patricia Monture-Angus (Mohawk) has a story
about how an editor once removed all the "I's" and the references to
her personal story in an article she had written on First Nations
women and violence. She writes, "[The editor] had created an academic
piece for me and I think he felt very good because in his mind he had
somehow elevated the status of my work."[2] Monture-Angus points
out how this illustrates a key difference between Aboriginal and
mainstream academic approaches to knowledge:

> In academic writing, the rule is that authors do *not* identify their
> voices. They speak from a pedestal of knowledge. The individual
> speaking is not a central part of that knowledge nor is he or she
> actively involved in the knowledge he or she has produced. The
> knowledge is outside the self.[3]

Although feminist academics have challenged the objectification of
knowledge, this kind of thinking is still prevalent in mainstream circles,
as Monture-Angus's story demonstrates.

Native people have suffered a particular brand of this objectification. Ever the objects of study, we have been the bed and foundation

upon which many consultants and academic "authorities" have built careers. Many people have begun to rightly question the authority of these "experts," but this has often led to another problem — the silly expectation that, because one is Native, one can speak about everything pertaining to Native people. How many of us have sat as the lone Aboriginal student in a classroom, embarrassed by the demands placed on us by instructor and students to field all the queries about Indians? Although I think it is good to give people a voice, this questioning (once again) reduces the complexity of our experiences as individuals and as peoples.

I don't profess to be any kind of an authority on Native women. I never will be. What I do know I have learned from speaking to the forty women that I interviewed for this book; from reading the works of (and sometimes about) Native women; and from my experience as a member of the Native community in southern Ontario. The "authority" of this book is therefore very closely tied to my personal experience. Another woman could have interviewed the same people and written a very different book. For this reason, I think it is important that the reader know something about me.

Native teachers often begin by introducing themselves; I was reminded of this when I went to interview Ojibway midwife Carol Couchie. Although Carol had some specific knowledge related to birth that she wished to share with me, she spent more than half of our interview introducing herself. Her personal background was important, she said, because it would allow me to better understand any of the more general observations that she was to share with me. We reflected on the practice that teaching in our communities often begins with the teacher telling us something of her/himself. In many cases, the teacher's story *is* the teaching.

I hope this section demonstrates how my interests, biases, abilities and perspectives play into how I assembled the stories of the interview participants to create *A Recognition of Being*. Finally, I would like to preface the personal by saying that it is a difficult task to make one's personal journey public, and I appreciate the courage of all of the interview participants for their sharing. Like the women I interviewed, I offer a small piece of my story in the spirit of Aboriginal teaching and sharing practices.

## CHAPTER ONE

# STORY OF THE STORYTELLER

❖

MY MOTHER IS a white woman of predominantly English Protestant ancestry. She was raised in Vancouver in an upper-middle class family that is several generations Canadian. My father's parents were both of mixed Cree and Scottish ancestry, and we also have some French and Saulteaux ancestors on his father's side. My dad was raised in a working-class family in Portage la Prairie, Manitoba. My parents met and married while working in Ghana, and then raised my brother and me in a white, middle-class neighbourhood in a rural area outside of Ottawa.

Like many Native people, I struggle with my identity. Because of racism, cultural genocide and policies that have encouraged Native people to abandon their heritage, many of us have come to feel ashamed, confused or embarrassed about identifying ourselves as Native. From this confusion, we must struggle to re-name ourselves and to understand what that means.

I currently define myself as a Cree/Métis woman. I am not sure if I will rest with this label indefinitely as identity language is complex and constantly changing for Native peoples. Because of our past, naming is politically and emotionally loaded. In my case it is complicated by the fact that I was not raised in the territory of my ancestors. Much of my development as a Native person has taken place among the Ojibway and the Iroquois. With the exception of my father, these are the people that have raised me in the Native way.

I have chosen the combined Cree/Métis label for a number of reasons. I am Métis as my father is of the Métis people of Manitoba. I am also Métis in the sense that I am a mixed-blood person and I wish to acknowledge my mother's Euro-Canadian ancestry. I further define myself as Cree as this is the language of my Native ancestors and I am a descendant of many different groups of Cree people, people who were born in places as far apart as Moose Factory, Ontario, and Cumberland House, Saskatchewan. Through all of this moving and mixing of peoples, I have concluded that Cree/Métis suits me best.

As a child, I acknowledged that "my dad is an Indian" without ever really thinking about what that meant. I went to a rural school where everyone was white. Issues relating to people of non-Euro-Canadian, non-Christian races and cultures were marginal to our thinking. I transferred to the city for high school, but there was similarly no acknowledgement of race or culture in that setting. I had no contact with Native people in my early school and community experience, other than with my father's extended family (the two siblings who lived in town and the others who made periodic visits from western Canada).

Because I spent my childhood and teen years deprived of Native community, I grew into adulthood without a grounded sense of identity as a Native person. The gaps in my emotional, mental and spiritual experience eventually caught up with me, taking me by surprise when they did. I trace it back to an incident that took place in the early 1980s. I was nineteen and living in Montreal when, one day, I found myself crying irrepressibly after getting into an argument with one of my university classmates about the Native characters in Margaret Laurence's novel *The Diviners*.[4] My classmate, a white woman from Alaska, had been arguing that the young Native character, Pique, retreats to the bush in Manitoba at the end of the book because the only alternative to assimilation is withdrawal from mainstream society.[5] This touched all sorts of buttons about my own position as an assimilated Native person, and brought on a hurricane of emotion. I surprised my classmate and myself with the explosion that was my reaction. Underneath that explosion, I discovered a profound sadness.

I now see my experience as a lesser version of the "adoption breakdown" syndrome that so often happens to Native teens who have grown up in white adoptive families. At some point our loss makes itself known, and it can be a heavy realization. Why does this happen? Part of it comes from gaining consciousness about the persecution of Native peoples, but much of it is emotionally, spiritually and physically driven. Sylvia Maracle has suggested to me that my experience was the manifestation of blood memory.[6] Many Native cultures teach that we carry the memories of our ancestors in our physical being. As such, we are immediately connected to those who have gone before us. We live with the trauma that has plagued the previous generations. We know their laughter, but also their sorrows.

It is clear that whatever had been repressed in my consciousness came to the surface that day. I was crying for the losses experienced by my ancestors, but I was also crying for my own loss of identity. I have since seen many Native people cry in sharing circles for the same reasons. Some Aboriginal people have always maintained a strong Aboriginal identity, but many of us have not, and at some point we must begin to reclaim ourselves. The incident with my classmate marked the beginning of my journey to "recognize my being": to *recognize* by working through a spiritual and physical remembering, and to *re-cognize* via a mental and emotional constructing. It was the start of a conscious decision to discover what it meant to be a Native person.

My first step was to locate the Native community that I had never known as a child. I told my brother about my sadness, and over the course of the following year we both began to seek out Native people through community organizations in Toronto (where we had moved). In this sense, I consider myself to have been raised up through the urban Aboriginal organizations of Toronto and the people connected to them. There I found a sense of community and belonging, and an incredible wealth of knowledge about the possibilities for a contemporary urban Native person. Those Native grandparents, sisters, brothers, aunties and uncles have helped me to shape an identity in defiance of the argument that my only choices as an Aboriginal person are to assimilate or to go back to the bush.

Along this journey, I have to continually work through lots of doubts, notions and stereotypes that challenge my legitimacy as an Aboriginal person. Ironically, we have gone from trying hard NOT to be Native, to trying hard TO be Native. Even though I realize this is just two sides of the same cultural genocide coin, the pressures are so insidious that I still have moments where I feel that I do not measure up to some kind of standard of Indianness.

One of the ways this insecurity has worked into my consciousness is through the overarching stereotype of the "vanishing Indian."

Plains Cree/Métis professor Emma LaRocque explains the vanishing Indian as "a white construct that comes from a combination of old history, old anthropology and the civilization/savagery paradigm that informed much of western intellectual tradition." She points to the resulting meta-narrative, that we must remain as we were 500 years ago in order to be considered truly "Native":

> There developed a notion that Native people were savage and primitive, and, as such, were static; had frozen cultures. Change was always seen as assimilation or vanishing. In other words, our cultures became ossified, and the definition of our cultures was that change was impossible. The moment we change, we are no longer Native.

Thus the "assimilation or vanishing" argument that I began with my classmate is alive and well. Those most critical of my Aboriginal status are, not surprisingly, white people, many of whom are quick to pronounce that I am "not really Indian," or inadvertently quantify my existence by asking, "Do you have Indian blood?" Some white people will question whether I am "really Native" because I didn't grow up on reserve or in a Native community; some will call attention to the fact that I am "only half"; others will interrogate me about my urban status. I still feel uncomfortable with this kind of cross-examination, but now I see it as part of a (conscious or unconscious) continuum of assimilationist practices aimed at making Native people disappear from this country called Canada. Once we are "only half," or once we become urbanized or non-language speakers, many non-Native people feel inclined to tell us that we no longer exist. We are no longer Natives.

In the Native community, we struggle with our own version of the vanishing Indian. I think many of us feel insecure because we lack the knowledge that was ripped away from our ancestors. We have internalized the belief that we are "less" Native because we can't measure up to some kind of quintessential "Native experience" whereby we grow up on the land, speak our language and are well versed from an early age in Native ways. In our neediness, we, too, are susceptible to what Emma LaRocque has called "the craze for the authentic Indian." LaRocque has noted a tremendous pressure, particularly among young people, to adopt a Native identity. Those of us who do not have a land-based culture to inform us often turn to symbols of traditions, ceremonies and a pan-Indian approach. Whereas this movement is generally helpful to us, we must guard against the tendency to "ossify" tradition, and we must question the benefit of calling on these things as a yardstick for Native identity. Absurdly, many of us, young and old, have now experienced shame or embarrassment because we are not conversant in the various traditions and ceremonies that have only recently come back to our communities. "Tradition" and "ceremony" can thus be damaging if we use it in a static or fundamentalist way to interrogate how "Native" we are. For those of us who have lost so much, these traditional lifestyles, values, customs and languages might serve us better if we see them as ideals and tools with which we reconcile our Native lives as they have come to be.[7]

I had to think about this to come to an understanding of what makes me a Native person. What is my "Native" experience? My first, most basic realization was that *all* people of Native ancestry have "Native experience," because, unfortunately, part of our experience as Native peoples includes being relocated, dispossessed of our ways of life, adopted into white families, and so on. All Native peoples have experienced loss to one degree or another because of these policies, and as a result we have to work at making sense of our identity. For many of us, part of being Native is feeling like we aren't!

When I look at my family, I can't point to a great knowledge of "ceremonies" to claim our place as Indians. But, recently, talking to Ivy Chaske (Dakota) I could begin to see how some of the positive parts of our Native heritage have maintained themselves through the generations. During a conversation about "ceremonies" and "traditional Indians" Chaske pointed out:

> How you live your life is also ceremony. I have met many people who do not have the language, don't know any ceremonies, don't know anything about who they are as an Indian person, but they are the most traditional people I know. They are loyal, they are honest, they have integrity, they are caring, they know how to be respectful, *they are all of those things that made our people who they are.* All of those things that those ceremonies are meant to be.

Chaske's comments help me to challenge pat notions that link our identity to how much knowledge we have of Indigenous customs. I want to be clear that we must recognize, honour and uphold the distinct Indigenous perspectives that come from life lived on the land and that are embedded within our languages and ceremonies. We need to call on people who have this knowledge to help us forge our identities and our futures, but we can also call on other, more subtle parts of a Native "tradition" that are fully operational in our families, communities and nations.

In my own case, I can point to inherited values and ways of relating. My dad doesn't know how to wave a braid of sweetgrass around, skin a moose or conduct a sweatlodge ceremony in Cree. Growing up at the time that he did in Manitoba, there was no taking pride in these parts of a Native heritage. He was not raised with explicit Native customs and traditions; many of these had to go underground, and did not resurface until the 1960s. He was taught to be ashamed of his heritage and to fear speaking his Indigenous language. His identity was forged in a small urban centre, saturated with internal and external pressures to become white. In spite of these pressures to "kill the Indian"[8] in him, however, I believe his Native heritage continues to define him. I think something of a Cree/Métis upbringing managed to slip through the cracks of the cultural genocide to make him the person he is: a kind, generous and respectful man; and one that deals with women in terms of equity and respect. I believe these are some of the things that he learned from his mother. Perhaps these are some of the things that she salvaged from her upbringing. Whatever the case, Ivy Chaske helped me to understand that, because of who my father is, he has taught me a great deal about traditional Native culture. With his gentle ways, my father was my first Native teacher.[9]

While negotiating these aspects of my father's tradition, I have had to work with the further complication of being a mixed-blood person. This can add to the layers of confusion, and I am still in the process of sorting it out. Although this book does not get into the question of defining a mixed-blood identity, I offer some preliminary thoughts about my mixed-blood journey here, as it is an important part of my biography.

As a mixed-blood who arrived late into the Native community, I initially felt fear to identify as Native. Did people see me as white? As I became more involved, I began to feel more comfortable because no one seemed to question that I was a Native person. Of course, there are many debates about the place of mixed-blood people, particularly when it comes to band membership, where blood quantum and other measures become significant. The complex path of a mixed-blood individual can be greatly affected by factors such as one's appearance, location and the political climate. I lived in Toronto for many years where there are people of all colours and appearances and no doubt my appearance has helped me to be accepted in many circles. It has allowed me to "pass" both as white and as Native, depending on the group and the context. When I was struggling to find my legitimacy as a Native person, however, the thing that I found most helpful was the way I saw elders look at me. Many seemed to look right through the barriers, the politics, the boundaries and the status debates. Reflected in their eyes, I began to see myself as a granddaughter, a member and a relation.[10] I think this is the way it used to be, when our societies freely adopted members of other nations, before "Indian blood" was invented, before people were seen as *parts* of one thing or another.

While I can build an identity as a Native person, I must also remember my additional duty as a mixed-blood, to honour, explore and nurture my Euro-Canadian heritage. This need is different from my need to explore a Native identity, likely because Euro-Canada is the dominant culture and I have been well schooled in those ways. We don't need to work at discovering western culture; it is all around us, and increasingly all around the world. Western hegemony ensures that everyone knows and practises pieces of western culture, and that we are rewarded for doing so. I was taught both directly and indirectly about what it means to be an Anglo-Canadian. I spent eighteen years in a school system that promoted the perspectives of the white western male mind. While some of this information is inspirational to me, other things I find problematic.

Maybe what I do need to do at some point is to find productive ways to be critical, find new ways to be inspired and fit those interpretations of western culture into what I am now learning from

Native culture. When I criticize Euro-Canadian attitudes and values (as I do throughout this book), I have to look at how they are also mine, and then find a way to work through them. As a mixed-blood person who wishes to explore my Native female identity, I must re-look for the positive gifts that the Europeans brought to my Native ancestors, and find forgiveness for those things that were and continue to be destructive. As difficult as it sometimes feels for a person learning about the direct effects of racism and colonization on her family, I must walk with my Euro-Canadian ancestors to find the richness of that culture and to find a place within Euro-Canada that is comfortable for me.

Western culture has typically not promoted, documented or explored the culture(s) of its women. I therefore also have a role to play in recognizing and honouring those ways. I was reminded of this when I interviewed Cree/Métis educator Myra Laramee, who talked about the need to recognize our non-Native grandmothers. Laramee, who has Scottish and French ancestors, has now come to a point where she can work with both Native and white grandmothers in her delineation of an enlightened womanhood. She encourages other women to do the same. When non-Native women come to Laramee seeking counsel, she tells them to return to their own grandmothers. She told me the story of a Hungarian woman who, upon receiving this advice, replied that she didn't have any grandmothers. Laramee's response was, "Oh, yes you do. That's part of the problem with your culture — you close that western doorway. Your grandmothers are standing there waiting for you to ask the question. You are just arrogant enough not to ask." Even though western culture does not encourage us to work with our ancestors (especially the dead ones), that doesn't mean they don't have anything to offer! Laramee thus introduced the idea that in my search for a positive female identity, I have much to learn from walking with my Scottish, English and French grandmothers. In learning about resistance to patriarchy, I can also reflect on the tremendous things that have been given to me by my mom.

A significant part of my Euro-Canadian heritage that I cannot overlook is the privilege that it has afforded me. Even something such as writing this book is related to the privilege that comes out of my Euro-Canadian race, my class, education and upbringing. In negotiating my position of privilege, I call on a story that Catherine Martin told me while I was interviewing her for this book. Although it is a story about the privilege of having lighter skin, I find it useful in helping me to effectively apply all of the privileges I have been given. Catherine and I were talking about the classic line that many of us often hear from white people: "Oh, but you don't look Indian." One time this happened to her in the presence of a Penobscot Elder. He offered this response to the woman who had made the remark:

> She is that way for a reason. She can go to places we can't go. She can speak in places we can't speak. People like her have been part of our culture ever since time began. We have always had people like her to do the work we can't do.

This story is a good way of explaining how I see my privilege related to my purpose. I don't want to speak for people, but maybe I can work some of the corners where I find myself to build bridges and raise awareness of our collective experiences as Native people. What I do with my privilege will, I hope, be of benefit to both my Euro-Canadian and my Native relations.

I have raised these points because my race and class privilege separates me from many Native people in terms of lived experience. I am a privileged Native person in that I have no lived experience of violent or *overt* racism, poverty, abuse and family breakdown. I am grateful for this, as these are things that no Native person need have inherited. It is telling that many of the things that I have experienced as *privilege* as a Native person are really just basic human rights. What does this say about the position of Native people in Canada?

Although our life situations may differ dramatically, the lives of all Native peoples intersect at the juncture of state-sanctioned assimilationist policies and genocidal attack. In spite of the smooth path that I have been given, I share the need with many Native people to reclaim my Native heritage. In finding solace, acceptance and solidarity among the urban Native population, I have found my place in a community-based healing process that revolves around reclaiming and defining a Native identity. My journey as a Native person, my recognition of being as explored in this book, is one way of telling the assimilation-makers that it didn't work. We may be struggling, but we are still here.

With this process of reclaiming a Native identity well underway, I need to further explore what it means to be a Native woman. This has only really taken place over the last few years because until recently my approach to gender was on a separate course from my struggle with race and culture.

My consciousness of the oppression of women began at puberty, a time when I began to recognize and experience threats of sexual harassment and violence from men. Rather than the sadness I felt about race, my primary emotions around gender were those of anger and fear. It was the anger that gradually drove me to become more analytical about the oppressive experiences of women in general. As a young woman, however, I did not participate in women's struggles, choosing, rather, to work in general forums of social justice, and often with men. I suppose I was taking the approach that I could simply move into any territory and operate as a genderless person. This was my way of seeking equity, in the way that it is so often proposed by mainstream culture.

When I began to reclaim Native culture, I was faced with many teachings that do not allow one to operate as genderless, and so I had to start to examine what that meant. I listened to the Elders[11] speaking about the different responsibilities of men and women, and tried to make sense of it. I attended ceremonies where there were specific roles for women and men, and I took my place on the women's side. I also worked for both Native women's and men's organizations in Toronto, learning slowly from them. What really jolted me into consciousness about a woman's struggle, though, was the experience of becoming a mother.

In truth, I may not have even approached motherhood had it not been for Native teachings that encouraged me to see the power and the beauty of it. I had held nagging assumptions that children are a burden to women, or that they are the outcome of participating in a dull linear life-plan narrative. When I heard Elders talk about how children are sacred gifts that are the heart of our communities, I started to appreciate the privilege of having a relationship with children, and the honour of taking responsibility for them. According to our teachings, I didn't need to produce my own children to participate in this society, as everyone has a responsibility and a relationship to the children. I could easily have become an auntie, a sister and later a grannie without bearing children. It so happens that my path brought me into a healthy, child-friendly relationship at a certain time, and so I became a mother first.

With this experience I stumbled onto the realization that I could no longer live the pretence of a genderless existence.[12] Along with the power and the beauty of motherhood, I acquired an immediate appreciation of how really difficult a woman's life can be. My class, age, location and privilege may have shielded me from this realization beforehand, but my status as a mother tore down all the disguises of western patriarchy. I gained a tremendous respect for women and their bodies, and then reflected on how the sanctity of this is never recognized or promoted in mainstream culture. I gained a genuine appreciation for the "women's work" of bearing and raising children, and reflected on how problematic it is that mothers are generally isolated and not recognized for the heavy responsibilities they carry. I started to think that the only way mainstream society can appreciate anything distinctly female is when it serves the greedy or lustful appetites of the consumer.

I knew that Native culture had a different vision for women and for mothers, but I had a hard time piecing this together. In the process of embracing Native culture and community, I had been troubled by the sexism that is as alive in "Indian country" as it is elsewhere. I had to wonder: *In light of the many positive aspects of Native culture, how is it that women are generally so poorly situated within their societies?* My community work in child welfare further provided me a glimpse of the kind of dire situations that many Native women face, the struggles that are reflected in the statistics placing Native women at the bottom of the Canadian socioeconomic hierarchy. I wanted to trace what had happened and look for alternatives.

There are many other events, relationships and lessons that have shaped my feminine consciousness and influenced my Native identity to date. However, I think what I have discussed here offers enough of a background to my research interests and how I came into my questioning. Aside from my own personal overview, there are two essential notions that figure prominently in my theories and in this book and which I discuss in the next chapter: "tradition" and "culture."

CHAPTER TWO

# WORKING WITH NOTIONS
# OF TRADITION AND
# CULTURE

❖

THERE IS A LOT of talk about "tradition," "traditional ways" and "culture" in our communities. Because of the cultural genocide that we have experienced, we have a real need to recover ways that are distinct from Euro-Canadian tradition. We look for "tradition" and "culture" that is free of the influence of the colonizer as we move through our processes of decolonization. We want to return to things that we may truly call our own.

I work with "tradition" and "culture" in a good part of this book because I think reclaiming our Indigenous ways is the only way we will recover ourselves as individuals, families and nations. I feel a need, however, to clarify my use of tradition and culture, because I am aware that simplistic notions of these dynamics can be problematic. Our losses and our need to reclaim our original ways can lead us down the dangerous path of romanticizing, generalizing or essentializing our heritage and traditions. We may unwittingly seek to lodge ourselves in a perceived golden age of our ancestors. We must therefore be attentive to the incredibly complex nature of tradition and how we use it.

My first reminder to myself and to the reader is that "tradition" and "culture" are living entities, subject to constant change, as are people. I agree with Laguna writer Leslie Marmon Silko, who challenges the static notion that is often applied to "traditional" people. She says:

> I understand now that human communities are living beings that
> continue to change; while there may be a concept of the "traditional"

Indian or "traditional Laguna Pueblo person," no such being has ever existed. All along here have been changes; for the ancient people any notions of "tradition" necessarily included the notion of making do with whatever was available, or adaptation for survival.[1]

When we look for Indigenous "traditions," therefore, we must be aware that everything we are looking at was constructed to fit a certain reality of the people who were living it at the time. When speaking about Indigenous traditions, we must be mindful of the hundreds of different nations across North America that have all participated in developing their own cultures to suit the different times and environments they have been through. Our traditions were oral and had the ability to adapt and change to the situations as necessary.

How, then, do we find something tangible in tradition and culture if it is always changing? Native Hawaiian educator Haunani-Kay Trask has suggested that we focus on the values and symbols that have persisted over the generations.[2] This helps us not only to find the common threads through the ages but also to see and draw upon the common threads of the multifarious Indigenous nations of the Americas (and, indeed, the world). Laguna Pueblo/Sioux scholar Paula Gunn Allen has summarized a few of the characteristics we share as Indigenous peoples:

> ... although our traditions are as diverse as the tribes who practice and live within them, they are all earth-based and wilderness centered; are all "animalistic," polytheistic, concerned with sacred or non-political power, and incorporate patterns that many in the western world identify as profane.[3]

As traditionally land-based peoples, we can uncover many common values about how we relate to the earth and all of creation, including how we define our human relationships. These values are distinct to Indigenous people in spite of, and sometimes because of, colonization and a continuous process of change. When we say "tradition" in our communities, we are referring to values, philosophies and lifestyles that pre-date the arrival of the Europeans, as well as ways that are being created *within* a larger framework of Euro-Canadian culture, or *in resistance* to it. The values and symbols that we use as we move through these processes can be as true today as they were five centuries ago.

In seeking a positive vision of Native womanhood, I have identified some approaches to gender and gender relations that are common to Indigenous peoples. Section II, "Looking Back: The Colonization of Native Womanhood," documents traditions of gender equity as they occurred in various Native nations. Although I realize that Native women were not equally valued, placed or conceptualized in their various societies, my study corresponds with Paula Gunn Allen's conclusions about the feminine in Native American tradition. She says, "The tribes see women variously, but they do not question the power of femininity. Sometimes they see women as fearful, sometimes peaceful, sometimes omnipotent, and omniscient, but they never portray women as mindless, helpless, simple or oppressed."[4]

The Sections of the book entitled "Resist," "Reclaim," "Construct" and "Act" document how we call upon our various traditions of womanhood to help us construct something that is positive in our modern lives. I think we can be selective in our use of tradition because, like our ancestors, we must work with those things that suit our present reality. This is particularly important for women, situated as we are so squarely within patriarchal boundaries. Many of the "traditions" we now know stem from Euro-Christian patriarchal ideals, and many of our own Indigenous traditions have been twisted to meet western patriarchal hegemony. I think Emma LaRocque has articulated some necessary questions we must ask ourselves:

> ... as women we must be circumspect in our recall of tradition. We must ask ourselves whether and to what extent tradition is liberating us as women. We must ask ourselves wherein lie our sources of empowerment. We know enough about human history that we cannot assume that all Aboriginal traditions universally respected and honoured women. (And is "respect" and "honour" all that we can ask for?) It should not be assumed, even in those original societies that were structured along matriarchal lines, that matriarchies necessarily prevented men from oppressing women. There are indications of male violence and sexism in some Aboriginal societies prior to European contact,[5] and certainly after contact. But, at the same time, culture is not immutable,

and tradition cannot be expected to be always of value or relevant even in our times. As Native women, we are faced with very difficult and painful choices, but, nonetheless, we are challenged to change, create, and embrace "traditions" consistent with contemporary and international human rights standards.[6]

When we begin to reclaim our ways, we must question how these traditions are framed, and whether they are empowering to us. The gendered nature of our tradition can be extremely damaging if interpreted from a western patriarchal framework.

The clearest examples of this can be found in the way we are reviving our spiritual traditions. Lakota anthropologist Bea Medicine has written about how what is interpreted as "tradition" can further be used by Native men to build and maintain the sexism they have learned from the colonizer. She points out that "male orientation in the revitalized Native belief structure is strong," as is evident in the way some men have reactivated ceremonies such as the Sun Dance and Uwipi to assume male importance.[7] Whereas the Sun Dance and other such ceremonies can be powerful affirmations of our womanhood (as I demonstrate later), we must be wary of when they are not. When I interviewed women for this book, I heard several examples of how men use "tradition" and "culture" to exclude women, render them invisible, or to shame them by twisting traditions that are related to female power. Barbra Nahwegahbow, an Ojibway who lives in Toronto, told me about an experience that pertains to the Ojibway tradition that women are expected to sit with their legs to one side while in the sweat lodge. Although this practice is meant to be an acknowledgement of the power that comes from a woman's centre, it is often left unexplained. Nahwegahbow told me, "I was in a lodge one time at ceremony and they had this guy going around saying, 'You have to sit in a certain way.' And he was walking around tapping women who he felt weren't sitting properly. I mean, that's unacceptable! It's an unacceptable thing to me." The failure to explain the values behind certain practices and the way in which some traditions are enforced can alienate women.

Our ways of dealing with taboos around menstruation are perhaps the most common example of the need for better education and a critical practice of tradition. Ojibway Grandmother Vera Martin remembers once having to correct a Sun Dance leader who was explaining that menstruating women are "dirty." Native people have always thought about menstruation as the sacred manifestation of a woman's power, which is why we must abstain from participating in certain practices and ceremonies while "on our time." Although few Native people would make the mistake of calling a menstruating woman "dirty" these days, Martin's example shows how our traditions can get distorted, filtered or interpreted through Christian notions of sin as it relates to womanhood. We still feel these interpretations today, sometimes subtly, and sometimes not! I had to chuckle in agreement when Myra Laramee asked: "How many times have you been in a ceremony where some man stood up and said, 'Okay, you women who are on your time ... now get out of here!'" We can be made to feel alienated, embarrassed or excluded when we are simply or abruptly told to leave ceremonies because we are menstruating. The way we deal with these situations is especially pertinent to women of our era because so many have grown up in residential schools where they were taught that they were dirty and evil. Cree Elder Kathleen Green now laughs when she remembers feeling a need to run away and hide while "on her time." The nuns taught her that menstruation "is the time when you are the evilest!"

I imagine that many Native women have stories like the one that was told to me by Laverne Gervais-Contois, a Sioux/Ojibway/Cree woman currently living in Montreal. Gervais-Contois recalled for me the feelings that she had the first time she ran into a menstrual taboo: "I was at a workshop, and I was told not to go to the room where the circle was being held. I felt totally ostracized, that I was being punished for something. I didn't participate." Her story provides a good example of how traditions around menstruation can be oppressive when they lack context and the related teachings are overlooked. I think it might help to work with menstrual taboos, for instance, by offering alternatives to exclusion, because until we do, menstruation during ceremonies can be experienced as disempowering. In Section IV, "Reclaim," I discuss how people are creating spaces where, for example, menstruating women *can* go during ceremony.

I believe that if we can revive the female teachings behind menstruation and other common practices and traditions we will regain our sense of purpose. We will be able to eliminate disempowering Euro-Christian messages such as, "You are a menstruating woman. You don't belong." We are making progress in this regard, as Vera Martin, an Elder who has been part of the Aboriginal healing movement since its infancy in the 1970s, points out: "When I started following the culture, in the beginning we wouldn't do anything unless we were told by the men! And we even questioned a woman when she said, 'You have to do it this way' in a ceremony." I would like to help with this progress by working with tradition and culture in a way that reaffirms the feminine as we move into the next stage of our development as Aboriginal peoples.

## CHAPTER THREE

# LITERARY AND ORAL
# RESOURCES

❖

ONE OF MY DRIVING PRINCIPLES behind writing about Native women was to include the words, perspectives and insights of Native women themselves.[1] My choice of background literature reflects this principle, as I have tried as much as possible to reference material that is written *by* Native women. Too often in the past, Native peoples have been misrepresented and appropriated on the page by outsiders. Native women have been erased, distorted or subjected to the "princess-squaw" perversion through historical records, literature and anthropology.[2] Non-Native people have typically been considered the "experts" about our Indigenous lives, families and nations. Patricia Monture-Angus gives a good example of how this occurs in the field of law:

> The great majority of Aboriginal law courses are offered by non-Aboriginal scholars who have developed an expertise in the area of Aboriginal rights as they are understood in Canadian law. I have often wondered how women professors would respond to the suggestion that men can, could, and should teach courses about law and feminism. It is so apparent that this would create quite a controversy. But when non-Aboriginal people teach courses on Aboriginal people and how Canadian law is applied to our lives, this is somehow unrecognizable controversy.[3]

It is true that we are so accustomed to accepting the opinions, studies and research on Aboriginal people by non-Aboriginal people that we don't question this practice. Often this is seen as more valid, somehow, than the words of Aboriginal people. I try to imagine a Women's Studies department filled with male faculty and fuelled by men's writing. This would be considered unacceptable. Why, then, do we find it okay to read about what non-Aboriginal people have to say about every element of our Indigenous lives, including our womanhood? To counteract these practices, I have made a conscious effort to use Indigenous writing and to validate these voices by referencing the nation of each Indigenous author in the bibliography.[4]

This being said, I have also used literature written by non-Native people and, in some cases, non-Native men. I have done this primarily because we still do not have enough material out there that is written by our own people. Native access to education and publishing is improving, but in the meantime, the majority of "Native studies" is still that: study of "Natives" by the outsider. I have found useful material in the work of non-Native scholars, but in working through the material, I called on a few factors to assist me in my critical approach. I asked myself, Who wrote this? What were their values? What was their understanding of women? What was their relationship to Native people? These are not easy questions to answer, particularly in scholarly work, where there is an expectation that the author remain hidden from the text. While sorting through anthropological and historical works, I tried to find literature written within the last twenty-five years. I had been warned that, up until the 1960s, most of what was written about Native women was framed within the princess-squaw mindset.[5] I looked for signs that the authors were taking a definite stand against patriarchy, and that they displayed some consciousness of the genocide that state and church policies inflicted on Native peoples. I looked for contradictions in the texts that would indicate biases or impositions on the part of the authors. I considered the time period of the studies, and wondered how the cultures being written about had adopted and were manifesting traits they had learned from living in a patriarchal world that demands assimilation.

I will illuminate my approach by discussing one text in particular — the text that I could not ignore — Ruth Landes's *Ojibwa Woman*.[6] Although this book was originally written in 1938 (and therefore not fitting with my criteria for more recent material), it seemed extensive enough that I needed to consider it. Eleven of the forty women I spoke with are Ojibway, and there is very little written about Ojibway women. I thought it might provide some evidence of traditional gender equity and Ojibway understanding of women. Some of the information in the book is useful, but there are contradictory passages throughout. Many of Landes's findings concur with the arguments supporting the existence of gender equity in Native societies — that divorce was common, that women deserted men in abusive marriages, that women hunted and doctored as men did, that women acted as warriors and shamans, that widows could support themselves rather than remarrying. However, Landes seems to seek out and present contradictory information to prove that Ojibway women were as oppressed, or more oppressed, than white women at the time.[7]

There may be a few reasons for this contradictory evidence. It is possible that Landes was, in fact, recording the influx of western patriarchal practices as they began to creep into Native society and that the contradictions in her book are reflective of changing worldviews as one culture moved into the other. It is, moreover, quite likely that Landes was interpreting Ojibway society from a western patriarchal framework, and that she therefore misunderstood the practices that she witnessed.

When I considered the work in terms of the author's agenda, it seemed to me that Landes was determined to show how the Ojibway women were oppressed in comparison with Ojibway men. Landes explains that the puberty ceremony for boys and girls is the difference between "a striving for broader horizons" for the male and a "conscious withdrawal from her malignant self" for the female.[8] She tells horrible stories of rape, drunken sex orgies involving alcohol (a definite link to ugly behaviour learned from the colonizer), and how women and children are shamed as a result of "illegitimate" children. She attempts to prove that Ojibway women's work is not as valued as men's work.[9] She concludes:

> If men are considered inheritors of the culture's wealth, women are the dispossessed and underprivileged; if men are the material selected arbitrarily to be the finest medium for the expression of Ojibwa ideas, women are second-rate, or perhaps reserve material.[10]

I am not certain that, traditionally, Native societies achieved uncomplicated and complete gender equity. I have no doubt that Landes, visiting at the time that she was, was witness to the beginning of the social breakdown and dysfunction that we are currently struggling with in our communities. Yet, upon studying traditions of gender equity for my book, and in talking to Ojibway women, I can conclude that the kind of patriarchy described by Landes in *Ojibwa Woman* is undoubtedly more of a reflection of her culture than that of the Ojibwa culture she purports to represent. Finally, in consideration of the significance of relationships, I am sceptical when I read that Landes's analysis is the result of several *months* of field work in the Ojibway community.[11] How does this compare with a lifetime of lived experience? What types of relationships did she build that could have given her any insight into the culture?

I came across a few anthologies of interviews with Native women while I was looking for contemporary Native women's voices in print. I have used these books with an awareness that they can be problematic as well. My concerns are around relationship, research methodology and editing techniques. One such book is *Wisdom's Daughters: Conversations with Women Elders of Native America*,[12] edited by Steve Wall. I will begin by noting that the editor of *Wisdom's Daughters* is non-Native. This is controversial insofar as Native people have identified that they have difficulties in accessing publishing grants and opportunities.[13] I was unable to find a collection of this kind that is produced by Native women.[14] In terms of voice, one wonders how a book of Native female voices can get funded and go unquestioned when edited by a white male, and why there isn't anything of the sort by a Native woman? These concerns aside, I would like to focus on the approach taken by Wall in *Wisdom's Daughters*.

Whereas some might interpret Steve Wall's enthusiasm for the "wisdom" of Native women as a positive affirmation of an ally, it turned sour on me as I glanced through his preface. I felt violated by Wall's explanation of himself as a "journeyer, a crosser of boundaries":

> In my crossing of two boundaries at once, the gulf between man and woman and the boundary from white to red, I have finally traversed frontiers from which there is no return, for I have learned, much to my surprise, more about being male than being female and more of what it means to be white than Indian.[15]

Perhaps, to Wall's credit, he admits to learning more about his own subject position than that of Native women. But we need to ask: *Who gains from this experience?* and *Why should it be a surprise to him that the process of writing the book is more about his self-discovery?* What better example of a modern-day colonial process could there be? The white male "journeyer" seeks to cross the "frontier" as represented by Native women. He sets out, he states, "looking for secrets." Colonial exotica spring to mind, the erotic therein corroborated by an experience he describes in the foreword of being sexually aroused by the "mystical" workings of an Elder (who supposedly demonstrates her spiritual power by sexually arousing him without touching him). The "secrets," which turn out to be "open, freely given truth," he finds transforming. In true colonial style, the transformation made available through engaging with Native peoples is ultimately to the benefit of his white male self. The shameless manifest destiny of Wall is apparent in his final comments:

> Now the work continues. I find myself off to the Andes seeking the way of the condor among the indigenous people of South America. More journeys to make, more boundaries to cross.[16]

To this I would add: *More cultures to appropriate, more "Others" to consume.*

This "eating the Other" syndrome is prevalent in a lot of writing about Native peoples, and has been a factor in my decisions about what to avoid in terms of literature. I now read books about Native people with these words of bell hooks in the back of my mind:

> … mass culture is the contemporary location that both publicly declares and perpetuates the idea that there is pleasure to be found in the acknowledgement and enjoyment of racial difference. The commodification of Others has been so successful because it is offered as a new delight, more intense, more satisfying than normal ways of doing and feeling. Within commodity culture, ethnicity becomes spice, seasoning that can liven up the dull dish that is mainstream white culture.[17]

Wall certainly seems to fall into this category of seeking desire from "difference," but I decided to use his anthology anyway, with the hope of finding something in the words of the women that he had recorded. There were other books that I turned down because the "eating the Other" seemed to eat into the entire text.

One good example is a book called *Women of the Apache Nation*.[18] The author's biography plainly states that she has been "fascinated with Apache culture since her youth." Standing at the library shelf, I flipped to the foreword, which is written by someone named "Dan Thrapp." Thrapp tells us how the (white) author of *Women of the Apache Nation* was at first shunned by the Apache women she wanted to interview. He describes how she "overcame" this, and offers proof of this achievement by calling up a scene from her concluding chapter in which she dons a shawl and participates in a traditional Apache dance. At this point, Thrapp states, the formerly shunned white author was able to conclude, "At long last, I felt part of the ancient, sacred ceremony," to which he adds, "Finally, she was Apache. The triumph of her study, the conclusion of her research, the end of her pilgrimage. She had arrived — and the account of it is in this remarkable book."[19] Upon reading this, I shut the book and returned it to the shelf. I didn't need to read any more to know that this book would be fraught with the desire not only to *eat* the Other, but to *be* the Other!

This critical approach to anthologies and recordings of Native female voice must now be turned inward, on myself and my own work, so I can demonstrate the way I have applied the voices of the women I interviewed. I am no different from Wall or any other editor/writer in that I operate from a very specific subject position in putting together this book.

## Oral Resource: Use of Women's Voices

I was interested in using interview material because I think the validity of the oral knowledge in our communities has been underestimated. As a young Native woman seeking information about my identity, I don't need to rely on a body of questionable literature: I can go and ask the aunties and grannies of my community for their perspectives and insights. This is the approach I took when I wrote the master's thesis that preceded this book; I interviewed only local women. I saw it as a traditional way of generating knowledge, one that is oral, collective and based on ongoing relationships within a community. The answers to my questions about Native womanhood lie within the stories, philosophies and visions of my friends, women I work with, people I meet in the community, workshops I attend. No one of us has the "line" on Native womanhood, and no one of us has "solved" the question of our identity, but collectively our experiences begin to tell a story.

My relationship with the interview participants has been really important to me. We exist because of and for the relationships we hold with everything around us. Knowledge is therefore of no use if it does not serve relationships. My goal has been to write a book that would serve Aboriginal people, but also a book that would grow from and evolve within the context of my relationships as a member of the Aboriginal community. I was much more comfortable with the original interviews I did for my thesis because I felt that those (local) women would be able to have more confidence in how I use their knowledge. They know me; they know my work in the community; they will be able to guide and direct me in the future; and so without hesitation they gave me their time and their stories.

When I decided to interview women nationally, I felt awkward and uncomfortable having to approach people I didn't know, and with whom I have no established relationship. It seemed to go against my need to work with material that is based on relationship. However, I made the decision to interview women across Canada because I thought that the book might then be more accessible to people in other communities, who could then relate to their aunties and grannies who appear in the book. I wanted a broader Indigenous perspective that would be accessible to members of the Aboriginal community overall. I tried as much as possible to find interview participants through word of mouth, so that there were some links, but in some cases I called upon Native organizations to give me contacts with women in their territories. I offered each interview participant tobacco and asked them to share their knowledge in the spirit of helping all of our people. I have not met all of these women in person, but I intend to make a connection with each one of them over my lifetime of work in the Aboriginal community. In total, I interviewed forty women, although only thirty-nine are presented in the book as I could not reach one participant at the time of publication to receive her consent about the final material. The interviews took place over a three-year period between the summer of 1996 and the summer of 1999.

The socio-demographics of the women are evident in their biographies (see the Reference List/Participant Biographies at the back of the book). I tried to get a cross-section of nations, but there are a majority of Iroquois and Ojibway women because these are the people that live in the area where I live. Most of the women I interviewed were between the ages of forty-five and sixty. This may be because they are the most accessible and most prominent leaders in our community. The age trend was also partly due to my choice of participants; I interviewed very few young women, having the bias that elders or women with more life experience would have more to offer. However, close to the end of the interviews, I was reminded by Michèle Audette (the twenty-eight-year-old president of the Quebec Native Women's Association) that the future is built by a collaborative vision of youth, elders, and all of the men and women in between. This was a good reminder to me that I need to think about the voice of younger people in future work.

The profiles in the biographies will give the reader some idea of where the interviewees are coming from. In addition, the following age chart will help the reader to better understand the experiences and historical contexts that stand behind their voices. For instance, women aged forty and over are likely to have attended residential school and would have witnessed the Aboriginal cultural and spiritual revival that took off in the1960s. Likewise, they have witnessed the many changes that have occurred as a result of feminist activity during this period. Women over fifty will likely have been raised close to the land, and women over sixty may have come through childhood with very little contact with non-Native people. Women who are younger will have had experiences that are shaped by these periods that preceded them and they may have had more experience walking the line between tradition and mainstream society, from the time that they were children and youth. The youngest interview participant was

Michèle Audette (at twenty-eight), and the oldest was Lillian McGregor (at seventy-five):

| 30-40 | 40-50 | 50-60 | 60-70 |
|---|---|---|---|
| Carol Couchie | Simona Arnatsiaq | Jeannette Armstrong | Marlene Brant Castellano |
| Valerie King-Green | Gertie Beaucage | Melanie Corbiere | Maria Campbell |
| Sandra Laronde | Andrea Chrisjohn | Ivy Chaske | Shawani Campbell Star |
|  | Diane Eaglespeaker | Laverne Gervais-Contois | Kathleen Green |
| Michèle Audette | Diane Hill | Monica Ittudsardjuat | Jan Longboat |
| (28) | Ida LaBillois-Montour | Emma LaRocque | Vera Martin |
|  | Nena Lacaille-Johnson | Edna Manitowabi | Dorris Peters |
|  | Myra Laramee | Maggie Paul | Shirley Williams |
|  | Lee Maracle | Lila Tabobondung |  |
|  | Sylvia Maracle | Helen Thundercloud | Lillian McGregor (75) |
|  | Catherine Martin |  |  |
|  | Ruth Morin |  |  |
|  | Barbra Nahwegahbow |  |  |
|  | Katie Rich |  |  |
|  | Theresa Tait |  |  |
|  | Wanda Whitebird |  |  |

Although I did not know many of the women I interviewed, they were all surprisingly forthcoming with their life stories, insights and perspectives. Overall the interviews were quite personal, but there were a few interviews that were quite theoretical, philosophical or sociological. With the women I knew, I was able to ask more direct questions about their work. Mostly, I just let the interviews take their course. I transcribed each interview, and from that material, I picked out those parts that spoke to me about Native womanhood. I used the interview transcripts in the same way I used the literature: as text that would allow me to build the vision and theory of my book. In the spirit of validating the oral knowledge of our women, I have tried to mix the literature and the interview text together, without discriminating between one and the other.

I hope that this section has made my work more transparent for the reader to be able to make her or his own critical analysis of my text. The other half of that critical process involves being able to analyse her or his own position as a reader in a particular subject position. This is something that I like to call "reader response-ability."

## READER RESPONSE-ABILITY

As a precaution against this work contributing to further misrepresentation of Native peoples, I ask that the reader consider her/his "response-ability." I take this concept from a talk by Ojibway poet and professor Kimberly Blaeser. In her presentation at a conference entitled "Talking on the Page: Editing Oral Aboriginal Text,"[20] Blaeser talked about the reader's responsibility to respond to the text. She pointed out that the way any text is read depends on the ability of the reader to respond to it. She related this to traditional oral practices in Native cultures, where it is assumed that the listener has as much a part in the creation of the story as the teller. In this way, the listener also carries responsibility for the knowledge that is transmitted.

One of the goals of this book is to create alternatives to the negative stereotypes of Native women as they have appeared in print. I have a job to do in writing a text that will hopefully deconstruct some of these stereotypes, and the reader also has a job. Before she or he engages in the text, I ask of them: What is your ability to respond to literature written about (and by) Native women? What kind of education and experience do you bring to this text? I think this is particularly important for the non-Native reader. This is not to suggest that every reader needs to be well versed in Native women's issues before approaching the work. It demands, simply, that the reader examine her/his own assumptions and approach the text accordingly. Are you hungry for the "Other"? What stereotypes inform your decision to read the book, and what do you expect to find? What will you do with the knowledge you have gained?

In addition to challenging stereotypical expectations (that is, looking for "wisdom" or "spirituality" from Natives), we must further consider our abilities as readers to shift out of a mainstream paradigm when reading about Native women. Paula Gunn Allen provides an example of discrepancy in the ability of the reader to respond. She offers a traditional story as told by a Keres man, and then presents two different interpretations of it: one from a mainstream feminist perspective and an alternative from a "feminist-tribal interpretation."[21] In the first interpretation, the women in the story seem greatly oppressed; in the second, the story is clearly a demonstration of the central role that women play in tribal life. The location of the reader thus shapes the interpretation of the story greatly, and in this case can foster ideas about the place of Native women that are unfounded.

The discussion of male-female division of responsibilities in this book could be read from a western perspective where such division almost certainly involves gender oppression. I have tried to help the reader to process the work contextually, and to see that the division between genders in Native traditions is more reflective of a need for balance, complementarity and reciprocity. In some cases, I worry that the English language and the concepts embedded within it will not convey the vision that the interview participants offer. When women, for instance, speak of a need for self-sufficiency, what the western mind is likely to engage in is a concept of western liberal individualism. This runs contrary to values typical of Native cultures, where a sense of self and the individual is grounded within a sense of responsibility to community and relationships. When the participants speak of a need to love and nurture oneself, they do not divorce themselves from responsibility to community, as with the "me first" western ideal. It may be that when Indigenous concepts are translated into English, they run the risk of being misinterpreted. It is likely that words such as "self-sufficient," "nurturing" or even "motherhood" are loaded with negative western connotations that impede an Indigenous understanding. Emma LaRocque has suggested that we seek new concepts and new words so that we do not get caught in the old patriarchal paradigms, and I think that there is a lot of work that we could do in this area yet. In the meantime, I have tried, as Paula Gunn Allen suggests, to frame these concepts in a "feminist-tribal perspective."

In her interview, Lila Tabobondung (Ojibway/Pottawatomi) made a comment about her "text" that serves as another good example of reader response-ability. Lila had just told me a lengthy story of how she received her "spirit name." She had been in a tipi where the spirits had visited, and she compared it to a shaking tent ceremony. When she finished her story she said, "But you would never tell that story to a white person, because they would say 'Oh, it was just the wind,' or whatever." In saying this, she acknowledged that I had the necessary background to respond to her story, but that others may not. It may be that she felt that the ability of the "white" mind to respond to her story is limited by a general rejection of belief in the spirits, the intrusion of science and empirical thinking and ethnocentrism. In any case, it is apparent that she felt this story would be misunderstood regardless of presentation.

I would not ask that anyone suspend their own frame of reference. I merely caution readers to acknowledge their personal abilities to respond. I ask that they resist the temptation to "claim" the text, and that they be open to new interpretations, paradigms and meanings.

From here, we can move together through this book.

*II*

# LOOKING BACK

## THE COLONIZATION OF NATIVE WOMANHOOD

❖

# LOOKING BACK

## The Colonization of
## Native Womanhood

❖

As Native peoples entering a new millennium, we have much to celebrate. The fact that we still exist, that we are living and working within our own communities is in and of itself an achievement. We have many strong women and men who are capably leading us as we rebuild our families, communities and nations. We have elders who will guide us, and children who give us our motivation.

We are also aware that we carry the struggles of the past five centuries into the new one. I have heard many people say, "It took us five hundred years to get into this situation; we are not going to fix it in fifty!" Poverty and violence are some of the heavy burdens that Native women are still carrying. In 1991, 33 percent of Native women were reported to have incomes that fell below the poverty line,[1] and we can only imagine that things have gotten worse in the current economic climate for the poor. Violence against women is so prevalent in our communities that it has become an "ordinary" part of everyday life for many Native families, and Native women who have not experienced some form of family violence are seen to be "the exception, not the rule."[2]

Over half of the women I interviewed indicated that they had endured relationships where they were physically, emotionally or sexually abused. Their needs have been considered secondary in partnerships with Native men as well as white men. Having lived through some of these things, many spoke frankly about the sexism that is operating within many contemporary Native families, communities and organizations. In the midst of these gender disparities, however, it is uncommon to hear Native women simply blame men for their condition. I think many Native women are aware that the social problems that hit them the hardest are the outcome of colonization. The struggle, then, becomes a struggle against the systems, policies and institutions that were enforced upon us by the colonizer. It is not a simplistic struggle against men or individuals.

In my introduction I described the distress I experienced in listening to one woman tell her story of abuse. The question that has driven me to write this book is, *How did this get to this point — where violence is so commonplace, and women and children are so disrespected? How did this happen?* In learning about the power that pre-contact Indigenous women held in the economic, political, spiritual and familial forums, and about how this was systematically dismantled by the church and state, I have been able to put a historical framework on the oppression that we see today.

## CHAPTER FOUR

# THE DISMANTLING OF GENDER EQUITY

❖

*I don't believe that sexism was thoroughly unknown before the Europeans came here. I have to figure that we had the same capacity for the "isms" in our original societies that we have today. What was available, however, were systems by which to balance that.*

— Gertie Beaucage (Ojibway)

THERE ARE CONSIDERABLE differences between the Indigenous nations of the Americas. Nonetheless, the values, lifestyles and systems that existed in our communities prior to the arrival of Europeans generally secured the status of Native women. Many Native cultures, values and practices safeguarded against the kinds of abuses permitted — and often encouraged — by western patriarchy. We had ways that protected us against the "isms" — sexism, racism, ageism, heterosexism. Our cultures promoted womanhood as a sacred identity, an identity that existed within a complex system of relations of societies that were based on balance.

In my personal exploration of Native female identity, I have looked at some of the ways our cultures traditionally promoted womanhood, and I discuss some of those traditions here. I think this is information that every Native woman should know. We should be aware that every Indigenous society had a sense of a woman's power and position within the community. Some societies, however, matrilocal or matrifocal societies, more readily demonstrated the status of their women. It is also important to know that life was certainly not always good for all Native women. Yet what we shared was a common sense of power, a power that was not part of the European woman's experience.

In my analysis, I have used examples from various nations across the Americas to compare the traditional status of Indigenous women to that of western women. I then look at the process that took place when western patriarchy infringed upon and altered our various understandings of womanhood. The Europeans who first arrived in Canada were shocked by the position of Aboriginal women in their respective societies. It was not long before they realized that, in order to dominate the land and the people that were occupying it, they needed to disempower the women. Indigenous systems that allocated power to women were incompatible with the kind of colonial power dynamics that would be necessary to maintain colonial power.

Colonization is a process that began five hundred years ago, and it continues today. The dismantling of Aboriginal womanhood took place all along this path, and at different times for different peoples. For this reason, I provide examples from a historical period covering that five-hundred-year span. Rather than speaking of "pre-contact" societies, which implies a finite culture of the past, I use the term "traditional." "Traditional" societies for the purpose of this section imply land-based cultures that have had minimal contact with Euro-Canadian society. For the peoples of eastern Canada, "contact" largely happened in the 1600s, and change from "traditional" lifestyle began then. Peoples in British Columbia have less of a history with Euro-Canada, as their "contact" has mostly occurred within the last century. For some northern peoples, the shift from a land-based culture has only occurred within the last twenty years.[3] We are all living with various degrees of "tradition," and it is therefore not easy to draw a historical line to mark the change in our status as women. Whether the date was 1578 or 1978, the colonial process and the consequent decline in status of Aboriginal women has been the same. My examples point out how this same process has happened at various junctures along the path of five hundred years of colonization, and I frequently shift between past and present.

I have also used some examples from contemporary cultures to show that many elements of "traditional gender equity" are still at work in our communities and to support my contention that "tradition" does not vanish, it merely changes over time. I move between the past and the present in an attempt to avoid the typical pitfall in writing about Native peoples, as if we were all dead, merely artifacts to be examined for the illumination of others. Native womanhood is not dead, but it has certainly been through a time of intense attack, which I trace through the following chapters.

## GENDER DIVISION OF LABOUR
## AND ECONOMIC AUTHORITY

When our societies were land-based, the division of labour was gendered. Men worked outside the community as hunters and warriors and women within, in the areas of childcare, agriculture, food preparation and housing. These divisions accommodated the work required for a land-based lifestyle. In the words of trapper Kaaren Olsen: "The divisions of labour were based on practical needs. Because women are reproducers as well as producers, their labour consisted mainly of work at the home. It was the men who procured the necessary items which were then turned into food, shelter or clothing."[4]

Although men and women had their spheres of work, they were not restricted from engaging in each other's work, if it became necessary. Maria Campbell remembers how this applied to her own community: "Those old guys lived in the bush, and you don't always have a wife out there to do the cooking for you. You have to be able to do it yourself, which is what my dad used to say." Similarly, women had to provide for themselves and their families in the absence of a man. Native women had to learn essential trapping and hunting skills, and many contemporary women recall watching their grandmothers hunt, fish and trap. Some women I spoke with remember learning these skills as girls. Michèle Audette (Innu) pointed out that this knowledge allowed each gender to have respect for the work that was typically done by the other. Many nations also had greater flexibility around the gendered work roles. For example, there have always been a small number of Native women warriors in the various nations. In some societies, neither women nor men were restricted from doing each other's work if they felt they were more suited for it, or if it made better use of their natural abilities.[5]

Within our land-based systems of labour, Native men's work was never considered to be more valuable than Native women's work. Native women were oblivious to the public/private split that Europeans brought with them. The incoming European division of labour trapped our women within the limitations of the western domestic role. Such a system, in which men were to go out and do the "real" work, while women had to play a secondary, supporting and inherently less important role in the home made no sense to our people. Our ancestors understood that the work of every individual was necessary for the well-being of the family, the community and the nation. There was, therefore, no concept that those involved in domestic labour were "not working." "Women's work" was highly valued.

Because their work was valued, women were given authority over the community's most precious resource: food. Although men were primarily responsible for hunting, "women's work" was essential for converting the raw materials into resources for the community. In the case of the Chippewa, it has been noted, "The finished product is what leads to status, influence and reputation. Rotting flesh, poorly dried meat, or raw hides gain a man little."[6] Women also had economic power because of their role in agriculture. Women were the farmers in many traditional Native societies — Cherokee, Choctaw, Hurons, and Iroquois — and were often directly responsible for providing food for the community. The Iroquois acknowledged that the strength of the tribe was only as strong as the work of women in food production.

In addition to producing the food, Native women were also responsible for food distribution. In Iroquois culture, stored food was considered wealth and was completely controlled by the women. Because they controlled food distribution, Iroquois women could hinder or prevent war parties by holding back the supplies.[7] In many nations, men would procure meat, but it took a woman to distribute it. Clara Sue Kidwell has noted this practice in Choctaw society: "A man who killed a deer would leave the carcass and walk home to tell his wife where it was. She would take the family horse to carry home the meat, and she thus assumed the right to distribute it as she saw fit."[8] Europeans were amazed by the control that women exercised over food — something they saw as property. Historian Carol Devens writes:

After spending the winter of 1633–34 in the bush with a Montagnais band, Paul LeJeune described this exchange with amazement: "Men leave the arrangement of the household to the women, without interfering with them: they cut, and decide, and give away [meat] as they please, without making the husband angry."[9]

Devens concludes, "A woman's distribution of meat to families within the group established her autonomy and her authority to control food while reinforcing a sense of community and interdependency among households."[10]

Sto:lo/Métis writer Lee Maracle maintains that traditional female economic authority extended to all of the materials that men brought into the community: "Goods coming into the village belonged to the women. It was determined what was essential to the survival of the nation, and then the excess was handed over to the men, to engage in trade." In some nations (among them the Ojibway, Winnebago, Sauk and Mesquakie), women engaged in trade themselves, both for their own goods and for those of their families.[11] Whatever their relationship to the outside world regarding goods, women in many nations were accorded jurisdiction over how the goods were distributed. In Maracle's estimation, this system allowed both men and women to participate in the "economic development" of the community.

Women also had authority over issues of property. Native people were never property owners in the western economic sense, where property is private and may be bought and sold; yet there was a concept that Native women had rights to the tools and products of their work. Women were often responsible for lodging, and so traditional housing, like the tipi, was considered to be the woman's property.[12] Juaneño/Yaqui scholar Marie Annette Jaimes states, "Among the Lakota, men owned nothing but their clothing, a horse for hunting, weapons and spiritual items: homes, furnishings, and the like were the property of their wives."[13] In nations where women worked the land, this too was considered to be within their authority. Land ownership has traditionally been attributed to the women among the Iroquois.[14] Anthropologist Joy Bilharz writes: "Because women were horticulturists, their more intensive use of land established their rights to it. In this context, men merely cleared the land for them."[15] The authority of the women over the land was even enshrined in the Great Law of the

Iroquois of the fifteenth century: "Women shall be considered the progenitors of the Nation. They shall own the land and soil."[16] Traditional Plateau[17] societies were set up so that women and men were completely independent in terms of authority over personal property. Neither husband nor wife could claim the property of the other.[18]

Property ownership was much more equitable in traditional societies. In the wake of colonization, however, this too began to shift. As European settlement took hold, the western relationship towards private property and capital was forced upon all Native people.[19] Across the continent, Indigenous societies were barraged with the foreign concept of private property — land, livestock, housing — all of which inevitably belonged to individual men. The split between public and private labour and the introduction of the moneyed economies were devastating to the traditional economic authority of Native women.

Carol Devens has traced how this loss took place during the fur trade of the seventeenth and eighteenth centuries.[20] As the trade evolved, Native women were displaced from their role in the disposal of hides and furs. They lost the status they had previously known as critical producers in the economy. Their loss was compounded by the fact that Native communities began to buy merchandise from the European traders. This trade replaced goods that had traditionally been produced by Native women.[21] The shift from subsistence to production-for-exchange economies marginalized Native women from economic participation and the authority that went with it.[22]

Colonization further robbed Native women of their traditional economic relationship to land and property. The first president of the United States, George Washington, succinctly described his plans for "civilization" as follows: "to turn Native men into industrious, republican farmers, and women into chaste, orderly housewives."[23] These instructions were completely incompatible with societies in which the women were traditionally the farmers. Native women's economic status was also devalued through the relentless policies of church and state, which insisted on granting exclusive title and rights to the land to men. These policies dramatically affected the Iroquois, as Sally Roesch Wagner writes:

> Missionaries insisted that women's sphere was the home and that Indian men should take up farming. When accomplished, this

change would not only take away women's economic independence, leaving them as dependent as white women; it also tore at the very fabric of the culture, which held that women, who produced life, were the only appropriate group to bring life from the soil. Despite resistance, Indian land, of which women had been the keepers for the nation, was often divided up among Indian men as "heads of the family."[24]

In the midst of this tremendous pressure, however, traces of traditional female economic authority continued. For example, in some societies, as men became wage earners, the Native women maintained control of the household economy. In a 1914 study of the Tlingit, one startled anthropologist noted, "The husband's earnings are wholly turned over to his wife. She is, therefore, the banker of the household. If he desires to make a purchase, he must appeal to her to get her consent."[25]

As Native societies began to participate in the settler economy, the idea that women were responsible for managing finances was most protected in matrilocal societies. Certain matrilocal peoples transferred control of capital to the women who held authority. In the farming economy of the Navajo, women secured economic power through control of vast herds of sheep.[26] This practice continued through the generations. Emmi Whitehorse, a contemporary Navajo artist, explains: "In my family, the female owned everything. They owned the land and the sheep. They nurtured and carried the family."[27] Okanagan educator and artist Jeannette Armstrong talks about being raised in a family where her grandmother was in charge of a ranch with 400 head of cattle. Her father and her uncles worked the ranch where her grandmother was not only the manager but also the owner of all the property.

Shifts in gender relations have been traced as recently as the 1970s among the Cree of Northern Ontario and Alberta. In their study of women's employment among the James Bay Cree Jennifer Blythe and Peggy McGuire point out:

> The notion that men be primary wage earners and senior partners in their families developed among them as a result of European influence. Yet, in most families that continued trapping in the

bush, considerable autonomy remained with the women. The flexible complementarity of gender roles traditionally enjoyed in Cree families became eroded after women's unpaid work in the home became less valued than work outside the home. This did not occur until after the Cree became urbanized.[28]

Rosemary Brown has written about the changes in gender relations experienced by the Lubicon Lake Cree of Alberta.[29] The Lubicon were forced to abandon traditional economy based on hunting, trapping and gathering in the late 1970s as a result of oil and gas exploitation in their territory. This radically changed the economic authority of women, who were no longer able to engage in complementary roles with men around the production and distribution of food, and of furs, hides and leather goods for the market. Euro-Canadian hegemony continued to demand that Native families become individual units of consumption, with women "dependent" on men for access to the purchased goods that replaced traditional foods and supplies.[30] Brown points out that women were also restricted from engaging in the new economy while looking after their children. Previously, women had been able to work collectively on processing meat and hides, for example. This permitted them to "work" and look after children at once. Wage labour economy had the inevitable result of increasing the gap between the private and the public domain.[31] With the settler economic system, Lubicon women have been forced to either work outside the home, or "not work" and stay at home with the children. Their economic status has plummeted as a result of this system.

The authority given to women as the centre of the home and community has been turned upside down by western ideas of the roles of women in the home. Native women who once made decisions about home and community finances were expected to turn this authority over to the men who participated in the western economy.

Practical reasons for gendered division of labour are disappearing with modernity, but some families have held onto the principle that women manage the economics of the family and community by virtue of their relationship with the children. Jeannette Armstrong explains: "The female needs are where the family needs are. The female needs to take care of the children; make sure they have enough, and make sure they grow up. It isn't for her. And the way she organizes is in that capacity." Armstrong contends that economic decisions that centre around the children safeguard against policies that are "always about material wealth and power, but never about home and health and security and wellness."

## WOMEN'S ROLE IN POLITICS

*Where are your women?*

*The speaker is Attakullakulla, a Cherokee Chief renowned for his shrewd and effective diplomacy. He has come to negotiate a treaty with the whites. Among his delegation are women "as famous in war, as powerful in the council.".. .*

*... Implicit in the Chief's question, "Where are your women?" the Cherokee hear, "Where is your balance? What is your intent?" They see the balance is absent and are wary of the white man's motives. They intuit the mentality of destruction.*

*I turn to my own time. I look at the Congress, the Joint Chiefs of Staff, the Nuclear Regulatory Commission ... to the hierarchies of my church, my university, my city, my children's school. "Where are your women?" I ask.*

— Marilou Awiakta (Cherokee/Appalachian )[32]

Marilou Awiakta clearly demonstrates the contrast between western and Indigenous political systems. Native women were not traditionally excluded from decision making, as has been the case for women in western politics. Native women had political authority because our nations recognized the value of having input from all members of society. The inclusion of women in decisions was critical for the security of the nation. Like her Cherokee ancestors, Awiakta points to the mentality of destruction, which sees nothing wrong with excluding 50 percent of the population from positions that are politically powerful within the nation, the community, the church, the school.

There are a number of ways that our women traditionally exercised political power. Any one of our Iroquois sisters and brothers can attest to the fact that their women had (and still have, albeit to a much lesser degree) political power, and there are a number of written works that confirm this.[33] Iroquois women had a role as leaders vis-à-vis the outside world, as is evident in their role in negotiating some treaties.[34] In traditional Iroquois systems of governance, women's political authority extended to choosing and deposing the chiefs.[35] Chieftainships were determined and managed by matrons of certain families who held meetings with other clan women to make these decisions. Iroquois women also exercised their political authority through participation in community meetings:

> [Iroquois] women often addressed councils; their opinion was asked and heeded. When tribal or village decisions had to be made, both men and women attended a meeting. Though the chiefs normally did the public speaking, women at times stepped up and, by their authority as owners of the land and their concern for the future of their children, took an active part in telling sachems what they should do.[36]

The Mohawks also had a women's council that would bring their issues to the Grand Council or to all of the people, if necessary. According to Sylvia Maracle, a women's council still operates. It travels between various Mohawk communities to hold public meetings. Although these women may have some influence on the modern-day political system, they no longer hold the official status or authority they did before the introduction of an elected chief and council.

Other Native societies had similar political systems that ensured the participation and influence of women. Sto:lo Elder Dorris Peters recalls her grandmother telling her "women were able to choose the chiefs, and women were able to fire the chiefs." Like the Iroquois, the Cherokee had women's councils whereby women had direct input into political decisions.[37] Some nations had elders' councils that were comprised of men and women. Simona Arnatsiaq, co-ordinator of the Women's Program for the Qiqiktani Inuit Association, points out that traditional Inuit politics were dealt with by both female and male elders who would discuss and decide on matters pertaining to the community. She confirmed that informal leadership of this nature is still operating in many Inuit communities today. Monica Ittusardjuat is an Inuk currently living in Iqaluit, Nunavut. She describes how women were generally called upon to deal with matters related to community harmony and wellness, but qualifies, "there was no rule that said it had to be a woman. It was according to ability and what people did."

Some societies had both male and female chiefs. Wit'suwet'en chieftainships, which are still in place today (but not universally respected or recognized), are hereditary. Leadership positions can fall on a male or a female child, and everyone takes direction from the wisest and the eldest (male or female) chief.[38] In Plateau societies, both women and men filled the role of chief. The wives of male chiefs also served as advisors, or as chiefs in the case of a husband's absence or death.[39] The Algonkian and the Sioux had similar practices.[40]

If formal political systems did not include women's voices, then women found the authority to voice their opinions through the influence they exercised over their male partners. This type of indirect evidence has been noted among the Blackfoot and the Sioux.[41] Be-te Paul points out that in Maliseet society, "the elder women were the ones to hold places in council and to guide the men ... We had chiefs, but the elder women were behind the men; they were listened to and held in high respect."[42] Inuit women, too, influenced politics by stating their opinions to their husbands. These opinions were taken seriously, as they were a way of accessing the collective opinion of the women of the community. In public gatherings, older women were likely to voice opinions about policy decisions. Their status as elders secured their authority, as it still does today: "Position in the age hierarchy protects old women from recrimination and retaliation so that they are in a position to insinuate the 'women's vote' into what would otherwise be an all-male 'caucus.'"[43]

It may seem incredible that this territory we know as Canada once hosted societies that afforded significant political power to those currently most marginalized: older women. Yet in "Indian country" the political authority of older women is not so far in the past. Many contemporary women can describe the political authority their grandmothers held in their families and societies, even after the introduction of western political systems. Jeannette Armstrong (Okanagan) recalls that "it was traditionally always women who made decisions about resources, who made decisions about land, who made decisions about the wealth, and who carefully constructed a balance of power in the family, and a balance of work and task making and so on." Armstrong grew up in a family where her grandmother played the role of decision-maker. Maria Campbell's great-grandmother held a similar role. Campbell points out that the authority of her grandmother was based on her relationship to the children:

> My great-grandmother was the head of our family. No decision was made without her first giving her blessing. My dad and uncles would sit down and talk to her when they were going to do something. If she said no, nobody questioned it. They trusted her, because her primary responsibility was to the children. Her decisions were based completely on the children. They didn't question that.

It becomes clear when we listen to these women that their societies understood the significant roles, responsibilities and skills involved in being the primary caregivers of children. Their societies upheld the people who held these roles and gave them the power to make decisions about their families, communities and nations.

In spite of the fact that many families and societies held on to traditional female political authority, Native women on the whole experienced a tremendous loss with the introduction of European political systems and laws. *The Gradual Enfranchisement Act* of 1869 decreed that Native women who married non-Native men lost their status, and that Native women who married Native men from other bands lost their rights in their home communities. This *Gradual Enfranchisement Act* was followed by the *Indian Act* in 1876, which defined who was an Indian and what Indians could and could not do. The Act legally took away long-established rights for Native women and left them with fewer rights than Indian men. Native women were categorically denied the right to vote in band elections. They could not hold political office, nor could they speak at public meetings.[44] The Act also prevented Native women from voting on issues of band territory. It was not until the 1950s that Native women regained the right to participate in these public and political affairs. Revisions to the *Indian Act* gave status Indian women the right to vote in band elections, but they were not permitted to vote in provincial or federal elections in Canada until the 1960s.

The *Indian Act* not only dispossessed women of community/communal authority, it very severely dismantled their authority within the family through the imposition of patriarchal marriage and property rights. Kathleen Jamieson has written extensively about the losses Native women experienced. In the following passage, written in 1978, she points to the inequities that Native women *were still living with at that time:*

> The woman, on marriage, must leave her parents' home and her reserve. She may not own property on the reserve and must dispose of any property she does hold. She may be prevented from inheriting property left to her by her parents. She cannot take any further part in band business. Her children are not recognized as Indian and are therefore denied access to cultural and social amenities of the Indian community. And, most punitive of all, she may be prevented from returning to live with her family on the reserve, even is she is in dire need, very ill, a widow, divorced or separated. Finally, her body may not be buried on the reserve with those of her forebears.[45]

These laws were not repealed until 1985. For over a century, Native women were shut out of their communities and families. Women who kept their status were shut out of political and economic decision-making because they were restricted from owning property. Even on the death of their husbands they had no inheritance rights: "On the death of an Indian, his 'goods and chattels' and land rights were to be passed to his children. The wife was excluded, her maintenance being the responsibility of the children."[46]

Catherine Martin, a Mi'kmaw from Nova Scotia, points out that the removal of women from the political process was part of a deliberate dismantling of the culture overall. When the colonizer came, she says, "they saw a society where women were respected and children were respected, and this was very much against the colonialist or the patriarchal world that they came from." The *Indian Act* banished Native women who married white men, while at the same time awarding Indian status to white women who married Native men. Martin comments on how this may have been part of an assimilation strategy:

> In order to break down and destroy a culture, you have to get to the root of it. The heart of Aboriginal cultures is the women, as givers of life. So it makes sense to start making policies that would banish the women, the givers of language, culture and life. They are the ones who bring Native children into this world and teach them their way. It made sense to make a policy so that white women could come in and take over that role and start teaching the white ways. This was a form of cultural genocide.

Whatever the intent, the patriarchal provisions of the *Indian Act* removed Native women from their roles as decision-makers and teachers and robbed them of their voice in community affairs. Once active participants in the management of community affairs, they were forced into positions that held little power. This deliberate state action imposed on Native women the devalued position of women in western society. White women had no power to vote, they did not hold political positions and were not included in decision-making on matters ranging from the family, to community, to nation. Native women who held political power were a threat to this kind of a system. They could effectively be put in their place through assimilation or by making them the same as white women, as Janice Acoose explains:

> Indigenous women's political powers (including and especially the freedom to exercise control over their bodies and relations with others) were almost completely eradicated while their energies were channeled into less threatening activities, such as ladies' auxiliary groups, church rituals (marriage, baptism, confession, communion, confirmations and funerals), as well as far less important social activities such as church sponsored teas, bake sales and bazaars.[47]

For the first time in our history, our women found themselves on the margins, in the ghettos of the evolving culture. The exclusion of our women from decision-making in important political and community matters not only disempowered the women, it also disempowered

Indigenous cultures. Another fundamental part of this process was the dismantling of Native female spiritual authority.

## SPIRITUAL POWER OF WOMEN

Spirituality has always played a significant role in our cultures. Even now, many Native peoples do not divorce spirituality from politics, business, education, health or social organization. Native women's roles in traditional spiritual practices, ceremonies and beliefs demonstrate that Native women held positions of esteem in their societies.

Creation stories strongly influence culture. They often form the foundation for economic, family and political relations. Many Native creation stories are female centred, and there are many stories that speak about the role of women in bringing spirituality to the people. The Iroquois attribute the beginnings of the earth to a female, rather than a male.[48] Among the Sioux, the White Buffalo Woman is recognized as the culture bearer, as she brought the sacred pipe, and thus elemental ritual and ceremony to the Sioux people.[49] Paula Gunn Allen has researched the centrality of female spiritual figures in a number of Native traditions, including the Keres Pueblo, the Hopi, the Navajo, the Lakota and the Abenaki. "Certainly," she writes, "there is reason to believe that many American Indian tribes thought that the primary potency in the universe was female, and that understanding authorizes all tribal activities, religious or social."[50]

Creation is understood to be within the realm of the female because of the profound understanding that women bring forth life. Traditional Cree/Métis teacher Myra Laramee talks about "womanspirit" as the "first truth":

> When Creator called for the universal energies to come together in that sound, that vibration, what came forward were the universal energies to create Mother Earth. Womanspirit is more than Mother Earth. It is those universal energies that come together. The manifestation of the physical form of her behaviour is woman. We emulate everything that she teaches the universe must be. So it isn't just Mother Earth. It is how we are connected.

This understanding of womanspirit is radically different than the Judeo-Christian stories that are male centred. In these stories, the creator is a white male, an authority figure standing above all others, as opposed to being part of our interconnectedness. Patriarchy is dependent on that ultimate (white) male authority figure, and it is this patriarchal consciousness that now shapes much of our world. If God is a white man, who created the first man, and then later created a God-son (who comes by way of a virgin), our social relations reflect a male-centred version of both creation and authority. Where is the creative power of woman in this story? Male-centred creation stories negate the creative/spiritual power of woman, something that is often prominent in Indigenous creation stories.

In male-dominated religions, women have no significant spiritual role to play. Within the spiritual structures of many traditional Native societies, however, women held significant authority and esteem. They acted as shamans and medicine people, which made them doctors, teachers, leaders and workers for the people.[51] If they did not act as shamans, Native women often played critical roles in sponsoring[52] or supporting spiritual ceremonies.

We continue to honour many of these practices today, as many ceremonies cannot take place without the input of women. The Sun Dance has been called an "obvious manifestation of the superior spiritual power of women." This ceremony is led by women and "cannot be held if no woman is willing to undertake the arduous fasting and heavy responsibility of the Holy Woman role."[53] Blackfoot Sun Dancer Diane Eaglespeaker confirms the critical role women play in the contemporary ceremony: "In our Sun Dance culture here, the head person is a woman. When the holy woman puts up her Okan (her lodge), the Horn Society Sun Dance starts."

Many Native spiritual traditions emphasize balance between men and women and structure ceremonies in ways that require equal input from men and women. This teaches us about equality and the need for one another. The late Ojibway Elder Art Solomon referred to women as the intermediary between man and the Creator: "She takes from both and gives back to both."[54] Through their ability to bring new life into the world, women play an intermediary role between life on earth and in the spirit world. This role is exemplified in ceremonies where the woman appears to be a helper to the male medicine person, but is, in fact, acting as the intermediary. Professor Alice Kehoe describes this role in Blackfoot ceremonies:

> Women are seen as the intermediary or means through which power has been granted to humans. This crucial role appears in medicine bundle openings: only a woman should unwrap and re-wrap a holy bundle. She hands the powerful objects inside to a male celebrant. It is important to note that the woman sits quietly behind the man and to European eyes seems to be the servant. The Blackfoot see the woman as more powerful than the man, who dares not handle the bundle entire and alone.[55]

Birthing children is also seen as the manifestation of the woman's role as intermediary. Childbirth can be a dangerous and life-threatening time for both the mother and the baby, and it is the doorway through which all people enter life. Betty Laverdure (Seneca) talks about how this physical experience is an affirmation of a woman's spiritual essence:

> They say that medicine people have certain requirements, near-death experience. Some even have out-of-body experiences. Go into the spirit world and they have constant communication with the spirits. But the woman does this each time she gives birth. It's a near-death experience.[56]

The "near-death" experience of birthing a child can be equivalent to other forms for spiritual enlightenment. It is a time when women are involved in bringing life from the spirit world to the earthly world, and it may be a time when she herself is at risk of re-entering the spirit world. As both birth and death are passages between the spirit and the material world, childbirth is a time when women are intermediaries between spirit life and life on earth.

The equation of women as creator and intermediary is also evident in the sweat lodge ceremony, which is often referred to as a symbol of a mother's womb.[57] People go into the sweat lodge to communicate with the spirit world, and the lodge, like mother's womb, is a place of transformation. The lodge is also a place for purification. Some women, like Ivy Chaske (Dakota), believe that women do not need to go into the sweat lodge because they have the ability to cleanse and purify themselves through menstruation.

Traditional understandings of menstruation were central to the understanding of creative female energy, and the power that it carried. As with birth, menstruation was perceived as a spiritually charged occurrence. Taboos that called for the isolation of menstruating women were common among Native cultures. Such practices were not (as has been propagated) a reflection of their cultures' thinking women were "impure" at this time.[58] Rather, the menstrual period was understood as a time in which women exerted a phenomenal amount of power that precluded them from taking part in certain ceremonies.[59] This belief holds true among traditional thinkers today. Women who are on their "moon time" do not participate in many traditional ceremonies, and this stems from a recognition of their power. In an interview with journalist Diane Meili, Cree Elder George Kehewin explains:

> Women are far, far ahead of men. It's quite hard to understand, but when you start living in the Native culture, you will. You are like Mother Earth, who once a year in the spring, washes herself down the river to the ocean. Everything ... all the debris is washed away. Same thing with a woman, except it's every month. It's that power you have. You cannot enter a lodge or a spiritual gathering because you will kill all the prayers and offerings in there. You are more powerful than all of it, and if you come in you can't fool the spirits. At Sundances, if a woman in her time comes near the lodge, the singers and dancers know. I have to tell the older women to tell the younger ones not to stay around if they are like that. It's not because we don't like them, it's the power they have. They're way ahead of me.[60]

Myra Laramee (Cree/Métis) says that in her culture, every time a ceremony was happening, a moon lodge went up. It was the job of the women who were "on their time" to go to the lodge and pray that any negativity could be filtered through their blood and back into the ground so that it could be neutralized through Mother Earth. This was an affirmation of women's power during the menstrual period.

The power attached to menstruating women allowed them in some cultures to have control over certain functions in their societies, as exemplified in this description of the Pomo of California:

> This form of extraordinary power gave women a certain secular
> power in the sense of controlling the group's activities. If a number
> of women were menstruating simultaneously, there could be liter-
> ally no hunting, fishing, ceremonial dancing, gambling or war.
> The captain and other professional men such as hunt or fishing
> leaders had to design their tasks around their women's periods.[61]

Whatever the traditions, menstruation was a sign of the incredible
power of the feminine.

Contact with Europeans was to change this thinking. Judeo-Christian culture saw menstruation not as a manifestation of female power,
but as a manifestation of female sin, contamination and inferiority.
Missionaries did not understand menstruation as a sacred gift; rather,
they taught women to see it from western eyes, as a "curse." Between the
mid-1800s and the 1970s, up to a third of Native children spent their
childhood in residential schools.[62] By the time residential schools had
reached their peak in the 1930s, almost 75 per cent of all Native children
in Canada between the ages of seven and fifteen were attending them.[63]

The majority of Native girls during the residential school era
had to pass through puberty in these institutions. Ceremonies around
menstruation were replaced with, at best, no recognition of this passage.
Cree Elder Kathleen Green recalls being terrified when her first
menstruation occurred. Green was a residential school student at the
time and thought she was dying until some older girls explained
what was happening. In many cases, there were definite menstruation "rites of passage" based in shame and sin. Ojibway professor
Shirley Williams recalls learning that menstruation was very "dirty,"
which contradicted what she had been taught by her parents — that
puberty was a sacred time. Mi'kmaw writer Isabelle Knockwood has
documented the menstrual experiences of girls who attended the
Shubenacadie Indian Residential School in Nova Scotia in the
1930s, '40s and '50s. Girls at this school were subjected to an "inspection" that was intrusive and undignifying. It is described here by
residential school survivor Nora Bernard:

> I don't know what Sister Wejuipsetamite'w's [the sniffer] problem
> was, for instance, she used to have us girls form a line and take

the crotch of our panties and spread them on the palm of our hands as we all walked by her so she could see if they were dirty. She told us that she didn't want us going to church smelly but why didn't she have all of us take a bath or a shower before church?[64]

Another residential school survivor from Shubenacadie remembers this inspection as "the most degrading experience of my life." She explains that the girls used to immediately wash the stains from their underwear and wear them wet, adding, "We didn't know why we were afraid."[65] Knockwood demonstrates the overall punitive approach to menstruation in this passage:

> During the 1950s the nun in change of the girls' side decided that the girls would no longer be provided with sanitary towels at night. Only those with exceptionally light periods were able to avoid bleeding onto the sheets. Every morning the sheets had to be held up for inspection. Some girls remember being sent to wash out the bloodstains. Others were beaten as well. For some girls, being beaten four days out of every month became a routine event.[66]

Knockwood recalls her sister's "rite of passage" following her first menstruation. She was unprepared and unaware about menstruation, and the nuns ended up shaving her head and telling her "Go to bed, you dirty girl."[67] Shirley Williams recalls a similar type of treatment that took place at the residential school that she attended in Spanish, Ontario. She remembers that if girls had an "accident" by failing to realize the onset of menstruation, they would be made to wear their soiled panties around their head as they were marched to the wash-room to wash. Williams states "This action told me to be ashamed of my bodily functions and I came to hate myself as a woman." The residential school "rites of passage" related to menstruation were almost the inverse of Native menstrual traditions, such as among the Ojibway and Cree where girls receive extensive teachings about puberty and womanhood while having their hair bathed in cedar water by their grandmothers (an act of love and beauty).

The shame-based interpretation of menstruation plays into the spiritual dislocation of Native women with the arrival of Christianity. With the coming of the Europeans, the male creator displaced the primacy of the female creator.[68] Women's spiritual identity was limited to the troublesome role of Eve or the impossible role of the Virgin Mary. This radically changed how Native women were treated in the community by Native men. It began from the earliest points of contact. As sociologist Karen Anderson points out, it was already evident in seventeenth century Huron society as a result of their interactions with the people of New France:

> With Christianization a great deal of anger was directed towards women. Women were identified as responsible for any unpleasantness, insecurity, or danger that the members of society, especially the men, found themselves in. A great deal of energy was directed towards controlling women and they became the legitimate brunt of hostility — both of their own self-loathing, and of men's loathing and mistrust.[69]

Women became devalued spiritually and devalued by their male counterparts. Missionaries pushed the idea that everything to do with Native spirituality was evil, and specifically that women were evil. What had been traditional sources of power were converted to danger, and then turned inward to destroy the cultures. In his essay on "The Female Spirit in Native American Religions," Jordan Power asserts that "the fact that the primary healing spirits were female must have also been a factor in the reversal of traditional values."[70] Females were equated with evil, and their important roles in Native spirituality fitted conveniently with the missionaries argument that Native spiritual ways were evil.

Overall, the church played a major role in "introducing the repression and exploitation of women as sexual objects, [and] as reproducers,"[71] and those who resisted conversion to Christianity were further problematized. Women were troublesome, and the power they held needed to be put in its place. By using Eve to create an image of woman as evil, and by calling upon the image of a passive and domesticated Mary, the missionaries were able to accomplish their goal of wresting traditional power from Indigenous women. The loss of spiritual power was felt in every aspect of Native women's lives and was connected to a loss of their political power. Among the Carrier, this loss was directly tied to the introduction of Christianity:

Christian proselytizing eroded women's sources of autonomy and authority. As clan-based trade and exchange disintegrated, women lost opportunities for trading independently among themselves ... Women were hampered even in their efforts to be indirectly included in community affairs. For, not only did priests explicitly forbid women a public voice in church or village affairs, they also ridiculed and berated men who took guidance from women.[72]

As the church replaced Native spirituality and became a powerful agent in the structure of Indigenous communities, Native women's loss of both political and spiritual authority was achieved. The political power held by the church made no room for women, and the missionaries sought to impose an order that would augment the priests' power and put white men in charge of authority. To accomplish this, church and state worked together until they had "established local political hierarchies that explicitly excluded women and that were empowered to uphold Catholic notions of patriarchy."[73] In a departure from traditional ways, Native men were encouraged to assume exclusive positions as community leaders and heads of families. Saskatchewan Métis women aptly summarize the role for Native women in the newcomers' spiritual tradition: "Church is run by priests and men, women get to put the flowers on the altar."[74] Through colonization and the work of missionaries, women were excluded from and handed a marginal role in the spiritual life of their communities, which went hand in hand with the eradication of their political power.

## CHAPTER FIVE

# MARRIAGE, DIVORCE AND FAMILY LIFE

❖

TO DISCUSS THE CONCEPT of marriage as it existed in pre-Christian Native societies is difficult, as there were so many different traditions regarding this type of union. Women made autonomous decisions about these partnerships in some cases, but many societies practised arranged marriages. Polygamy was acceptable in many societies prior to Christian influence. Some societies expected that the union of two people was a lifetime arrangement but in others "divorce" or separation was common and in others still "marriage" was viewed as a primarily economic relationship that had nothing to do with sexual fidelity or loyalty. Native women's status and experiences with marriage were therefore not uniform. Like the people of western society today, partnerships were formed, but the expectations of those partnerships were very different from nation to nation.

Regardless of these differences, Native women typically had power, respect and recognition within their families. As part of a family unit, a Native woman was interdependent, yet in many nations her autonomy as an individual in this unit was also respected. It may be that the principle of non-interference which was prevalent in many Indigenous nations was helpful to Native women in the arena of marriage. The principle of non-interference meant, among other things, that no one person had the right to tell another what to do.

This principle was honoured by the Hurons in New France: "The Huron, unlike the French, had an overwhelming commitment to individual freedom. There were no institutional mechanisms available to limit that freedom from extending to women as well as men."[1] Marriage for the Huron woman did not mean that she had to give up the freedom and autonomy as a Huron individual. As such, there was no concept of obedience to a husband. This was a major difference between seventeenth-century Huron marriage relations and Christian marriage relations. Christian marriages established institutional control of men over women, as wives were expected to be subservient to their husbands.

In the matrilocal societies of the Navajo, Seminoles, Cherokee and Iroquois a woman's autonomy in marriage was even more pronounced. The central position of the woman in the family was sustained by living with her own kin. There was no way for men in these societies to assume the position of "head" of the family; rather, they became part of the interdependent family unit that ensured the central role of the mothers. The man joined the woman's family to assist with the survival of that family; he would work for the well-being of the family that had descended from the mother's line. As Jeannette Armstrong points out, this meant that the woman's property was handed down through a line of women, and that women were assisted by the men.

Some traditional Aboriginal marriage practices would not be desirable by today's standards and some were disadvantageous to women. For instance, the Choctaw and the Inuit had arranged marriages. Apphia Agalakti Awa, an Inuit who was born in 1931, describes her arranged marriage at the age of fourteen as "a really unhappy time for me." She was married before she had her first period and, despite her resistance, was forced to go and live with a man who was much older than she was.[2] There are examples from other societies, however, in which a woman was not forced to take a man she did not want. In Choctaw tradition, the marriage ceremony "consisted of a ritualized pursuit in which the young man chased the woman. If she allowed herself to be caught, the marriage was confirmed. If not, the disappointed suitor withdrew."[3] In Plateau custom, the parents arranged first marriages of both male and female children. Children could then choose subsequent marriage partners. If the child wanted out of a marriage, she or he simply left. Plateau individuals could have several spouses in a lifetime.[4]

A number of societies (such as the Inuit, Lakota and Siksika) practised polygamy. Some Native women argue that polygamy can not be considered according to western/Christian standards of marriage.

In fact, it may have provided a better life for women. Virginia Driving Hawk Sneve writes, "Polygamy — a practice that most whites found reprehensible — lessened an individual wife's duties. The more wives a man had, the more skins could be tanned for the comfort of the lodge; however, the more women in the lodge, the more they controlled the man."[5] She reports that Sioux women who married white men found themselves in monogamous marriages that increased their workload:

> Indian wives of white men soon found that their lives were filled with drudgery if there were no "sister-wife" to share the household and conjugal duties. A single wife gave birth more frequently and over a longer period of time, and, as a result, suffered more in childbirth.[6]

Native women were not always happy with these arrangements. As anthropologist Mary Shepardson points out, there were "ambivalent reactions" to polygamy in Navajo culture: "We knew of cases in which the first wife drove off the interloper and others in which the first wife herself was chased out of the hogan."[7] There were options for women who wished to leave polygamous marriages. In Sioux culture, "many left their men, taking with them their possessions and children (who were considered to 'belong' to the mother). Such a woman was usually welcome to return to her parents' home, where her father, if able, provided for her. If he could not, the woman's brothers or male cousins assumed the responsibility until she remarried."[8] Yet some women chose suicide as a way out of polygamous marriages.[9] In Siksika culture, as writer Beverly Hungry Wolf reports, suicide was not uncommon among young women who were betrothed to older men and in love otherwise.[10]

Polygamy may not have been the most ideal situation for women, but it may have offered some advantages. If marriage is understood as a primarily economic relationship, it is possible that polygamous relationships served some particular needs for Native women. However, we need more research to better understand women's positions in these marriages. For example, what were the sexual liberties of women? How did they relate to the other wives? Were these marriages simply thought of as work-teams or socioeconomic units, and how was this at odds with European notions of love?

There were many types of unions in traditional societies, and many of these relationships could be ended quite simply. Separation from one's partner was not complicated by the religious and legal ramifications of western society. In numerous Indigenous nations, "divorce" was uncomplicated, commonplace and could be initiated by either the man or the woman.[11] In Navajo culture, for example, either the woman or the man could decide to end the marriage:

> Divorce is easy for both men and women in the Navajo way. The woman "puts the man's saddle outside the hogan" and he gets the message. If the man wishes divorce, it is said, "He went out to round up the horses and he never came back." A woman keeps the children within her extended family, and the man returns to his family of origin until he marries again and moves to his new wife's hogan.[12]

In our communities today, women are afraid to divorce because of the threat of poverty. Many Native women did not have the same worries, because divorce did not necessarily result in the devolution of their economic status. In matrilocal societies, it was the husband who left, while the woman stayed with her children among her kin. She therefore did not experience any change in her social or economic status. Among the Plateau peoples, who were typically patrilocal, divorce did not result in economic deprivation for either the husband or the wife, as both had the opportunity to move in with their own kin or to live independently. With this system, women could gather food and trade it for fish and meat to support herself and her children.[13] The extended family systems within Indigenous societies ensured that women were not trapped by "wedlock" or left destitute should they decide to leave the marriage. This security extended to abandoned or widowed women as well, who were able to live comfortably with their families and continue their labour within that structure.[14]

"Divorce" was easier in many Native societies largely because of the understandings of property. As with the understanding that one can't "own" land, there was an understanding in most Indigenous cultures that one can't "own" people.[15] This meant that a man could not own his wife, nor could parents own their children. The family was not the property of the man. In this way, a woman was more free to marry or divorce as she saw fit. With relation to the principle of non-interference, the wife had autonomy and respect. This enabled her to make decisions on her own behalf.

Whether single or in a partnership, motherhood accorded Native women tremendous status in the family, community and nation. Motherhood was an affirmation of a woman's power and defined her central role in traditional Aboriginal societies. This stemmed from the reverence for women's innate power to bring forth life. Yet this power belonged to all women, regardless of whether or not they biologically produced children. Indigenous societies highly valued their children and both biological and non-biological mothers were honoured for their work. Pre-conquest women, Paula Gunn Allen writes, "were mothers, and that word did not imply slaves, drudges, drones, who are required to love only for others rather than for themselves, as it so tragically does for many modern women."[16]

With colonization, this powerful role of mother and the position of woman in the family came under attack. Social, economic and political power was ripped away through the imposition of the western family structure. European "family values" were a keystone in the conquest strategy. From the outset, missionaries were instructed to change Aboriginal family structure as part of their project to convert Native peoples. The Jesuits of New France, headed by Father Lejeune, introduced the patriarchal family structure, "with male authority, female fidelity, and the elimination of the right to divorce."[17] "Field matrons" were sent out to Native communities to "civilize" and "educate" Native women so they could meet the patriarchal ideals of wife and mother.[18] In order to be civilized, Native women needed to learn how to obey. Residential schools taught Native women to be compliant to their husbands and prepared them for the domestic role that was expected of white women at the time.[19] The intent was to break down extended family and clan systems, considered by the missionaries to be a degraded state, "the outcome of looseness of morals and absence of social restraint"[20]

The patriarchal nuclear family model was strategic in the fight against these "loose moral values" which allowed women to divorce easily and make their own decisions in the family. More importantly, the patriarchal model would help the state seize economic control from Indigenous communities. Pre-contact systems of communal ownership were dismantled and in their place the male head of the family was given ownership of everything. This rendered women dependent on the men, made divorce more complicated, and ultimately stripped women of economic freedom. As "heads" of the household, men were encouraged to think as individuals and see themselves as owners of the property. The state encouraged this type of thinking, as property is easier to wrest from individual owners than from inter-dependent communities.

The new family structure severely damaged women's roles. As Mohawk midwife Katsi Cook puts it, "The nuclear family has been the moral equivalent of the nuclear bomb!"[21] It isolated women from one another and broke down family and community systems that once empowered women. Mary Crow Dog describes the destruction of the Sioux extended family unit, the tiyospaye:

> The government tore the tiyospaye apart and forced the Sioux into the kind of relationship now called the "nuclear family"; forced upon each couple their individually owned allotment of land, trying to teach them "the benefits of wholesome selfishness without which higher civilization is impossible."... The civilizers did a good job on us, especially among the half breeds, using the stick and carrot method, until now there is neither tiyospaye — nor a white style nuclear family, just Indian kids without parents.[22]

With the diminishing family structure, the respect for women and children vanished, and men's responsibilities shifted dramatically. In her essay on the criminalization of single, destitute mothers, Lakota scholar Elizabeth Cook-Lynn relates family and social breakdown to the destruction of traditional values. Before contact, men had natural and ethical responsibilities towards children. Men who dishounoured women were not accorded political, spiritual or social status and were often physically attacked by women. Today, this is no longer true: "men who are known to degrade women and abandon children now hold positions of power, even sometimes sitting at the tribal council tables. They are directors of tribal council programs, and they often participate unmolested in sacred ceremonies." Women were also traditionally held accountable for their actions in the case of irresponsibility towards children, but they were not singled out and placed "at fault" alone, as they are in the increasingly popular "single-mother" bashing of today's society.[23] With the loss of their traditional responsibilities and the honour accorded to their position, Native women have in many cases become oppressed by a role that was once a great source of strength and power.

## SEX AND SEXUALITY

Attitudes towards sex and sexuality were complex, and varied extensively among the nations. One thing they held in common, however, was the acceptance that sex was something natural for both women and men.

The sexual mores that came with colonization and the introduction to Christianity changed sexual behaviours of both Native women and Native men. Missionaries were horrified by Native attitudes towards sexuality. They remarked, in particular, on the sexual conduct of the women. The seventeenth-century Jesuit superior Lalemant was shocked that sexual encounters were initiated by women or men, and expressed disgust at the "libertinage at which the girls and women abandon themselves."[24] The partriachal/Christian attitudes dictated that a woman's expression of sexuality be more shame-based than a man's, a social stigma that was notably absent in many Native societies.

According to many Native peoples, women's bodies, by virtue of their capacity to bring forth life, were powerful and celebrated through all their cycles. Respect for their bodies was related to the respect and responsibility they commanded in their families, villages and nations. Because of this respect, women were not seen as "sex objects," and as well they had a great deal of individual control over their own sexuality.

In many societies, standards or sexual norms were often applied to men and women equally. Among the Sioux, virginity was prized in both young men and young women.[25] In societies where multiple partners were acceptable, the situation applied to both women and men. Sexual freedom was equally accorded to men and women in a number of nations of the Great Lakes region.[26] In the Blackfoot and Muskogee societies, women and men enjoyed sexual freedom until marriage and then fidelity was expected, although the standards were often unequal between men and women. For example, Blood educator Diane Eaglespeaker has told me that, whereas promiscuity and pre-marital sex were traditionally frowned upon for both genders, it was more enforced for the females. In traditional Muskogee society, women enjoyed complete sexual freedom until they were married, at which point fidelity was expected. Although fidelity was also expected of married men, the punishment for them was less severe.[27] In other nations, fidelity was not a condition for men or women who were married. Perhaps this was due to an interpretation of marriage as a socioeconomic union, an interpretation still prevalent in some Navajo marriages: "Marriages traditionally are primarily economic arrangements, so they are not expected to fill all of one's sexual desires."[28] Laguna writer Leslie Marmon Silko also identifies marriage as a socioeconomic union that allowed greater sexual freedom:

> Sexual inhibition did not begin until the Christian missionaries arrived. For the old-time people, marriage was about teamwork and social relationships, not about sexual excitement. In the days before the Puritans came, marriage did not mean an end to sex with people other than your spouse. Women were just as likely as men to have a si'ash, or lover.[29]

Attitudes towards marriage, sex and love were so different that it is hard to imagine traditional Native marriage relations from a contemporary western viewpoint. However, if one considers that people married young into arranged marriages that were based on economic development for the families, it is not hard to imagine that there was acceptance of this type of sexual freedom in marriage. Jeannette Armstrong (Okanagan) says the existence of post-marital sexual freedom among her people is a practice that still exists in some families today.

The fear of unwanted pregnancy was also absent among Native women. Children were always welcome, and because women were esteemed for having children, pregnancy was a natural part of the sexual cycle. Nor did children born out of wedlock have the stigma that later came with European ideas about "illegitimacy." Women were not punished for having children out of marriage. Leslie Marmon Silko asserts: "New life was so precious that pregnancy was always appropriate, and pregnancy before marriage was celebrated as a good sign."[30] There was no such thing as a "single mother," because children were accepted into large kin-based or clan-based communities, with all the supports that accompanied this. Ironically, many Native communities ended up raising white children who were abandoned. With tongue in cheek, Mohawk Elder Ernie Benedict points out: "Children of white people born out of wedlock were either put aside, abandoned … or given to Indians!"[31] Mi'kmaw filmmaker Catherine Martin explains how the practice of caring for white children in her society was possible because of Indigenous understandings about the sacredness of children:

> Our ancestors raised pure Irish, Scottish, and English children from the 1600s through to the 1900s. We raised them as Mi'kmaq people, speaking and being Mi'kmaq, because in those times the Scottish and English and Irish were ashamed if their daughter became pregnant out of wedlock. They would drop their girls off to our reserves. The girls would have their baby. They would come and take the girl back, and we would raise the babies. We did this because we treat all babies as sacred. It doesn't matter what the colour is. And it doesn't matter whether their mother was married or not, we maintained the fact that they are all sacred. Because of that, we always took in those children that the Scottish and English and Irish were ashamed to have in their families.

The idea that all children are welcome, regardless of where they come from, is such a persistent value in Native societies that it still exists today, even in communities that have been heavily Christianized. Myra Laramee says that teenage pregnancy does not carry the same stigma in the Aboriginal community, "because a child is a sacred being, and it doesn't matter how it gets here."

Despite children always being welcomed as sacred beings, it appears that Native women did have access to birth control. Beverly Hungry Wolf has recorded Siksika elder Ah'-dunn (Margaret Hind-Man) talking about the traditional knowledge and practice of birth control. Ah'-dunn says:

Some had the power to "tie" women so that they'd never have children again. I've always suspected my old mother-in-law had that power and used it on me. When I was young I just had my one daughter, and after that the old lady said, "I don't want her to have any more children."[32]

Ah'-dunn never did have any more children. While the power to make decisions about childbearing was still out of her hands, Ah'-dunn's experience nonetheless demonstrates that there was a body of traditional female knowledge related to birth control. Blood educator Diane Eaglespeaker told me that "in the old days they had medicines when a woman had an unwanted pregnancy," and Valerie Mathes has written about the evidence of birth control among the Chippewa:

> This situation was particularly apparent because of the often noted fact that Indian families had only two or three children whereas white families had thirteen or fourteen. Indian women could, under certain circumstances, prevent sexual intercourse. A Chippewa woman, if she wanted to avoid sex with her husband, simply left the tent and moved to a menstrual hut. Furthermore, in almost all tribes a woman did not have to have intercourse during menstruation.[33]

I imagine that it was unthinkable for men and women to engage in sex during menstruation because of the taboos surrounding it. Likewise, there were taboos around sexual activity during various ceremonial times of the year, and there are suggestions that women had choices about whether to engage in sex when pregnant or nursing an infant.[34] Native individual self-expression and self-esteem were nourished by sexual freedom and acceptance, which contributed to women's spiritual power and celebration of the body.

The sexual freedom and fluidity of sexuality included homosexuality in many Native societies. Anthropologist Sue Ellen Jacobs has identified eighty-eight societies with documented references to gayness. Eleven other societies have denied the existence of homosexuality, and these societies were "in areas of heaviest, lengthiest, and most severely puritanical white encroachment."[35]

The fluidity of gender was inherent in Native cultural views of the world. Some Native cultures understood that there were four genders rather than two: man; woman; the two spirit womanly males; and the two spirit manly females. A wide variety of Native American languages have words to describe people that are a combination of the masculine and feminine.[36] Current literature suggests that two-spirited people were not traditionally understood as they are now; for instance, it was not as socially sanctioned to have sex between people of the same gender (i.e., man/man), but people could have sex with an individual of another gender, regardless of whether they were the same sex (i.e., man/two spirit womanly male). The prevalence of this across Native societies and the acceptance within societies was such that people could marry members of the third and fourth gender.[37]

The Yuma would change gender roles according to dreams. For example, if a female dreamed of war weapons, she would take on the male role of warrior. Among the Mohaves and Cocopah, children took on the gender orientation of the toys and playmates that they chose.[38] Inuit may also take on different gender roles as children if they receive a "soul name" that is different from the gender usually related to their sex. When I spoke with Simona Arnatsiaq, who was named after her deceased brother Simon, she recalled that, "traditionally I was brought up as a boy. I had a boy's haircut, boys' clothes. I had a dog for hunting ... Right through that time, I believed I was a boy." She added, "Having been brought up without gender biases, I've always found it very difficult to understand sexism against women. My early childhood formative years were proof that we are all equal without borders because of sex." Leslie Marmon Silko writes about this fluidity among her Laguna Pueblo ancestors:

> Before the arrival of Christian missionaries, a man could dress as a woman and work with the women, and even marry a man without any fanfare. Likewise, a woman was free to dress like a man, to hunt and go to war with the men, and to marry a woman. In the old Pueblo worldview, we are all a mixture of male and female, and the sexual identity is changing constantly.[39]

Although these practices may not necessarily imply homosexuality, they do indicate a lack of homophobia in the societies that would allow such gender fluidity.

Homosexuality was highly regarded in some cultures. Odawa Elder Liza Mosher states that homosexual men were traditionally considered special because they could do "women's work" such as taking care of children or cooking for feasts when the women were on their moon time.[40] Dakota Sioux Elder Eva McKay remembers:

> Yes, they had people who were homosexuals. They were special in the way that they seemed to have more skills than a single man or a single woman. He doesn't harm nobody, he has skills like a woman and he would also have the skills of a man. He is two persons, this is when people would say they have more power than a single person. They were treated with respect. There are some here like that today. They could be a niece or a nephew, so what, they were born that way and we cannot do anything about it.[41]

As supportive as she is, McKay's conclusion that "we cannot do anything about it" is reflective of the larger ambivalence within contemporary Native communities. Teachings about homosexuality in our societies are not readily available, and what little information there is almost always pertains to male homosexuality. Some elders say that they never heard of homosexuality until recently,[42] and many Native people consider homosexuality an abnormality. We really need to speak more to our own people about these traditions, particularly because much of the information about homosexuality in our societies has been appropriated by the non-Native lesbian and gay community in an effort to bolster their own struggles. Native tradition has been called upon as proof that homosexuality was once widespread and universally accepted. M. Annette Jaimes (Juaneño/Yaqui) has contested this, saying that Native homosexuals were deeply revered and accorded status because they were relatively rare. She takes exception to non-Native activists who try to impose the idea that everyone engaged in homosexuality, and that homosexual people are therefore more "traditional."[43]

I have concluded, from talking to the women that I did, that homosexuality as with other aspects of Native sexuality, was considered the private affair of the individual, and up to her/him to determine.

Jeannette Armstrong remembers an experience from her childhood, when she questioned her aunt about two women who were living together. Her aunt replied, "Well, they like each other. Why shouldn't they be together?" According to Armstrong, homosexuality was traditionally a "non-issue."

With European contact, homosexuality, the open sexuality of women, and the acceptance of children out of wedlock immediately came under attack. In short, sexuality that did not fit into the patriarchal model was unacceptable. Pregnancy out of wedlock, for example, was condemned as shameful and sinful. Jane Willis, herself an "illegitimate" Cree child born in 1940 on the eastern shores of James Bay in Northern Quebec, remembers when the village priest held court to condemn two "sinners" who had conceived out of wedlock. He castigated the young couple in front of a packed church audience as a means of instilling shame. When the baby was eventually stillborn, he remarked: "It was God's punishment to this sinful woman that her child be born dead. And the child, without the cleansing of its sins by baptism, is doomed to eternal hell for the sins of its mother."[44] The contrast between the church's interpretation and the traditional Aboriginal interpretation, which would see both the woman and child as sacred, the father remiss in his responsibilities, and the terrible loss of a spirit, is stunning. This radical shift in values opened up the conditions for the epidemic proportions of violence against women in Aboriginal communities.

Homosexuality was viewed as the ultimate sin. Algonquin educator Helen Thundercloud explains: "We honoured two-spirited people because they brought gifts to our communities that were very important. And all of a sudden the Christians came along and said, 'Oh you can't do that. That is a sin against God.' Over the years we took those beliefs, and that has destroyed our people." Where God was not enough to regulate homosexuality, the state stepped in. The *Indian Act* institutionalized heterosexual marriage (and heterosexuality) as it was the only way by which an individual would be able to pass on Indian status and rights.[45] Whether by way of the church or the state, Euro-Christian attitudes about homosexuality have borne their bitter fruit, as homophobia has now found a place in every Native community.

Of course, Christian ideology condemned women's sexuality. It became shame-based and subject to scrutiny and punishment by the church. Barbara-Helen Hill recounts the puritanical teachings around sex that replaced our traditional teachings. Native women, she writes, were told that sex is "a man's thing; men enjoy it; it's a woman's duty; it's dirty; save yourself for your husband." Traditional teachings which encouraged a healthy sexuality were erased:

> With colonization and "churchianity" we stopped talking about sex. Parents listened to the church injected doctrines of the Puritans and sex became a taboo subject for discussion. The church spoke often of the sins of sex and the sins of the woman temptress. Respect for women was lost, and with that loss, came the loss of the natural teachings.[46]

I believe that the most tragic and devastating impact on both Native women and Native men's sexuality came during the residential school era, when sexuality and sexual expression were suppressed, distorted and perverted. Schools were either all male or all female, as the churches believed that Native students were likely to be more sexually active than non-Natives. Historian J. R. Miller speculates that this fear that led to the "fanatical segregation" of the sexes "might have been based on a misunderstanding of the greater autonomy and control of their own bodies that females in some Native communities enjoyed."[47] It could be that the missionaries confused Native children's personal control of their bodies with open sexual license. Whatever the cause, Native children suffered the consequences by being chastised and even beaten for even attempting to communicate with members of the opposite sex, who were often their siblings and relations.[48] Shirley Williams recalls the policing of sexuality and the hysteria associated with it at St. Joseph's Residential School. She remembers that girls were accused of improper behaviour when they tried to make contact with boys: "We were called boy crazy." These attempts at contact were usually not sexually driven, but the attempts of lonely little girls who wished to speak to their brothers or cousins. Their excitement at catching periodic glimpses of family members was often met with anger from the nuns, who accused them of sexual behaviour.

At residential school, girls were taught that the female body was a locus for shame. Miller describes the measures taken by the nuns at the Blue Quills Residential School in Alberta to conceal the female body: At Blue Quills, school girls had to wear "this real tight binder" so that their growing breasts would be flattened, and at all ages they had to wear "a bathing suit" that resembled "a grey flannelette night-gown" when taking a bath. Other schools demanded that boys wear shorts in the shower, but "females had a greater obligation than males to be modest in dress, chaste in behaviour, and free of pregnancy. Their heavier burden was part of the misfortune of being a woman."[49]

Shirley Williams knows too well the sense of worthlessness and the denigration that came out of these policies. She remembers that girls in her school had to wear clothing that was loose, "because you couldn't show your shape of your body":

> Any kind of clothing was up right around your throat. That was because to show your flesh was sinful. Many times they talked about that, so we began to feel that there was something wrong with our bodies; that because we were Indian girls, we were dirty. That was the way they talked.
>
> So, as you are growing, you begin to think that you are not worth anything, being Indian. Being an Indian woman is dirty. Being Indian was to be told that you are not worthy. You are less than. You begin to feel this low self-esteem.
>
> I think we came out of there so pitiful.

Residential school priests and nuns fanatically instilled the dogma that sex was the most punishable of offences, while at the same time sexually abusing the children in their care. The prevalence of rape, sexual assault, induced abortion and sexual/psychological abuse is well documented,[50] as are the outright and horrific pillaging of Native sexuality:

> The residential school did virtually nothing to foster healthy sexual development among the aboriginal children consigned to their care. Instead, all kinds of behaviour was sexualized. Sto:lo grand-mother Mary Chapman recalls the shaming punishments meted out by the Sisters of St. Ann when she was a student in the 1940s and '50s at Kuper Island Residential School. "When girls were caught doing something like stealing food or talking

Halq'emeylem, the nuns would make them stand in a long line in front of the whole school, then lift their skirts right up. They had to stand there in front of everybody, naked, with their genitals exposed."

The fact that the people meting out this abuse were the de facto "parents" or figures of authority for lonely, vulnerable aboriginal children only served to compound the damage. Children subjected to this kind of treatment came to believe they were only sexual objects, a devastating blow to their self-esteem expressed later in their lives through compulsive sexual behaviour, promiscuity, sex addiction, prostitution, and an inability to found relationships on love rather than lust. [51]

Residential school survivor Shirley Williams says that she left residential school "starved for love." Presumably, this was the case for many residential school survivors. When these feelings were coupled with abusive and degrading teachings about sexuality, they had the potential to wreak havoc on Native individuals, families and communities.

## FAMILY VIOLENCE

*From an Anishnabe perspective, striking out against a woman is like striking out against everything we hold sacred, our life, our future, our customs, and beliefs, because our women represent the power which is contained within all these concepts. By weakening women, we are weakening our people.*

— Calvin Morrisseau (Ojibway)[52]

The traditional respect accorded to Native women made it unthinkable in Aboriginal cultures to practise violence against them. Although some writers contend that violence against women existed in early Native societies,[53] there is overwhelming evidence that such behaviour was offset by strong taboos and severe punishment. Sylvia Maracle writes, "Our elders tell us that incidents of violence — be they sexual, mental, emotional or spiritual — were rare and swiftly dealt with in our communities prior to contact with the Europeans."[54] Patricia

Monture-Angus asserts that "violence and abuse (including political exclusions) against women were not tolerated in most Aboriginal societies." She cites the journal of Mary Jemison, a white woman who spent sixty-nine years among the Iroquois:

> From all history and tradition it would appear that neither seduction, prostitution, nor rape was known in the calendar of this rude savage, until the females were contaminated by the embrace of civilized man. And it is a remarkable fact that among the great number of women and girls who have been taken prisoners by the Indians during the last two centuries … not a single instance is on record or has ever found currency in the great stock of gossip and story which civilized society is prone to circulate, that a female prisoner has ever been ill-treated, abused, or her modesty insulted, by an Indian, with reference to her sex. [55]

The absence of violence in Iroquois society was totally perplexing to the eighteenth- and nineteenth-century patriarchal settler society of Upper Canada, whose laws legalized both marital rape and wife beating.[56] Other Aboriginal societies throughout North America, with their strict approach to violence against women, must have also shocked the settlers. Among the Sioux, wife beating was seen as a blight on the community. Violence against women was contrary to Lakota values and was the breaking of social law.[57] For their part, Native peoples must have been shocked at the acceptance of violence against women in settler society.

When violence against women happened, there were systems to deal with it. Abusers could be met with violence in return, often at the hands of the women. Lee Maracle recalls her grandmother physically beating a cousin who had been violent with his sister. In the Plateau societies, the women meted out punishment to rapists:

> Rape occurred in traditional Plateau societies, though informants insisted that it was an unusual crime and was not condoned. Two narratives of punishment of rapists were collected in the field. Both involved turning the man over to a group of women who physically molested him and publicly humiliated him. He was then ejected from the village.[58]

The Sioux also had practices to guard against wife battering:

> Once a man battered his wife, she was free to make him leave her lodge if they lived among her tiyospaye. From then on he could never marry again. Brothers were obliged by social law to retaliate by speaking to him, or even killing him. If the couple lived among the man's relatives, his parents were obligated to get her away and return her to her tiyospaye.

> A man who battered his wife was considered irrational and thus could no longer lead a war party, a hunt, or participate in either ... The wife batterer could no longer own a pipe ... A man who killed his wife was thought to be not Lakota anymore ... His name would never be spoken again. He would cease to exist.[59]

Among the First Nations of British Columbia, abusers received severe punishment. Tsartlip Councillor Manny Cooper recalls, "In traditional culture, they would put [a rapist] in a canoe and ship him out and he wouldn't come back. Or they would tie you to a reef, and if you drowned, you were guilty." Other First Nations would scar abusers and even burn them to death for repeated offenses.[60] The severity of these punishments indicates the severity of the taboo of violence against women in these societies.

There were also ways of dealing with the sexual abuse of children, which was not unknown to Native societies. In a 1992 consultation, a number of different nations in British Columbia testified that there were traditional sanctions and laws against child sexual abuse, and that the clan system did much to eliminate or control these crimes.[61] In my conversation with Maria Campbell, she told me that Métis and Cree culture had stories that warned about pedophiles, and precautions were taken to keep children away from unknown men. Men were expected to socialize in a house away from the children, and old women had the responsibility to watch over them. Among the Sto:lo, watchmen elders could send their spirits through the walls of an extended family's house to make sure the children were safe. They were called upon to work with visions about what was happening to a certain child. Guardians who were suspected of child abuse were publicly identified and punished with banishment, segregation from children, and even death.[62] The protection provided by the extended family, clan, and community systems was lost with the introduction of nuclear family models. As the "head of the family" male sexual predators were handed control over their wives and children, a role that shielded them from public scrutiny.[63]

Colonization in and of itself is a violent process. It brought many untold forms of violence against the women, children and men of the Americas. Today, we are faced with epidemic, lateral violence in our communities. State and church policies started this vicious cycle by instilling violence in children who were placed in residential schools and abusive foster homes, and by degrading women sexually, politically and socially.[64]

Abused Native boys and girls have grown into adults who abuse or who accept abuse as part of a relationship. If the cycle of violence is not broken, adults can pass violence on to their children. Instead of being positive role models, they risk teaching children violent behaviours.

Colonial practices also stripped Native men of their autonomy and dignity,[65] and robbed them of their ability to "provide and protect." An Ojibway man once described to me the desperate frustration experienced by Native men who had to witness their children being taken away to residential schools and placed in the hands of the child welfare system:

> When they took our kids away and the women were yelling and screaming, the men, who were supposed to be the protectors, had to stand and watch it happen ... These men felt helpless and frustrated, and because they couldn't take it out on white people, because of the guns, or whatever, the frustration and anger was turned on someone weaker.[66]

Western patriarchal family structures enabled Aboriginal men to turn their violence inward: "Aboriginal men who had been deprived of natural authority through impoverishment and the theft of land were handed in exchange the weapon of absolute possession and control over their wives and children ..."[67] Frustrated and powerless men have exerted their anger in the only arena of power they were given by the colonizer: the power to dominate Native women and children. The introduction of alcohol and drugs exacerbated the violence. Our people have used (and continue to use) alcohol and drugs to fill the ugly gap left by the theft of our ways. Sylvia Maracle describes how this dependency has taken shape:

> As traditional ways continued to erode, our people became lost to the bottle, drugs and solvents. Addictions contributed to the downward spiral of learned violent behaviour. We saw violence all around us — it became part of our day-to-day interactions. We questioned our own self-worth as a people and began to internalize the anger, bitterness, resentment and poor self-esteem. More and more often, what we sought was to block out the pain. This situation was coupled with being poor and unable to participate in the social and cultural fabric of our community. There came a generation who had learned violence well and practised it as a way of life.[68]

The violence that has become a "way of life" for many Native women has crippled their well-being. It feeds into all the other mainstream messages about the worthlessness of Native women, and creates a vicious cycle of abuse that is passed onto the future generations. This culture of violence works in direct opposition to an understanding of woman as a sacred source. As Calvin Morrisseau suggests, "striking out against a woman is like striking out against every thing we hold sacred ..."[69]

Through my research and my conversations with women in different Native cultures, I have come to understand how the sacredness, power and beauty of Native womanhood was traditionally understood. The church and state have dismantled the philosophies, practices and systems that upheld our status as women, a dismantling that has been fed by a simultaneous process: the construction of a negative Native female identity.

CHAPTER SIX

# THE CONSTRUCTION OF
# A NEGATIVE IDENTITY

❖

*Drunken squaw.*
*Dirty Indian.*
*Easy.*
*Lazy.*

EVERY CANADIAN KNOWS THESE WORDS to commonly describe and identify Aboriginal women. Many Canadians are fooled by this construction of Native womanhood. This imagery is so ingrained in the North American consciousness that even Native people have, in dark times, internalized these beliefs about their grandmothers, their aunties, their daughters, and themselves.

Perhaps people begin to see alcohol abuse, sexual dysfunction and poverty through the lens of these stereotypes. There are many people in our communities who are still using alcohol to drown the shame and confusion that festers within such negative definitions of their ancestry. We have a lot of family and sexual dysfunction because of the imposition of Christianity, western morality and abuses endured in the residential school system. Yet, when we consider our lived experience, the drunken, easy squaw is not a character that Aboriginal people know. I would not describe my Native female relations as lazy and dirty. I don't know any squaws. So where did these images come from? How did they become so widespread, and how do they affect the day-to-day living of contemporary Native women?

As I began to explore these questions, I discovered how this negative understanding of Native womanhood was constructed. The dirty, easy squaw was invented long before poverty, abuse and oppression beset our peoples. She was invented and then reinforced because she proved useful to the colonizer. The "uncivilized" squaw justified taking over Indian land. She eased the conscience of those who wished to sexually abuse without consequence. She was handy to greedy consumers. Dirty and lazy, she excused those who removed her children and paved the way for assimilation into mainstream culture. She allowed for the righteous position of those who participated in the eradication of Native culture, language and tradition.

To me, these images are like a disease that has spread through both the Native and the non-Native mindset. In tracing this development, I hope to highlight a renewed understanding of Native womanhood that will help us to recover our strength, self-esteem and dignity.

## Roots of a Negative Female Image

In both western and Indigenous frameworks, Native women have historically been equated with the land. The Euro-constructed image of Native women, therefore, mirrors western attitudes towards the earth. Sadly, this relationship has typically developed within the context of control, conquest, possession and exploitation. The Euro-Canadian image of Native women has been constructed within this context and has evolved along with the evolving relationship of European people to this continent.

When they first arrived on Turtle Island in the sixteenth century, Europeans produced images of Native womanhood to symbolize the magnificent richness and beauty they encountered. This was the phase of the great mother, the Indian Queen. Cherokee scholar Rayna Green describes the personification of "America" typical to this period (1575–1765):

> Draped in leaves, feathers, and animal skins, as well as in heavy jewelry, she appeared aggressive, militant, and armed with spears and arrows. Often she rode on an armadillo, and stood with her foot on the slain body of an animal or human enemy. She was the familiar mother-goddess figure — full bodied, powerful, nurturing but dangerous — embodying the wealth and danger of the New World.[1]

"Exotic, powerful, dangerous and beautiful," this Native female symbol represented both "American liberty and European virtue,"[2] but as the European settler became more familiar with the land, the queen was demoted. Colonial claims to the land would only work if the queen became more accessible, less powerful, and within the grasp of the white man. Out of this need, the "Indian princess" was born. The queen was transformed from a mother-goddess figure to a girlish-sexual figure, for who can own mother or dominate the gods?

"Indian princess" imagery constructed Indigenous women as the virgin frontier, the pure border waiting to be crossed.[3] The enormous popularity of the princess lay within her erotic appeal to the covetous European male wishing to lay claim to the "new" territory. This equation of the Indigenous woman with virgin land, open for consumption, created a Native female archetype which, as Elizabeth Cook-Lynn has pointed out, could then be "used for the colonizer's pleasure and profit."[4]

The erotic image of Native female as "new" territory in the American narrative persists to this day. You need only to glance at posters of Walt Disney's *Pocahontas* to be confronted with a contemporary example of this archetype. We see a voluptuous yet innocent looking Native (but not too Native) "girl," who will soon become involved with an adventurous young white male. As Emma LaRocque points out, Disney's *Pocahontas* combines a lot of the overarching stereotypes about Native people. LaRocque sees a Pocahontas who is "so oversexualized, kind of crouching around, slithering around on the rocks," part noble savage, part princess, part loose squaw. This archetype has been perpetrated again and again throughout North American his-story. It has been promoted through other popular his-storical characters like Sacajewea, the Shoshone woman who led "explorers" Lewis and Clarke into the interior of the North American continent. In Spanish colonial history, there is la Malinche, the Aztec woman who birthed the mestizo children of Cortez and interpreted for Spanish troops.

It is possible to interpret characters like Pocahontas, Sacajewea and la Malinche as strong Indigenous leaders,[5] but the mainstream interpretation of these mythic characters is quite the opposite: Native women (and, by association, the land) are "easy, available and willing" for the white man.[6] This mythology ensures that the "good" Native woman who willingly works with white men is rewarded with folk hero or "princess status."[7] Racism dictates that the women of these celebrated liaisons are elevated above the ordinary Indigenous female status; they must be some kind of royalty. The ultimate "reward" for the Indian princess is marriage to a white man, providing her the ability to transcend into his world.

What, then, of the Native woman who does not comply with the colonizer?

As with other colonial his-stories, once Indigenous peoples began to resist colonization, the archetypes changed. Indigenous women worldwide became symbols of the troublesome colonies, and in the Americas the squaw emerged. Carol Douglas Sparks has traced the princess-to-squaw devolution in colonizer accounts of the Navajo.[8] The virgin-princess, so commonly found in white male adventurer records of the nineteenth century, is soon transformed. While the princess held erotic appeal for the covetous imperial male wishing to claim the "new" territory, the squaw drudge justified the conquest of an uncivilized terrain:

> ... Americans found squaw drudges far more comfortable than these outspoken and powerful women, whose presence defied colonial rationalizations. Not only could the squaw be pitied, but her very existence justified American intrusion into her land and society.[9]

In her book, *Capturing Women: The Manipulation of Cultural Imagery in Canada's Prairie West*, Sarah Carter demonstrates how both the Canadian state and the national press deliberately promoted "dirty squaw" imagery in the late 1800s.[10] At the time of settler invasion in western Canada, "dirty squaw" fiction was useful for a number of reasons. The uncivilized squaw provided a backdrop for the repressive measures against the Native population of the time. Like the men who were depicted as savage warriors, the women were reported to be "violent instigators of atrocities" (against whites),[11] thereby justifying colonial violence against Indigenous peoples. The image of the Native woman as the beast of burden in her society was drawn up to demonstrate the superiority of European womanhood and femininity (after all, women did not "labour"), and the necessity for replacing Native womanhood with European womanhood. This distortion of Native women's physical labour and contribution to their community is at the root of the longstanding "squaw-drudge" image. Rather than being seen as significant players in the economic structure of society, Native women were framed as drudges and beasts of burden.

As Native people moved off the land, and women lost their status and role as producers within the economic structure of their societies, they were cast as lazy and slovenly. Women were no longer able to provide for their families because they had lost the means to produce primary goods, such as clothing and food. They became dependent upon purchased goods and an economy in which they held no power. The dirty squaw emerged, conveniently taking the blame for the increasing poverty on reserve and deflecting attention from government and public complicity in the devastation of Indigenous peoples. If Native women were constructed as "squaws," dirty, lazy and slovenly, it was easier to cover up the reality of Native women who were merely struggling with the increasingly inhuman conditions on reserve:

> In the unofficial and unpublished reports of reserve life ... it was widely recognized that problems with reserve housing and health had little to do with the preferences, temperament, or poor housekeeping abilities of the women. Because of their poverty, the people were confined in one-room shacks, which were poorly ventilated and were impossible to keep clean because they had dirt floors and were plastered with mud and hay. One inspector of the agencies noted in 1891 that the women did not have soap, towels, wash basins, or wash pails, nor did they have any means of acquiring them. Similarly, it was frequently noted that the women were short of basic clothing and had no textiles or yarn to work with. Yet in official public statements, the tendency was to ascribe blame to the women rather than drawing attention to conditions that would injure the reputation of government administration.[12]

Similarly, if Native women were portrayed as poor parents, it was then excusable for the state to remove Native children and place them in residential schools and foster homes.

Native female sexuality was also transformed into the "squaw" who was "lewd and licentious" and morally reprehensible. This representation was projected onto Native women to excuse the mistreatment they endured from white settler males. Within the context of late-nineteenth-century morality, it was easier to blame Native women than to challenge the behaviour of the heroes on the frontier. The narrative espousing how "easy" Native women were was developed to cover up the fact that white males were involved in unmarried sexual activity and that state officials were perpetrators of sexual assault. This tactic is common in rape cases and is well entrenched in the western consciousness: blame women for the sexual deviance of certain men. As part of the Native woman-blaming campaign, the *Toronto Daily Mail* of February 2, 1886, railed, "The character of the men of this country has been assailed."[13]

The squalor of the media-driven uncivilized easy squaw was further intended to guard against interracial marriages, thus protecting racial "purity" in the new country: "There were fears that the Anglo-Celts might be overrun by more fertile, darker and lower people, who were believed to be unable to control their sexual desires."[14] The moral reform movement of the late 1880s in the West embraced images of the dirty squaw in an effort to keep the races segregated and to keep the white race pure.

The dirty, dark squaw not only justified the deplorable treatment of Aboriginal peoples, she also created a gauge against which white femininity could be measured and defined. Where Native women were powerful physical workers, white women were encouraged to be weak and frail. The Native woman thus was re-invented as a drudge. Where Native women had sexual liberty, white women were restricted from pleasure. The Native woman had then to be perceived as easy. Where Native women resisted the increasing restrictions and poverty of reserves, white women were expected to be models of domesticity, industriousness and obedience. The Native woman had to be reconstructed as deficient in order to prop up the image of the white woman:

> The particular identity of white women depended for its articulation on a sense of difference from Indigenous women. What it meant to be a white woman was rooted in a series of negative assumptions about the malign influence of Aboriginal women. The meanings of and different ways of being female were constantly referred to each other, with Aboriginal women always appearing deficient.[15]

Since contact with the European, Native women have been trapped within a western dichotomous worldview, where everything is either good or bad; dark or light; pure or corrupt. The Euro-constructed Indigenous woman with her dark ways, her squalor and corruption makes the construction of whiteness all the more attractive. In the absence of white women, Native women can represent both characters: the "Indian princess," bathed in a sublime light (and well on her way to becoming white), or the "easy squaw," hunched and wallowing in her darkness. In terms of female identity, the Native woman must endure the western framework of virgin-whore, which was translated to princess-squaw and slapped on top of the complex understanding of Native womanhood that had existed for tens of thousands of years. This his-story continues to interfere with the lives of contemporary Native women.

## GHOSTS OF THE SQUAW AND THE PRINCESS

The majority of Native women will tell you that, at some point in their experience they have been called a "squaw." Depending on the degree of overt racism in their environment, this will happen to a greater or lesser extent. Sometimes it is applied in the context of "friendly" joking; often in the form of a violent assault. Whatever the context, the "squaw" label has been applied to Native women right across North America; there are accounts from women of nations as widespread as the Mi'kmaq (Rita Joe) and the Pawnee/Otoe (Anna Lee Walters). [16]

Native girls begin to hear racial/sexual slurs from an early age, often before they even understand the terms themselves. Ojibway Professor Shirley Williams says she remembers hearing white boys singing, "Squaws along the Yukon aren't good enough for me." The boys would follow up with, "Would two dollars be enough?" playing on the myth that Native women are "easy." Williams states that she thought "squaw" must be an English word "because it sounded like something dirty." Laverne Gervais-Contois, a woman of Ojibway, Cree and Sioux heritage recalls the slurs she heard while growing up in Winnipeg. Typically, the images were (and are) steeped with degrading sexual innuendo. She recalls hearing Native women referred to as "dark coffee" which was implicitly sexual, as the boys would say, "Dark coffee is good if you like it good and strong."

When negative images of Native women are so ingrained in the Canadian consciousness that even children participate in using them, it is easy to see how Native women might begin to think of themselves as "easy squaws." Janice Acoose describes how these negative images affected her consciousness:

> I learned to passively accept and internalize the easy squaw, Indian-whore, dirty Indian, and drunken Indian stereotypes that subsequently imprisoned me, and all Indigenous peoples, regardless of our historic, economic, cultural, spiritual, political, and geographical differences ... I shamefully turned away from my history and cultural roots, becoming, to a certain extent, what was encouraged by the ideological collusiveness of textbooks, and the ignorant comments and peer pressure from non-Indigenous students.[17]

Many Native female writers — including Joanne Arnott, Beth Brant, Maria Campbell, Janet Campbell Hale, Beatrice Culleton, Paula Gunn Allen, Lee Maracle and Anna Lee Walters[18] — have provided accounts of how they or other Native women have fostered destructive and hateful attitudes towards themselves. This self-hatred is rooted in internalized racism that comes from the negative self-concepts of racist stereotypes. Internalized racism spreads like a disease through Native communities.[19] It makes us doubt the validity of the existence of our people, and thus ourselves. This results in self-destructive behaviours, including addictions and involvement in violent relationships.

Less destructive and overt but equally as false is the princess. This is a stereotype that I am more familiar with in my personal experience. My class, age and stature likely play into this interpretation of my being. The fact that I am half-white also helps. Remember, the Indian princess is well on her way to becoming white, so it follows that those of us who are more assimilated qualify for this racist nobility. Mixed-bloods have "exotic" appeal because we look "different," yet we are accessible to white people.

No one would ever call you a princess, but you can see it in their approach. Sometimes people glow all over you about your heritage; others want to use you as some kind of showpiece. It is a sexualized identity, which, in my case, has, for example, resulted in the humiliating experience of being called "my little Indian" as a measure of affection. I have felt stalked by Canadian and European men because of my Indianness, which, to them, was a "bonus" to whatever interest they had in me as a female.

When I read bell hooks for the first time, I felt a wash of relief to discover that I hadn't been imagining this syndrome; that, in fact, several people have written about it. As I discussed earlier, hooks provided me a name for it: "eating the Other." In an essay so named, she explains how it has become fashionable to "enjoy racial difference." She demonstrates, for instance, how advertising has picked up on this desire, and has used people of colour to sell products.[20]

People with a desire for "eating the Other" do not see themselves operating within a racist framework; rather, they think they are progressive in their desire to make contact. Hooks suggests that relations of this nature may further be used to assuage guilt and "take the form of a defiant gesture where one denies accountability and historical connection."[21] People need to believe that their desire to befriend an Indian or to sleep with a woman of colour is proof that we have all transcended the racism that plagues the Americas, and that in so doing we are tucking our racism safely in the past. But what is implied in this type of contact? What narratives are we replaying?

I see Pocahontas looming in the background. There is a desire to cross some kind of frontier, to be transformed by the experience and, finally, to take possession. Hooks relates her experience of hearing some white college boys talk about how many Black, Aboriginal, and Asian women they could "fuck" before graduation. To these boys, sex with the Other represents a rite of passage into a more "worldly" state. Whether overtly stated or covertly desired, transformation through contact with the "exotic" is played out in the forum of certain white-dark sexual relations. These attitudes reinforce colonial power relations, where the dark, earthly and sensual paradise is there for the enjoyment of the white newcomer.

Whether princess or squaw, Native femininity is sexualized. This understanding finds its way into our lives and our communities. Sometimes, it means constantly having to fend off the advances of people with an appetite for the "Other." It may involve a continual struggle to resist crass, sexualized interpretations of one's being, as in the experience of these (anonymous) women:

> I can't stand at night in any place by myself because all the men think that I am trying to pick them up. I am telling you, it doesn't matter where I am … They think that all the Native women in the world, we are there just to [have sex with them]. All the time — it doesn't matter where — poor area, rich area, it doesn't matter.[22]

❖

> I found that I was constantly, throughout my life, pestered by men who were drunk, alcoholics, feeling like they had a chance with me. I found this really insulting. I mean, I may not be rich, but I'm well educated, I'm hard-working, I'm not an alcoholic — you know, to me I've got a lot of positive things going for me, and I feel that I should have men who are at least my equal coming after me. And I've found throughout my life that I have not had that. I have them coming up for one-night stands. They don't want a relationship with me, they just want sex. And this is quite upsetting.[23]

This sexualized understanding of Native women can be seen in our communities, where, as Lee Maracle has observed, "it is nearly impossible for Native men to cherish the femininity of Native women. They have grown up in a world in which there is no such thing as dark-skinned femininity. There is only dark-skinned sensuality."[24]

In terms of overt violence, Plains Cree/Métis professor Emma LaRocque asserts that "the dehumanizing portrayal of the squaw and the over-sexualization of Native females such as Disney's Pocahontas surely render all Native female persons vulnerable."[25] After telling me, "Since childhood, I have had to walk through a maze of racist and sexist assaults on me," she told me a story that offered a striking image of the perceived worthlessness of Native female existence as it has too often been understood by the dominant society :

> My first experience of when I was conscious of this kind of assault happened when I was about ten years old. I was sitting in a café in my home town, reading a comic book, as I was wont to do.

Minding my own business. I don't know where my parents were, but I just remember a big, fat, red-faced white guy coming in. Leering at me. I don't even think I could identify what that look was, because I had been so safe at home and in my community. I had never been attacked, and I didn't know what on earth that was. This guy, he throws a quarter. I still remember, and I still see that quarter rolling right past my coke bottle. He threw a quarter and he said, "Want to go for a ride, little squaw?"

LaRocque acknowledges the danger she was in at that moment, and how racist stereotypes endanger Native girls and women: "To this day, I am profoundly grateful he did nothing else. He could have just picked me up and taken me away. Nobody would have known the difference." She asks, "Where do these men get off on attacking little children, teenagers, regular aged women and grandmothers? It has to come from some conditioning, some horrendous sociological, racist and sexist conditioning, to be so inhumane to your co-human beings. It is really stunning."

Negative images of Native women, whether in historical accounts, anecdotes, jokes, movies or Canadian literature,[26] are at the root of stories like that of Helen Betty Osbourne, a sixteen-year-old Native woman who was picked up by four white men and brutally raped and murdered in The Pas, Manitoba, in 1972. This story remains fixed in the consciousness of many Native women, as it demonstrates how mainstream society interprets violence against Native women, especially when it is committed by whites. In my conversation with Gertie Beaucage (Ojibway), she pointed out that Osbourne was killed because she was expected to be "easy," and yet she resisted the sexual assault of the white men who attacked her. As Emma LaRocque has further pointed out, "In the minds of 'good boys who did bad things,' it is not the place of 'squaws' to resist white power, especially power snakily connected to the male ego."[27]

The Osbourne case eventually received a moderate amount of publicity because of the injustices it represented. There are, however, many more Native women's tales that would reveal the minimal worth placed on Native female lives. In our conversations, Lee Maracle (Sto:lo) and Catherine Martin (Mi'kmaw) have demonstrated to me that the notion that Native women are there for the sexual taking has been acted out from one side of the continent to the other. Maracle recalls her childhood on the West Coast:

> In my village, every single weekend … men came into the village, picked up little children, took them to the gravel pit, raped them — sometimes killed them — and were never prosecuted. I personally was chased in automobiles by white men. And when I went to swear out a complaint, they said it was in my imagination. I had charged a white man with assault, and I was called not a credible witness. Those things happen in our personal lives.

Maracle attributes this to the "permission that white society gave to white men to enter our communities, murder, pillage, rape and plunder us at will, right up until 1963."

A Mi'kmaw from Nova Scotia, Catherine Martin recalls, "In my grandmother's time, during the war, during the time when the Indian Agent had total rule, atrocities happened to our women. I know that." This was a time when, in the absence of Indian men, women were even more subject to attack. But Martin knows that racist ideology was at work:

> Our women were raped. They weren't just raped back in cowboy and Indian days, they are still raped. But that myth or misperception about our women [being easy] is in the minds of the mainstream society, which is why our women end up being attacked and raped. The fact that we have been raped tends to make them think that we are easy. It is a way to excuse the rapist, or to ignore the race issue.

Hereditary Wit'suwet'en Chief Theresa Tait lives in central British Columbia. When I spoke with her about this issue, she told me that in the last decade there have been at least five Aboriginal women who have been killed in her local area. There is little investigation and next to no media coverage about these incidents. Tait contrasts the lack of attention to violence against Aboriginal females with cases involving white women who go missing in Vancouver: "There, you have the media, you have everybody on side."

Native women seeking justice against the violence in their lives are overshadowed by the image of the squaw. In her study of how race figures into sexual abuse trials, Sherene Razack notes that Aboriginal women are treated as "inherently rapeable" because of assumptions made about Native female promiscuity and the insistence that a rape victim who has passed out because of alcohol is considered to have suffered less of a violation.[28] A Native woman who is drunk is deemed particularly unworthy of human treatment, and Native women who are involved in abusive relationships may not feel comfortable calling police in the case of domestic violence because they may be seen "at fault," or deserving of the abuse.[29]

The construction of a negative identity can rule a Native woman's experience, as these women have described. The triangle of oppression, developed by the Doris Marshall Institute,[30] is a useful tool for analysing how the oppression functions:

### DIAGRAM 2: THE TRIANGLE OF OPPRESSION

*Dominant ideas, assumptions and values*
"EASY SQUAW"

*Structures, systems*
(courts, healthcare system)

*Individual behaviour*
(name calling, sexual abuse)

*Impact on Native women's lives*
(low self-worth
violence
sexual abuse)

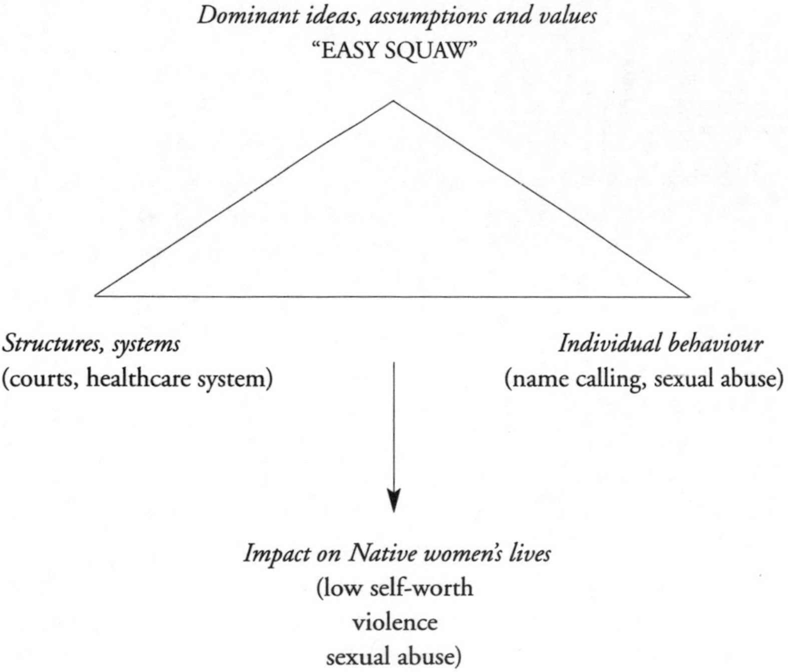

Each point of the triangle supports the others to maintain the oppression of Native women. If Native women are constructed as "easy squaws" and are locked into this imagery through the behaviour of individuals, they will continue to be rendered worthless in public institutions such as courtrooms or hospitals. If we treat Native women as easy or drunken squaws in the court system, we feed negative stereotypes that will further enable individuals to abuse Native females, and so on. Negative Native female images are part of a vicious cycle that deeply influences the lives of contemporary Native women. We need to get rid of the images, the systems that support them and the abusive practices carried out by individuals.

*III*

# RESIST

❖

# RESIST

❖

COMING FROM THE HISTORY THAT WE DO, Aboriginal women have had to become practised at resistance. Through collective resistance, Native women have worked hard to protect their cultures and sustain the social and political fabric of their nations. On a personal level, Native women have had to defend their identities. This has meant learning to resist stereotypes, imposed roles and negative definitions of their being, as well as learning to cope with the poor treatment from others that results from all of this.

When I look around our communities, I am amazed at some of the women I see. I have often wondered how they have managed to achieve such a strong sense of self, particularly taking into account all of the oppressive experiences of Aboriginal people. My exploration in this section thus comes out of my personal interest in how Native women resist negative definitions of being. In my discussions with the women who participated in my research, I looked for the common conditions that have helped them develop a positive sense of identity. I examined the interview material to identify the actions and attitudes that they have employed as part of this resistance. My intention is to map out a resistance that might be useful to other people, and I have drawn upon the women's stories to create this map.

Though often a very personal struggle, the individual resistance related to Native female identity also has national implications. By resisting negative definitions of their personal being, Native women question the imbalance and injustice that is encouraged by a colonial patriarchal society. This section demonstrates how resistance to a negative definition of Native womanhood is, at the same time, resistance to colonization itself.

## CHAPTER SEVEN

# FOUNDATIONS OF RESISTANCE

❖

ONE OF THE QUESTIONS that guided me in my exploration of Native female identity was "What has assisted Native women to take a position of resistance?" I did not ask this question of the women I interviewed for this book, but as they were telling me their stories I began to see patterns and common experiences that have made them strong. These "foundations of resistance," such as strong families, a sense of community and a close relationship with the land, provide the strength to defy the many oppressive experiences that an Aboriginal woman is likely to encounter.

## STRONG FAMILIES

Many Native women identify their original families as the foundation of their strength. Shame or denial about Native heritage is easier to avert when we come from families that insist on taking pride in tribal identity. Ojibway Elder Lillian McGregor "never had a problem" with her identity because her parents continually told her that she was "Anishnawbekwe," an Ojibway woman. "That's where you get your identity," says McGregor, who left her home in Birch Island, Ontario, at fifteen to go to school in Toronto. McGregor has held onto an Anishnawbekwe sense of self in spite of spending sixty years in the city.

Algonquin educator Helen Thundercloud asserts that early childhood reinforcement of identity can provide a lifetime of resistance. Thundercloud was raised by her grandmother in the Baskatong territory in Quebec until she was eight, when she was hospitalized for TB (and subsequently sent to residential school). She states: "Being with grandmother for those formative years gave me an incredible strength. She gave me all the self-esteem I needed for the rest of my life." This self-confidence enabled Thundercloud to survive the residential school system and all the negative messages she received about her identity.

A large or extended family is also a source of security. Women who were younger members of a family speak of the benefit of having "multiple"caregivers (parents, grandparents and older siblings). The many bonds and roles that occur within a large family can be powerful teaching tools. Girls who are the oldest often play a caregiving role, but girls who are younger members of the family have the benefit of having "many mothers." Marlene Brant Castellano, the eighth child in her family, says that her large family provided "that expectation that the world is friendly, that there are relationships to be made and people willing to help." Many women also mention that growing up in families where there are lots of girls and women can be empowering in terms of learning about womanhood through a community of women.

Aboriginal women who witness love, respect and equity between their parents when they are girls learn to resist the concept that women exist to serve men. Tasks were often divided along gender lines in the past, and in healthy Aboriginal families this exemplified a sense of balance between the male and female roles. Ojibway consultant Barbra Nahwegahbow describes how this worked in her family: "My mother had her role, she was happy with it, and my father had his. Together they kind of made a team. So there was never any sense in our family of inequality — that her role and function weren't valued." Many strong Aboriginal women have told me that their fathers were "supportive" and "devoted" helpers to their mothers. Myra Laramee and Emma LaRocque have referred to their fathers as "feminists," implying that they were men who did not question the respect that was due to their wives or to the work that they did.

The teaching relationship between fathers and their girls is also tremendously helpful. Katie Rich, former president of the Innu Nation, acknowledges that her father groomed her for politics from a young age, without apparent consideration of her gender. Sto:lo Elder Dorris Peters and Cree/Métis writer Maria Campbell value the considerable time they spent with their fathers as young girls. The father of Shirley Williams (Ojibway/Odawa) fought to keep her out of residential school until she was ten years old so that he and her mother could have more time to provide her with a Native education. Williams spent much of her childhood walking in the bush on Manitoulin Island (Ontario) with her father. His Native classroom provided her with invaluable lessons and a foundation for her adult work as a language and culture instructor. Through his own questioning of the rules of the church and the state, Williams's father taught her to be a critical thinker.

Strong, independent female role models provide Native girls with the sense that they can overcome whatever obstacles they will inevitably encounter. These lessons have traditionally been learned in a non-verbal way, by example, as in the case of Mohawk educator Marlene Brant Castellano. She remembers her mother's style of teaching:

> Without ever letting us know, without being ambitious for us or pushing us, mother held on to the belief that she had it in her to "be somebody." If there were any obstacles, she just barrelled them out of the way so that we could be whatever we wanted to be.

For Castellano, lessons around autonomy came from witnessing acts like her mother shouting a cattle drover off the family farm at Tyendinaga Mohawk territory (Ontario) because, as she told her children: "The only reason he comes on the reserve is to cheat the Indians because he thinks we are too stupid to know his game."

The bond between Aboriginal girls and their grandmothers is notably strong, and this relationship has taught many lessons about resistance. Those familiar with Maria Campbell's autobiography, *Halfbreed*, will recall the strength of her "Cheechum." This great-grandmother is an anomaly in Campbell's family and in the Métis community where they lived in northern Saskatchewan. She resists not only the government but also the church and its undisputed power over the people. Cheechum has an acute understanding of the destructive processes that colonization has put in place. She is not afraid to confront the men around her. In the midst of the drunken violence that takes over one of the community gatherings, Cheechum leads the women to lock the men in the dugout cellar. Campbell writes, "When they tried to climb out, Cheechum would hit them on the head with her cane."[1] In our conversation, Campbell told me that this great-grandmother is still a strong support for her. She says, "In times in my life when I have been frightened, or feel like I can't do anything, she is there. She is still there, and I can hear her. She was so independent and so strong, nothing was impossible for her; if she wanted to do it, she did it."

Other grandmothers that appear in the literary world include those of Anna Lee Walters and Leslie Marmon Silko. Says Lee Walters of her Otoe grandmother: "There were many facets to her that I found quite miraculous. She was able to wrestle snakes from the trees and sweep them out of the house, and work like a man bailing hay in the barn."[2] Marmon Silko depicts her Laguna grandmother as "unafraid of anything in the hills" (of New Mexico) and "the horse-woman who would ride any bronco."[3] This woman could move in and out of what western society has known as the male purview. Silko writes:

> My Grandma Lily had been a Ford Model A mechanic when she was a teenager. I remember when I was young she was always fixing broken lamps and appliances. She was small and wiry, but she could lift her weight in rolled roofing or boxes of nails. When she was seventy-five, she was still repairing washing machines in my uncle's coin-operated laundry.[4]

The contrast between the powerlessness of older women in mainstream society and the power accorded to some Native grandmothers is remarkable. Ojibway trainer Gertie Beaucage lived with her grandmother and knows this from experience: "I grew up always knowing that physical power and strength didn't equate with power." She adds:

> I think my grandmother was a very good teacher of that [understanding of power] because she was in a wheelchair. She was the *absolute final decision-making power* that I knew of. And it didn't

have anything to do with whether she could stand up and lean over you, or whether she sat back in her chair and said, "This needs to happen."

The authority of many Native grandmothers stems from their role as the head of the extended family. In such families, Native girls witness both the social and the economic decision-making power of older women in their communities. The foundation for Lee Maracle's understanding of gender roles is, as she says, based on the "remnants of seeing my great grandmother manage the social relations in the community." Maracle understands the authority of older women to "maintain discipline in the village" because she witnessed her grandmother leading the women and girls to confront violence in the community.

Jeannette Armstrong grew up around people like her grandmother and her aunt, both of whom commanded ranches of 400 head of cattle. Armstrong recalls a scene in which western expectations of women collided with the traditional way her family was going about the ranching business:

I recall some man coming to talk about the horses. My uncles and my dad were standing there, and they listened to him talk and so on. Then they told him, "Well, we have to go and talk to our mom. She will be the one to do the transaction with you ... She owns all the horses and all the cattle."

He didn't want to deal with her. He came out and said, "But she is a woman!! How can you guys let a woman decide? You guys can decide right here. Just tell her what you decided." And they were shocked that a man would say that.

Armstrong's tradition is matriarchal, in which women have clearly defined economic authority. This authority is not so clearly delineated in other Native traditions, yet grandmothers and mothers from various nations have exemplified a sense of economic independence. "Providing" for the family was part of the ongoing activity of many mothers, as Andrea Chrisjohn (Onya:ta'ka) recalls:

My mom cooked. She was a tremendous cook. She could cook, she could sew, she did housekeeping. But she also chopped wood, she'd do water, she took care of the garden. She didn't limit herself.

And none of us were limited either. It wasn't a job that one of the boys did, and another job that the girls did. We all did it. When my dad went out to the bush, we all went.

Gertie Beaucage not only witnessed her grandmother's strength, but was also influenced by her mother's:

I never remember my mother saying somebody should take care of me. My father was away for months at a time, off doing work, and he would bring home money after three or four months, but in between there wasn't any. So she did have to work, and she never had a "woe is me" attitude towards it. There was just always a notion that women work, and it never occurred to me that this wasn't the case for every one.

The "women's work" of these mothers, aunties and grandmothers taught these women about community interdependency and dispelled the myth that one gender is overly "dependent" on another because of certain tasks that they perform. Even though tasks were generally gender specific, individuals of both sexes were taught to value and practise all basic tools of survival, regardless of their gender association. They knew they had to learn the tasks that were typically done by the other gender because there would be times when their partners would not be able to fulfil their roles. Maria Campbell recalls how her father instructed her to take care in the bush: "What are you going to do," he asked, "if you are out in the bush and there is no man out there? Look at our granny, she is a better hunter than I am. If she had to go out there, she could shoot. So you learn to do it too." Kathleen Green remembers her father telling her brothers that they needed to learn how to cook, look after children and clean house.

Girls in such families learn that they have the ability to do any kind of work, and moreover, that they are *expected*, as members of their societies, to know how to take care of their basic survival needs. They grow up observing women who take on the family responsibilities of childrearing, the economic responsibilities of providing for the family and the community responsibilities of healer, teacher and community organizer. They also learn that jobs and tasks are not essentially linked to gender; rather, that the bottom line is about working together for the necessity of survival. Growing up in rural Manitoba in the 1950s, Laverne Gervais-Contois remembers:

> I wasn't told to stay away from the axe when we had to go and cut up some firewood. I was shown how to use it! If grandma was sick, then grandpa had to cook. If the kid needed his diaper changed, gramps got up and changed his diaper.

Strong families also teach more overt lessons of resistance. Although her grandmother's teaching was mostly by way of example, Helen Thundercloud remembers "one spoken lesson," given just before she was taken away to the tuberculosis sanatorium when she was eight. Her grandmother told her:

> I want to tell you something, my girl. You are going away and you are going to meet lots of people, white people over there. They are going to try to teach you things. You just remember one thing, my girl: people can teach you all you want, but you don't have to learn.

When Thundercloud was later scooped from the sanatorium and placed in a residential school, her grandmother's words were essential components in the foundation of her resistance to the dismantling and negation of her identity. Thundercloud resisted "learning" much of what she was expected to internalize throughout her ten years of residential schooling.

Gertie Beaucage's early political awareness was fostered by her mother. When she was twelve, her mother gave her a copy of the *Indian Act.* She was told to read it and to understand that "everything in [your] life is affected by that piece of paper." Her mother encouraged her to consider her position as a Native woman who, because of the patriarchal practices of the *Indian Act*, stood to lose a number of rights through marriage:

> She said it would probably not be a good idea to get married. That marriage in itself was primarily for the benefit of men more than women ... And she said, "Look in there further, and realize that if you marry somebody from another reserve, then you have to go over there. You lose your right even to be buried here amongst your own family." That's how much the *Indian Act* affected us.

The guidance that women receive from their mothers, aunts and grandmothers shapes the way they learn to understand themselves and their positions in the world. These teachings, these ways of working together as families build resistance. Women learn that they need to create their own worlds that oppose the hegemonic pressures of destruction.

## GROUNDING IN NATIVE COMMUNITY

Ties to community are as significant as ties to family in terms of bolstering a positive identity. Women who come from reserve communities have had to struggle to retain those ties, because so many were forcibly removed as children or had to leave as adults in search of education or employment. The removal of children for residential school resulted in the slow erosion of relationship to community and to the identities that were based in that community. Women who leave the reserve often feel displaced when they first leave home, experiencing feelings of alienation and isolation as a result of not fitting in with the dominant society while at the same time having a growing sense of removal from their home communities. They must find ways to maintain or replace that sense of community.

Those who have maintained contact but are unable to live in their home communities find ways to go there periodically as a method of grounding themselves. Ida LaBillois-Montour, a Mi'kmaw from Listuguj (Quebec), knows the importance of maintaining these ties. Although she has created community as a member of the urban Aboriginal population in Montreal, she has always found strength in being able to return "home" to her reserve community. Others, like Blood educator Diane Eaglespeaker, go back regularly to attend ceremonies or visit with family members.

Many urban Aboriginal people do not have the opportunity to return "home." In order to nurture their sense of identity, they must look for alternatives. They often begin to rediscover their sense of identity by hooking up with other Aboriginal people. Lillian McGregor recalls her experiences when she first moved off the reserve and went to Toronto in the 1940s: "I looked around for my people when I went downtown, and I met them. We all got together ... we knew just by looking at a person that they were Indian." Michèle Audette has created an Aboriginal community for herself in the city of Montreal. The connections this provides will sustain her until she can return to her community, near Sept Isles, Quebec. Whether these relationships are temporary or long-term, urban Aboriginal communities are the lifeline for many Native people.

Often these communities are built through organizations. Sylvia Maracle, executive director of the Ontario Federation of Indian Friendship Centres, points out that Native urban organizations provide Native people a degree of isolation that protects and fortifies them against an onslaught of demeaning messages from mainstream culture. She equates this with the geographic isolation of some reserve communities, which have protected on-reserve Native people in the same way. Interaction with the mainstream population can be tainted with sexist and racist definitions of Native being. Immersion into Native communities, whether on reserve or within Native urban organizations, both protects and builds a positive sense of Native identity.

For women who have come from dysfunctional families or communities, urban Aboriginal communities offer a place to heal and to build alternatives. Laverne Gervais-Contois recovered from the drug and alcohol culture of her upbringing by returning to the Native community. It was "a process of coming away from hating brown eyes to learning to love brown eyes." Her return was a return to love of self. After having re-entered the Aboriginal community in the urban context, she reached the point where she could say "Hey: I love me, and I want to have a relationship with my family. And this is who my family is today. That community. That Native community. I will go back and work and try to get things together." Gervais-Contois is now an active member of the urban Aboriginal community of Montreal.

Aboriginal people also find and create community through political activity. Urban and reserve-based people can work together as a community to fight political injustice and oppression, and in so doing they develop a political consciousness. The emergence of Indigenous political resistance movements has shaped the political identity of many Native women. Former Principal Chief of the Cherokee Nation, Wilma Mankiller, attributed her political awakening to the occupation of Alcatraz. This event took place in 1969, when a group of university students occupied the abandoned prison on the island of Alcatraz in the San Fransisco Bay. They stayed for nineteen months in an attempt to attract attention to the injustices faced by Indian people. Mankiller recalls:

> In most ways I was a typical housewife at that time ... but when Alcatraz occurred, I became aware of what needed to be done to let the rest of the world know that Indians had rights too. Alcatraz articulated my own feelings about being an Indian. It was a benchmark. After that, I became involved.[5]

Gertie Beaucage remembers Wounded Knee as a time when her aunt began to politicize her about both her rights and her responsibilities as a young Native woman. Beaucage was a teenager living in her home community of Nipissing First Nation in 1973 when members of the American Indian Movement took over Wounded Knee, South Dakota, and held a sixty-nine day siege. They asked that the US Senate fully investigate the conditions on reservations and demanded the return of the Black Hills to the Lakota Nation. Beaucage's aunt took the opportunity to inform her about her responsibilities to Indigenous people:

> I was politicized by my aunt, who woke me up one morning and said, "There's a lot of trouble going on at Wounded Knee. Wake up and pay attention!" With ten kids and a happy-go-lucky husband and all the rest of it, she had to wake me up and tell me: "There's things going on and you have got to pay attention, because you're young and educated. Use your brain!"

In Canada, many Native people refer to the Oka crisis as a turning point in their lives. This eleven-week armed stand-off began when Mohawks from Kanesetake (west of Montreal) erected a roadblock to protest the construction of a golf course on traditional Mohawk land. It soon turned into a national event, drawing Native people from across the country in support. It was a rallying point and an overt example that colonial warfare was still happening in 1990. It was a call to consciousness for many Native people about identity, as it renewed our awareness and resistance to the way in which Aboriginal people are treated in Canada.

The erosion of Native women's rights has also been a politicizing experience. The crisis experienced by women who were disenfranchised through the *Indian Act* was instrumental in sparking a critical consciousness about identity and inspiring resistance. When Mary Two-Axe Early (Mohawk) was evicted from her property on the reserve of Kahnawake in 1967 because she had lost her status through marriage, she began to organize the group Equal Rights for Indian Women. In the early 1970s, Jeannette Lavell, an Ojibway from Wikwemikong (Ontario), and Yvonne Bedard, an Iroquois from Six Nations (Ontario), went to court over the loss of their status through marriage. In the early 1980s, Sandra Lovelace, a Maliseet from the Tobique reserve in New Brunswick, took her case to the United Nations Human Rights Committee.[6] These critical events culled Native women's awareness of the discrimination they faced through the *Indian Act*. The Act was finally changed in 1985, and women (and their children) who had been disenfranchised began to re-apply for their status.

One politicization leads to another. The *Indian Act* alerted women to other discriminations they faced, whether they were status or not. It was a period of women beginning to speak out about the injustices they faced — not just from mainstream society, but also from within their own communities. For example, Ojibway Grandmother[7] Vera Martin was involved in taking the Lavell case to Ottawa. She remembers this time was significant: "That was a bonding on its own. Coming together." This bonding/awareness inspired local political action. In the late 1970s, several women of the Tobique reserve in New Brunswick took on not only the disenfranchisement but also the way in which women were being treated in general in the community. They raised awareness about domestic violence and how patriarchal property ownership regulations resulted in homelessness for women and children.[8]

The community of women in the 1970s saw a growth of women organizing politically, but there has always been a strong sense of community among women who support one another. Aboriginal women find a lot of strength and inspiration in the company of other women, if not through immediate families, then through their alternative families. Many women have experienced the security and comfort of being raised in large families of girls. Where women have not had mothers, grandmothers, aunts or sisters in their biological families, they have found and created families and communities of women for support and guidance. Some have done this through women's groups, and this has been helpful to them. Others have developed supportive relationships with women in a more informal sense. Lila Tabobondung remembers developing a critical consciousness through meeting women who were working alongside her in Aboriginal political organizations during the 1970s in Toronto. Discussions with co-workers helped shaped her perspective and understanding about her own identity, about the state of community development across the country and about the role of Native women within those communities. For Tabobondung, meeting other women politicized her and helped her become more active within community politics.

Vera Martin was raised by her father, but she talks about the many "mothers" that came to her along her path. As an adult she was adopted through ceremonies by a few older women. These women looked after her until they died, and they continue to care for her from the spirit world now that they are gone. Both Vera Martin and Carol Couchie have told me about women who were their "intellectual mothers," women who stimulated them by reading and discussion, which was particularly helpful at the time when they were at risk of being overwhelmed by childcare responsibilities and husbands who did not value their minds. Their experiences demonstrate the significant place of older women in our lives; whether biological or not, many of us have had aunties or mothers who have taken us under their wings, and mothered our spirits, minds, emotions and bodies. They have given us community.

## CONNECTION TO LAND

*I know that without my land and my people I am not alive. I am simply flesh waiting to die.*
— Jeannette Armstrong (Okanagan)[9]

The relationship with the land is critical to Native female strength and resistance. It is a relationship that usually begins in childhood. Many women have told me that, as girls, they went out on the land to seek restoration, solace and comfort from some of the dysfunctional situations they were involved in. Nena Lacaille-Johnson, a Seneca who grew up in Pennsylvania remembers her childhood: "I spent most of my time outdoors. That was my survival technique. I didn't have to be in the middle of most of the conflict that was going on within my family and within my community. I was out wandering around, catching frogs and climbing trees and playing horses." Valerie King-Green would go into the bush when she was a child to escape the abuse and violence that was happening in her community: "I don't know how long I would be back there, but I would come out really happy and re-energized to carry on. That's where I would release a lot of my frustrations, ever since I can remember."

Land as mother can provide both comfort and wisdom. As a child, Gertie Beaucage learned to see the earth and the moon as female relations:

> I learned from my grandmother that you always have your mother, and you always have your grandmother ... She referred me to the earth. The earth is always there; your grandmother [moon] is always there. And if you can't tell anybody else, you can always tell them. So I remember when I would be really upset with my family... then I would talk to her. I would go out and sit quietly, or take walks in the night-time under the moon, saying, "Here I am. Have you ever seen this happen?" Because I knew she had been up there for awhile.

Some women come to understand or remember the healing and nurturing qualities of the land as adults. One woman told me a story about how she turned to the land to help her deal with the anger she experienced as a result of domestic abuse:[10]

> I was scared. Scared, [I thought], *What can I do with this anger?* So I went down to my room and I tried to cry, but it was like I was empty. I had no feeling. I thought if I cried I would stop being so angry, but nothing came out. I thought to myself, I had to do something. And then I remembered, *Oh, men go out hunting, or on their skidoos, and nature heals them. Why can't we women do that?*

So I phoned up a friend and got a skidoo. I went and picked her up and we were driving around the mountains and the valleys, but I still had this anger in me. It was blocked ...

I don't know, but somehow it felt like the dam broke and I just started screaming and yelling in anger and frustration and humiliation. For about five, seven minutes. And then I started laughing, just laughing, and then I said, Whew, yippee, hallelujah, whatever. Hooraying and all that. Laughing and crying at the same time. Just so full of joy because I had released my anger and my frustration and my pain.

I think that is when I became a woman!

Grounding in our particular geographic territories is also significant in terms of maintaining one's Native identity.[11] For Melanie Corbiere (Ojibway), the teachings of her elders around geographic place have been key to her identity. She passes on these teachings to the younger generations, in spite of the fact that she now lives in an urban setting. She expresses the sense of belonging her people have always felt to Turtle Island (North America):

From when I was very little, I've had Native people, old people telling me all the time, "We were always here. We didn't come from someplace else. We might have moved around on this continent, but we were always here."

How can you change those words? You can't. "We were always here." They mean the same thing. They mean the same thing to my son and daughter as they did to me. That we were always here, that this was the place.[12]

## LANGUAGE

Women who have managed to hang onto their Indigenous language have found that it helps maintain and preserve their Indian identity. When Lillian McGregor moved to Toronto in the 1940s, she sought out her new community and kept her identity intact through language: "I always felt I was still Native because I spoke Ojibway."

Those who lost their languages because of residential school attendance or other pressures to assimilate have felt tremendous loss and separation from their people. When Monica Ittusardjuat returned from residential school, she felt like a "misfit in Inuit society" because she had lost her fluency in Inuktitut.

Language can support and promote the esteemed position of women, as in the Dakota nation. Dakota speaker Ivy Chaske explains that one can not say, "I am Dakota." This phrase is expressed in one word — which is, in fact, the word Dakota split apart, with the representation of the individual's existence inserted in the middle. Chaske continues, "What that tells you as you are growing up is that you are part of a nation of people." This can, as she points out, reinforce the identity and esteem of girls (in particular) who learn to see themselves as conveyors of the life force: "As a girl child, you are the centre of that nation, you are the life force of the nation."

Chaske also explains that Dakota women have their own language, which is a reflection of the traditional respect accorded to women. Dakota men understand the women's language, but they do not speak it. "This silence is a show of respect and awe," she says. "It is part of honouring the givers of life." The existence of a language particular to women is in accordance with traditional Dakota taboos that once prevented a man from speaking with his mother-in-law. Chaske explains why: "It is out of respect that he is not allowed to speak to his mother-in-law because he has such respect for the woman who gave life to his wife, who is now going to give life to his children."

The way in which various Indigenous languages are constructed can protect Native women from understanding themselves from a patriarchal world view. In the Okanagan language, for example, there are no pronouns for male and female. As Jeannette Armstrong describes, there is no way to refer to a person in a gender-biased way:

> You can't point to that person and say "she" or "he." You can only point to that person based on how they are related to us, or how they are related to other things. You could say "my aunt," or you could say "that person who is my teacher" or "that person who is selling me goods."

Nor is there a way to refer to women in a derogatory fashion in many of our original languages. Sylvia Maracle points out that when you want to insult someone in English, you use a term that refers to the female — bitch, for example. Negativity is thus equated with femaleness. Maracle says, "You can't do that in Mohawk. When you talk about a woman, you talk about Ista. That woman is your mother." She draws the parallels with Ojibway: "I think it's the same thing, in terms of Anishinabekwe. That concept of woman. [A woman is] not somebody's possession, not a belonging, not a negative concept. [You refer to her] in the purest, most respectful way you can." Catherine Martin explains how our original languages have helped us avoid negative body images: "In Mi'kmaq language, there are no swears. You don't use body parts to swear. You are taught to respect your body."

When Aboriginal women begin to speak English, the way in which they perceive themselves culturally, racially and as women changes, an experience that Maria Campbell can understand: "A lot of the bad things that happened to us happened when we started to speak English, and when we started school. Because there is a different way of looking at and thinking when you are looking at stuff in English as compared to when you are thinking and doing things in Cree or Michif all the time."

The use of Indigenous languages allows Native women to self-define outside of the misogynist paradigms that exist in the colonizer's language.

## STORYTELLING

Indigenous stories are significant because they are anchors of resistance. They are also ways of preserving the language and the power and meaningfulness of the spoken word. Our stories are unadulterated version of our history and creation. They are critical for Native people who seek a sense of identity founded within Native culture. As Laguna Pueblo/Sioux writer and professor Paula Gunn Allen articulates:

Since the coming of the Anglo-Europeans beginning in the fifteenth century, the fragile web of identity that long held tribal people secure has gradually been weakened and torn. But the oral tradition has prevented the complete destruction of the web, the ultimate disruption of tribal ways. The oral tradition is vital; it heals itself and the tribal web by adapting to the flow of the present while never relinquishing its connection to the past.[13]

Laguna writer Leslie Marmon Silko also recognizes how stories connect her people:

> When I was a child at Kawaik, in the Laguna Pueblo reservation in New Mexico, the old folks used to tell us to listen and to remember the stories that tell us who we are as a people. The old folks said the stories are alive, the stories are our ancestors. In the very telling of the stories, the spirits of our beloved ancestors and family become present with us.[14]

The respect accorded to Native women in many traditional stories provides the foundation for strong Native female identity and helps us retain an understanding of our power. Sandra Laronde, the artistic producer at Native Women in the Arts (an arts network for Native Women that operates out of Toronto), was taught that stories are an effective way to learn about womanhood. In her search to understand more about her female identity, Laronde has been told "Go back to the mythology. To the stories. To the archetypes that we have been given in our culture. That is where a lot of the information is."

Many Indigenous creation stories are female centred and reinforce the value of Native women in their societies. Stories like that of White Buffalo Calf Woman (who is credited for bringing ceremonies and behaviour codes to the Sioux) offer ways to resist the vision offered by religions where the law-giver is always male and the female is subservient. Kochininako, the female heroine of Laguna Pueblo stories has many adventures in which she displays her courage and strength. Leslie Marmon Silko finds that "Kochininako is beautiful because she has the courage to act in times of great peril, and her triumph is achieved by her sensuality, not through violence and destruction." Silko has found strength in these stories since childhood, and they have helped her to resist oppressive experiences.[15]

As a writer, educator and storyteller, Maria Campbell works with traditional stories. She understands their significance and their role in preserving traditional knowledge and in promoting a positive image of womanhood. Yet, as Campbell points out, we can also turn to our current lives and our everyday stories for these images. Campbell has always taken inspiration in the "no-nonsense" approach of her grand-mothers, who simply did the work they saw had to be done. She points out that we don't have to look far to find these women in our communities today, referring to a story she recently read in a local newspaper about a woman who had moved back to the reserve so she could look after her aging father:

> She got herself a saw and an axe, went into the bush and sawed and cut her own logs. Leasing a friend's half-ton truck, she hauled the logs home and built her own house. She mixed mud and grass and mudded her home just as her mother and grandmother had done befor her. She also planted a huge garden and hunted for her own meat. Now who says we are dependent on anybody? This woman is in her fifties. Old-time stories were full of this kind of self-determination, but we also have determination today. Women are strong; they can do anything if they have to.

## SPIRITUALITY

For most Native women, spirituality is the heart of survival, resistance and renewal. Some of the women I interviewed mix Christianity with Native spiritual traditions, but many have turned exclusively to Native spiritual tradition because it allows them to claim an identity that has been historically denied. Many Native women told me it felt like they had finally found something that was "ours" when they began to practise Native spirituality. The practice of Native spiritual tradition is, in and of itself, an act of resistance to all the conditioning that Native ways are "evil," "pagan" and "witchcraft."

Although Native women generally prefer to practise the traditions that come from their particular nations, they often call upon other Native spiritual traditions to help them with resistance and spiritual fulfilment. Simona Arnatsiaq calls upon Cree teachings in the absence of her Inuit spiritual ways. She must use a mixture of tradition because of all that has been lost:

There's something I have always found missing in my spiritual
world. What about a spirituality I can call my own? So I revert
back to Catholicism when I need it. I remember in Winnipeg
being at a pipe ceremony for Aboriginals with AIDS. I remember
saying, "Well I envy you. You have this spirituality, you have your
rituals, you have got the sweetgrass, and I don't have my own."
Whatever I have spiritually is begged, borrowed or stolen.

Arnatsiaq's comments demonstrate the importance of having
traditions that feel like they belong to us, even if they are borrowed.
Many women start out on their learning journey by participating in
ceremonies that do not come from their particular nation. In some
cases, this connects them to the spiritual ways of their own ancestors.
Theresa Tait has told me a story about bringing the (Sioux) Uwipi
ceremony to her (Wit'sutwet'en) community in central British Columbia. The ceremony inspired her to ask her grandmother "How did we
used to pray?" Her grandmother, also inspired by the ceremony, began
to remember traditional ways that Tait's great-great-grandmother had
practised. She told Tait, "I remember my grandmother was sitting by
the river one time, and she was using smoke from the fire, and she
had the pipe. She was blowing smoke up and she was praying. I was
just a little girl, and I was sitting beside her and all of a sudden she
started to shake. She fell to the ground and I knew she was in contact
with the Creator."

If women cannot access spirituality through particular ceremonies,
there are other ways that are common to many Native traditions.
Dreams, visions and the simple acknowledgement that there are spirits
all around us all the time have been helpful to many Native women.
Ida LaBillois-Montour doesn't smudge every day, but she listens to
dreams and works with the spirits that she sees and hears. Dreams
can be a powerful tool of resistance to oppression. Ojibway Grandmother Vera Martin says, "The dreams were what guided me when I
had nobody." She tells the story of trying to commit suicide when
she was with her seventh child. At this time, her grandfather came to
her in a dream and told her, "You have to go back. You have work to
do." Martin returned to her life and began a healing journey that has
involved helping other people to get well. Many women will talk

about the guidance they receive from their ancestors through their dreams.

Native women have hung onto their spiritual practices in spite of pressure to abandon these ways. Mohawk healer Diane Hill credits her ability to listen to spirits for "saving her from calamity." She relates that "many people tried to tell me that my experiences with spiritual energy, such as the movement of spirits in the house, were just figments of my imagination." Nena Lacaille-Johnson remembers how she used dreams when she was a child, stating that this helped her to survive the violence and turmoil that she was experiencing at the time: "If I was particularly troubled, I think it was my way of praying. I would ask for help for something, and I would get insights in my dreams." Unfortunately, she shared this at one point with a school counsellor, who crushed her ability to connect with her faith in this way. Lacaille-Johnson recalls this conversation:

> I told the counsellor, "Well, I just ask for help in my dreams, and it comes to me."
>
> The counsellor said, "Who are you talking to?"
>
> And I said, "I guess, God." I didn't have any other name for that, so I said, "I guess I am talking to God, and I get my answers in my dreams."
>
> So she took all the authority that those people in those positions can muster, and she said, "Now *you* know, *you* know deep in your heart that there is no such thing. You can't talk to God. He's not going to answer you in your dreams. You are just fooling yourself."

"Well, I was devastated," Lacaille-Johnson remembers. "That was the first time it dawned on me that it wasn't normal. And that maybe I was nuts!" The result of this experience was significant: "I quit dreaming until I was about eighteen years old. I had a real mental block about dreaming."

Through dreams and other experiences, many women experience connections with ancestral spirits. These experiences are helpful to women when they become discouraged or tired of struggling to improve their lives and the lives of others. Maggie Paul has made valuable contributions in the revitalization of Native culture. But there was a time when she just wanted to "throw in the towel." Her singing and telling of dreams were frequently met with, "Oh, she is too loud," or "I don't want to hear them dreams again. They are stupid. They are crazy." She finally reached a point of wanting to quit singing and sharing her dreams. During this period she was visited in the sweat lodge by a spirit, who told her, "I want you to keep singing because where we are, we know what you are singing. Keep on telling your dreams, because they are visions. Could be for somebody, could be for you. Don't quit." These words gave Paul the encouragement to continue on as singer and a cultural teacher.

However they work with their spirituality, a connection with the Great Mystery has been a significant factor in helping Native women resist oppressive experiences and redefine their womanhood. Taken in an Indigenous context, it is really a part of everything we do, and for this reason, it underpins a lot of the discussion in this book.

## CHAPTER EIGHT

# ACTS OF RESISTANCE

❖

WITH THE FOUNDATIONS FOR RESISTANCE in place, Native women may strengthen their sense of identity through various acts of resistance. With each act of resistance, Native women can further define and confirm a positive identity and challenge the oppression of Native people in general.

## CHALLENGING STEREOTYPES

The earliest act of resistance for most Native women is to recognize and then challenge negative stereotypes. As difficult and courageous an act as it is, it is a liberating experience. For many contemporary Native women, this was something that happened at an early age, often with the stereotypes they were faced with when they entered the school system. It may have been the first time they encountered non-Native people; the first time they were made to feel "different"; and the first time they felt a need to resist the racism that defined the new world they found themselves in.

Native girls have demonstrated various acts of resistance to the racism that comes from teachers and classmates. Racism against Native people has been so pervasive in the North American school curriculum that the majority of Native women have had to endure many years of racist schooling before naming it and calling for change. Fortunately, many eventually come to this consciousness. Marlene Brant Castellano reached this awareness in university:

> In school when I learned about the savage Iroquois and how they slaughtered the brave pioneers and priests, I made no connection between the textbooks and the Mohawks of which I was one. But

at university, people began to ask questions about my Indianness and I realized that I had been socialized into an identity that totally ignored my heritage and history. This was the beginning of my conscious efforts to sort out what it means to me to be an Indian in modern society.[1]

Janice Acoose, a Cree/Métis raised in Saskatchewan, says that she did not have the "political consciousness or strength of spirit" to allow her to challenge the racist assumptions of her high school. By the time she went to university, however, she had gained sufficient strength from the voices of other Indigenous peoples to challenge one of her professors.[2] Mi'kmaq poet Rita Joe's consciousness of the racism in history surfaced when her children began to criticize their high school history textbooks.[3]

One particular racist narrative that was popular in schools for a long time was that of the "savage" in need of salvation. This was particularly popular in religious schools, as salvation was the vocation of priests and nuns. There were many Native girls who resisted this narrative, even before they understood all the dynamics. Theresa Johnson Ortiz, an Ojibway who attended a private Catholic school in Toronto, has written about the expectation that she play the savage in a school play:

> The nuns told me to be an Indian in the school play. I was told to supplicate myself: get on my knees in gratitude before the founder of their order. My salvation was her reward; she had saved me from barbaric and evil ways. I was chosen because I was an Indian. I was to re-enact the subjection of my people. Their way of teaching perpetuated cultural genocide, the removal of our Indianness, demoralization and condemnation.[4]

The story of Johnson Ortiz shows that the school system asked again and again that Indians play out the part that had been devised for them by the colonizer. In this instance, Johnson displayed resistance by refusing to act the humble savage, in spite of the fact that she had not yet developed a full analysis of the situation at her young age: "The words that would have expressed my feelings of shame, powerlessness, and utter loneliness were not mine to share. They were unknown to me."[5]

If not through school plays, the narrative of the savage was inculcated through lectures at Sunday services and mass. Gertie Beaucage recalls an experience in which a visiting priest attended a mass at her boarding school, St. Joseph's in North Bay. He gave a special lecture that depicted Catholic priests as martyrs to the savage Indians. He did not limit this depiction to the historical, as Beaucage relates: "He said, to that day (which was about the early 1970s), he hadn't seen any real progress in terms of civilizing these savage Indian people, and that he kept going back and forth to these Native communities trying to civilize us." This school had both Native and non-Native students, and Beaucage recalls that there were about twenty-five Indian students in attendance. Her resistance to this treatment was to walk out of the lecture, and in so doing she inspired a number of the other students to follow.

Native females have been subjected not only to racist notions of the savage, but to the sexist notion of a debased womanhood. To be Native was uncivilized; to be female was inferior; but to be a combination of the two was particularly base. The residential school experience of Shirley Williams offers a typical illustration of this convoluted mix of sexism and racism that was taught to girls who attended these schools. Williams remembers learning history lessons about different alliances of Native people with colonial powers. Children would attempt to take pride in these alliances. But when they would say, "Our ancestors helped," the nuns would respond, "Yeah, but you are not them!" For Williams, this had a debilitating impact on her twelve-year-old consciousness, because the outright dismissal of her heritage and history jeopardized her connection to her ancestors. Her story offers an example of the kind of instruction Aboriginal children typically received, where anything that was good about being Native was dismissed. Anything female, such as the female body or menstruation, was even worse.

Williams's most decisive act of resistance to residential school misogyny and oppression was brought on, finally, when one of the nuns called her mother a whore. She told me the story, which began with her mother sending her a special dress for her sixteenth birthday. As a store-bought dress was an exceptional luxury in her family, Williams's mother had sent one that was slightly large. The intent was that her daughter could grow into it over the years. When

Williams went down to the sewing room of the residential school to try it on, the supervising nun pronounced the dress to be low cut and accused her mother of being a "whore" who was teaching immorality. Williams recalls, "I didn't know what a whore meant, other than it was something very dirty." She resisted by defending her mother, and for this act had to stand by a pole for three days, receiving only bread and water. This was a pivotal moment for her: "I think during the time that I was standing there, I thought to myself, 'I don't deserve this. I don't need this. I'll find some other way of getting my education,' and that's when I left." The incident marked the end of Williams's residential school experience. Soon after she went home for Christmas break, and never returned.

## WRITING AS RESISTANCE

*The purpose of my writing has always been to tell a better story than is being told about us. To give that to the people and to the next gen-erations. The voices of the grandmothers and grandfathers compel me to speak of the worth of our people and the beauty all around us, to banish the profaning of ourselves, and to ease the pain. I carry the language of the voice of the land and the valiance of the people and I will not be silenced by a language of tyranny.*

— Jeannette Armstrong (Okanagan)[6]

In the anthology *Reinventing the Enemy's Language: Contemporary Native Women's Writings of North America,* Native women talk about their writing as a tool of resistance against all the negative outcomes of colonization. Editor Gloria Bird recognizes the importance of this form of resistance: "One of the functions of language is to construct our world. We are the producers of this world who create ourselves as well as our social reality, and we do this through language."[7] Writing offers both a means to resist and an opportunity to reinvent.

Many Native women started writing because they wanted to re-spond to negative materials they encountered in school. Emma LaRocque describes her primary motivation:

As soon as I knew what writing was in grade eight, I wanted to do it. And mostly I think it came from a profound need to self-express because there was so much about our history and about our lives that, I quickly learned, has been disregarded, infantalized, and falsified. I think I had this missionary zeal to tell about our humanity because Indianness was so dehumanized and Metis-ness didn't even exist.[8]

Mi'kmaw poet Rita Joe, who began writing in her thirties, was also moved to write because of the negative stereotypes and the negation of Native history she found in school textbooks. Shocked by the history and science textbooks that were being brought home by her teenage children during the 1960s, she encouraged them to speak the truth. With each piece of her own truth-telling writing, she found more strength in her ability to define herself outside of racist paradigms: "I call my words a chisel, carving an image. Our image has been knocked down for too long by the old histories and old chronicles ... When I wrote my second book, and into my third, I didn't give a damn what the historians said about us."[9]

Writing also gives women a means of surviving oppression and a way to engage in a healing process. Anna Lee Walters points to the liberatory qualities she has experienced through this practice: "Writing released years of oppression. It made me whole and free." Expressing her voice also allowed her to stop trying to follow the mainstream ways and to stop denying her tribal essence.[10] This is true for many Native women — the process of writing creates a space where they can deal with anger, pain and sadness, and then begin to kindle positive feelings about their identity. As women heal and reclaim their identity, the overall healing movement for Indigenous people takes hold. Beth Brant, a Mohawk writer who has conducted writing workshops throughout North America, agrees that Native female writing heals "not just the individual, but the broken circles occurring in our Nations."[11] In writing about experiences with racism, sexism, colonization, loss of language and culture, Native women are able to fuel the healing process on both a personal and a national level.

The desire and demand for Native female literary expression, so absent in the past, is increasing as there are more opportunities for

Native women to publish. One of the major outlets for this literary production is Native Women in the Arts. Sandra Laronde, the NWIA founder, acknowledges that writing projects of NWIA have picked up at an incredible pace over the course of the three anthologies that they have produced. Native Women in the Arts has published over ninety new Native female writers in this time.[12] Projects such as these create a much-needed publishing space for Native women who wish to express and recreate the world as they see it. This in itself challenges the false representation of Native women so widely circulated in the dominant culture.

## CREATIVITY AS A SOURCE OF STRENGTH AND IDENTITY

The need for creative expression as a means of healing and identity recovery is crucial in many Native women's lives. Some women have had to fight for their right to express themselves creatively in their private lives. They talk about their husbands telling them they were no good at singing, no good at sewing, no good at dancing. The resistance comes when they begin to do it anyway, and for many this is the beginning of a journey of discovery about their Native womanhood. It is also a journey to reclaiming their voice in the private and public spheres.

Through her learning and her work as a singer, Maggie Paul (Mi'kmaw) has been able to achieve recovery, both at the personal and at the community level. As young women, Paul and her friends used to ask themselves, *"We are Indian people, but what is it? What do Indians do? Do they wear feathers? Do they wear leather? Do they sing and stuff like that, and drum?"* Now, she travels extensively as a singer and a teacher among Aboriginal peoples.

Edna Manitowabi, also a singer, describes the first time she heard the drum. The sound reached deep inside her. It was like "finding a great sense of peace," "coming home to where I belonged." It changed her life:

> That's really what I've followed since '74. Whenever there was a ceremony, I don't care how far it was, I would go, because of the sound of that drum and how it affected me.

The sound and the vibration of the drum triggered a very deep emotion in my heart that awakened my spirit. It allowed me to see life in a different way, in a spiritual way. The memory of my grandmothers and grandfathers, my ancestors, my historical memory, my blood memory was awakened in me.

It is not the sound of the drum. It's much more than that. It's not just any drumming. It's a specific drum, "the little boy water drum," a sacred drum sounding in a specific context, that of ceremony. The spirit of that little boy, speaking through the drum, spoke to my spirit and awakened it, and changed my life around.

Native drumming can help women dismantle negative definitions of being and lead them to places where they will find powerful affirmations of self and nation. Mi'kmaw filmmaker Catherine Martin acknowledges the drum as a teacher:

The drum has helped me to be a stronger Mi'kmaw woman and it has brought me into places where I have learned so much more. Brought me to funerals, or hospitals, or gatherings, or to conferences ... Everywhere I go I sing, and when I sing I receive people, friends, knowledge and sharing, and the drum just keeps teaching me what I need to know.

Music, singing and drumming are integral parts of Native cultures — banned by the colonizer, yet kept alive through the generations. Sewing is another form of creative expression that was once a vital part of our communities and part of a feminine identity. Through sewing, women created needed goods out of raw materials, and they often did so in an artistic manner. This creative form has also been lost and some women have reclaimed it. Monica Ittusardjuat says that for many years she felt that she was less of a woman by the standards of her culture as she lost the ability to sew in residential school. She explains how she reclaimed this ability:

It makes me feel good to create, to be creative. So I found a little closet, somewhere in my son's room. Whenever I want to sew, I close the door, put on some gospel music, and I am sewing away, and I sing with the music at the top of my lungs! [laughs] And I feel good about that!

Whether at the individual level or the national level, creative expression is essential for the recovery of our identity. During a conversation about the development of the newly emergent territory of Nunavut, Simona Arnatsiaq remarked, "How can we have self-government without joy, without arts? You can't have a building spring up one day — a government house with a whole bunch of politicians running around — without pride. You have to have arts. You have got to reclaim your identity. You have got to have song. And that is something I would love to see more of."

## RESISTING ASSIMILATION

Because of the overwhelming efforts to "kill the Indian" through assimilation policies in Canada and the United States, Native women have had to practise tremendous resistance just to maintain their identities as Native. The most overt assimilation tactics are now part of our dark history, and Native pride has improved considerably since the 1960s, but people are still pressured by everyday racist experiences which may force them to abandon their Native heritage and seek out a different identity. Lighter skinned Aboriginal people sometimes choose to identify as white. There are those among us who still dye their hair blonde — and now we even have the option of wearing blue contact lenses! Our darker-skinned relatives have, at times, identified with people of colour as a way of avoiding the pain of being Native. Laverne Gervais-Contois has family members who used to claim they were Mexican. Likewise, the protagonist in Richard Wagamese's novel *Keeper 'N Me* adopts a black identity before coming to a realization that he must make peace with his Native self.[13]

Native women who claim their ancestry in spite of pressures or "options" to deny it demonstrate remarkable resistance to racism and assimilation. Rita Joe has written about one such demonstration that took place in her youth. She was walking down the street with a few friends when some boys yelled "Squaw!" at one of her friends. Rita Joe, who had been mistaken for a white woman, swung her purse at the perpetrator of the slur and replied, "If you are calling my friend a squaw, we're all squaws, because we're all Native."[14] Rita Joe refused to disappear as a Native person by refusing the "option" to be white.

Native women have had to work hard to resist the underlying residential school goal of turning them into white people. Helen Thundercloud remembers the way she was presented the "option" to abandon her Nativeness. The nuns at St. Mary's Residential School in Kenora pitted her against the other Native students, by telling her repeatedly in French, "You are not like them, you are like us." They instructed her that "it would be best if you just quit seeing those people, because they are not for you." Thundercloud maintained her identity by complying with the nuns on the outside, while inside refusing to let go of her sense of herself as Native. She would dutifully take holy communion, but, she says, "In my heart I was a practising pagan." Her silent resistance was so effective that "the nuns thought I was the one they were going to save; that I would end up in a convent like them."

Some Native people start resisting the "option" to be white later in life, after having gone through a process where they have themselves denied or have been denied their heritage. Métis writer Joanne Arnott has written about her family's ongoing denial of Aboriginal ancestry and how hard it is for them to embrace their heritage. Even if they "know" they are Aboriginal, they can't quite internalize it:

> At this point, I am convinced that my father doesn't "know" that he is Native. I think perhaps one of his brothers, the most visibly Native of the bunch, "knows," but he has never spoken to me about it. My father's sister has been knowing/not knowing it for years, she has told and denied so many times that I get dizzy thinking about it.[15]

Arnott has been able to reclaim her Native heritage. The decision to "pass" as white, says Arnott, is "one of the very few options for survival of mixed-race people in a virulently racist society."[16] Rhonda Johnson (Métis) agrees, pointing out the difficulty and confusion that Métis people endure as a result of trying to claim their Indian identity. She states that many Métis people live in denial about their Indian heritage, and that they feel guilt about it. It is a struggle to accept the Native side of their ancestry, yet for Johnson, acceptance of her Native ancestry is a way for her to protest racism against Native people and the racism that fed her denial about her heritage. By embracing her Native identity, she finds power and voice as well as peace with herself.[17]

## Rebelling Against the Church

The church has been heavily implicated in all aspects of colonization and it played a critical role in undermining the role of women in Indigenous societies. Many Native female individuals develop a personal resistance to the church, both because of the way that they perceive it has governed their communities and because of the way it has violated their personal well-being as Aboriginal women.

Contemporary Native women can recall the days when Native communities were under the divided authority of the Indian Agent and the priest. As children, many began to question the hypocrisy of the church in relation to their poverty. In *Halfbreed,* Maria Campbell writes about her childhood impressions of the priest's visits:

> He always arrived when it was mealtime and we all had to wait and let him eat first. He ate and ate and I would watch him with hatred. He must have known, because when he finished eating all the choice food, he would smile at me, rub his belly and tell Mom she was a great cook. After he left we had to eat the scraps. If we complained, Mom would tell us that he was picked by God and it was our duty to feed him. I remember asking why Daddy didn't get picked by God. All through my childhood years that priest and I were enemies.[18]

A further hypocrisy Campbell notes is that the children were not allowed to "steal" the choice strawberries that grew in the churchyard, as they belonged to God — but she had seen the priest taking things from the Indians' Sun Dance pole many times.[19]

Sto:lo Elder Dorris Peters has told me about her early resistance to the church. Growing up in British Columbia in the 1930s and '40s, she had cause to question the inequities that she was encouraged to overlook. She states:

> I always questioned it, even when I was a little girl. When they came around with the collection plate, my dad gave all he had.

We had no shoes. I thought about this well dressed man in black, with shiny shoes and big rubbers that went over. He took the money from my dad. I thought, *What is the matter? There is something wrong with this picture.* And I questioned it, and you know, my mother said, "Shh ..."

Peters felt further alienated by the church when she was repeatedly denied confirmation because she didn't have the right dress. Three years in a row she was passed up by the visiting bishop because the cloth on the dress her mother had sewn was not pure white.

Gertie Beaucage offers a humorous story about her introduction to the discrepancy between church practices and Native poverty. At the age of eight, shortly after she began to speak English, Beaucage recalls attending a mass in which she discovered some lit candles. "People would come in and they would go and light these candles. Anyway, I thought, 'Boy, that looks pretty neat.' Well, I went over there and I was going to light a candle. And then some nun came up to me and said, *'You have to put your money in. Before you light the candle, you have to put your money in.'* Beaucage shrugs, "In my own logical process, I figured out that if you don't put the money in, God can't hear you. Well, I didn't have any money. So I figured out that I couldn't afford God. [laughs] It was the sort of down side of being Catholic. You had to have money. So I gave up on them right then and there."

Another point of resistance has been the regimentation of female sexuality that was imposed in residential schools and elsewhere in Christian teachings. In spite of her ongoing faith as a Christian, Rita Joe has acted in a rebellious way towards the church policies and values that oppressed her sexuality and spirituality in earlier years. She writes about how she rejected the option of becoming a nun, and how, after leaving the Shubenacadie Residential School at the age of sixteen, she did not go near a church because of the anger she felt about its regimented spirituality.[20] When she went back as a young adult to visit the church located at her former school, she presented her resistance by adorning herself in symbols of female sexuality:

I wore my red, red shoes and a beautiful dress. My hair was long and I had lipstick on, about an inch thick. I wanted to show the nuns: "This is me. You have nothing to do with it, with the way I look or present myself. You have nothing to say about it. I dare you to say anything about it." That was the attitude I had.[21]

Rita Joe's presentation is a powerful act of defiance to the multiple oppressions she endured as a colonized Native girl. She had been one of thousands of children who had their long hair cropped and doused in gasoline to get rid of (often non-existent) lice. Her long hair is thus an assertion of a reclaimed Native identity. The red shoes, beautiful dress, and heavy lipstick symbolize a sexual identity in defiance of the sexual mores imposed by the church.

Joe expressed a further act of defiance against the sexual mores of the church by engaging in sex out of "wedlock." She describes how she ran away to Montreal with a young man while still a teenager, returning pregnant. Her explanation for this is: "I had rebelled against the regimentation I had experienced at the Shubenacadie school and thought I could do anything; I thought I was my own boss."[22] Joe eventually had three children before marrying.

Some Native women have come to resist the church because of the role it has played in situating them in wrong or abusive marriages. Wanda Whitebird (Mi'kmaw) recalls the limited teachings of her Catholic school upbringing in Nova Scotia during the 1970s. "We were raised to be wives," she states. At sixteen, Whitebird married a white man, because, she says, "That was the thing to do back then: if you were going to be an Indian, you may as well marry one that isn't an Indian." Whitebird points out that, in a racist and sexist society, the apparent option was to "hide out in society" under the role of wife. The charade of the ideal white wife eventually proved itself to be unsustainable for Whitebird, as it has for so many Native women. She finally left her husband and the children with her husband. For Whitebird, this "totally unmother-woman thing to do" was an act of resistance and survival.

Ojibway midwife Carol Couchie also found herself in an unhealthy role as a wife. Couchie, a former born-again Christian, now sees that her relationship with the church came partly out of a need to cope with the stresses endured in her early years. She told me :

I got really religious at fifteen. I became a born-again Christian. That was *my* alcohol. Most of my siblings had drinking or drug problems. Or they married an alcoholic. That was the loop. So I married an alcoholic. And I got Jesus instead, which can be just as big of a problem, but it's a lot easier on your body!

Couchie married at age seventeen, and was encouraged to stay in the marriage in spite of the difficulties she experienced: "I really believed that if I prayed hard enough, that God would come and heal my marriage. Divorce was not in my vocabulary. For thirteen years I stayed because I really believed that I would go to hell if I left and got a divorce." When she eventually left the marriage, it marked the beginning of her resistance to the church and the patriarchy within: "When I left my husband, started reading more and got into school, it was the beginning of my sort of hate-on for the church and what it does to women." Couchie's liberation allowed her to unravel the particular church dogma that finds fault with a woman who does not sustain the role of an obedient wife, even at the expense of her own well-being.

Through these processes of resistance and rebellion, many Native women develop a consciousness that lets them see how damaging the church has been to their Native female identity. They learn to articulate and rebel against the sexism and racism that the church has propagated in their personal lives and to name the role that the church has played in the cultural genocide of Native peoples. Many speak about the church as the forerunner of assimilation; about the role of the church in stamping out Indigenous spiritual traditions; about the church execution of oppressive schooling; and, for women, about the critical role the church played in introducing patriarchy to Indigenous peoples.

## CHAPTER NINE

# ATTITUDES OF RESISTANCE

❖

IN THIS SECTION, I have looked at many different components that can build "foundations of resistance" with the hope that we might replicate some of these components and thereby make our future generations strong. The examples from the women who participated in my project and from Native female writers map out some actions and strategies of resistance. In this chapter, I look generally at some of the attitudes I uncovered when researching the strength of contemporary Native women.

When I looked for the source of women's resistance in my conversations with them, I discovered a strength of spirit that seemed to manifest itself in some cases right from birth. For example, in trying to explain why her mother had been so strong, Marlene Brant Castellano conceded, "It was just her gift, the spirit she was gifted with — because *her* mother was timid!" Castellano told me her mother was bold and upfront even as a child: "We used to hear the story when Grandpa Harry came in drunk and loud, the boys would hide in the barn. And my mother would greet him at the door and confront him." She had no fear, Castellano concludes: "She knew she could stand up to a man who enjoyed exercising his power."

When I heard Dorris Peters's stories, I was amazed at the unabashed way she would stand up to anyone, from employers, to church and government officials, to politicians, to men and women within our own organizations. Her attitude of resistance began in her childhood, as I discovered through a story she told me about protecting herself against sexual abuse from an employer. In this excerpt, she recollects a scene that happened when she was twelve years old and was employed as a carpenter's helper on the Canadian Pacific Railway in central British Columbia:

The day was hot. It was the first of July, in fact. My boss called me down, and I knew something wasn't right. I just knew it. He was in the house somewhere, so I came down. I swung down, just like a monkey, and I came in through the bathroom window. I had a carpenter's outfit with a hatchet and a hammer and all the nails. When I got in the window, he was there. I said, "Were you calling me?" He says, "Yes. C'mon in. I want to talk to you."

He turned around and he had his private parts exposed. Before he turned around, he said, "I know all about you." He says, "I know what the boys have been doing to you," and he says, "If you are good to me I'll be good to you." And he turned around and had himself exposed.

I was shocked. I had never seen that part of an adult.

He came towards me, and I just dug out my hammer. It's lucky I didn't bring out my axe. I said, "You come near me, and you are going to wear this, and then you are going to wear the axe." I backed up to the window. He backed up. I told him to turn around and walk away. He did. So I got on my ladder and went up to the roof. I stayed there until his daughter came home.

Shaken, the young Peters fled from the scene, but later returned with her sister to demand back wages from her employer, which she got. Her courageous acts refuted not only the sexual abuse of her employer but also the myth that Native girls are "easy" and that they are powerless.

Peters recognized her self-worth at the age of twelve. So many women don't reclaim this until later in life. One way of doing this is to focus on the positive elements of being Native. This does not imply that we should overlook all of the challenges faced by Native people, rather that we should look for the opportunities for resistance and change. Melanie Corbiere understands the importance of seeing the positive in Native experience, rather than accepting the identity of the downtrodden. Quoting her mother, she says:

If you allow yourself to be clouded by all the negativity, or all the negative experiences that you've lived through, you'd be broken down. A person would be really broken down, and you see a lot

of that in our nations. Women, especially, will forget that they
are mothers, will forget that they are grandmothers, and will forget
that they are aunties, and just smother and suffocate in negativity.
We need to see those good things, those things that we've
learned. An experience isn't good unless you've learned something
from it, whether it's a negative or a positive experience.

People say, "Melanie, you see life through rose-coloured glasses.
Why don't you take them off and look at the real thing?"

And I say, "Because I've lived through the real thing. Why should
I look at it again?" My anger and everything, I had to put down
to be who I am. I've had to put those away, and I've not come
through my life unscathed.

One of Corbiere's tools of resistance and recovery is humour. She
learned this lesson from her mother too, who said, "That's what
brings you out of depression, is laughter, nothing else. No pills will
do it … The more you laugh, the longer your life will be. If you cry
all the time, you shorten up your life, thereby depriving your children
of yourself." Similarly, Lila Tabobondung worked with Ojibway
Grandmother Vera Martin when she was beginning to reclaim a positive
identity as a Native person. Tabobondung remembers that residential
school killed the laughter in her, as she used to get strapped for
laughing. She credits Martin for bringing her back to her laughter,
and observes that there is always laughter in Indian groups and organizations. "Native women are always laughing, it seems to me," she
concludes (and I think many of us would concur).

With these foundations, actions and attitudes of resistance, we
can defend ourselves against the negative definitions of ourselves and
our people. The work that remains is to develop alternatives to what
we have had to resist. Speaking of the social movement in Indian
country that has been taking place since the 1960s, Emma
LaRocque has commented, "We have developed what we might call
an aesthetics of opposition. But now we need to develop an aesthetics of simply who we are." She challenged me to look for new ways
to interpret our traditions so that they can be empowering for
women:

Can we find entirely new constructs? Constructs that both build on wonderful values and traditions, and yet at the same time move us forward, I would say even past traditions, to the new world, so that my young nieces and nephews could build on something and yet have a sense of moving forward.

Emma's challenge related to some of her concerns about how concepts of "motherhood" and "nurturing" might not be the most empowering for us, given the framework they provide through mainstream society. Nonetheless, I will try to demonstrate how some of these traditions can be reworked, and how we can shape them into new constructs. In the next section, I show how women have rebuilt on the old by reclaiming those traditions, and from there, how they have reconstructed the traditions in ways that fit within their contemporary lives.

*IV*

# RECLAIM

❖

# RECLAIM

❖

IDENTITY RECOVERY FOR OUR PEOPLE inevitably involves the reclaiming
of tradition, the picking up of those things that were left scattered
along the path of colonization. This process is significant towards our
recovery because it involves reclaiming those things that were wrong-
fully taken, but also because many of our ancestral traditions, customs
and lifeways are better for us than the western practices that were
thrust upon us in their place. Certainly for Native women, reclaiming
tradition is the means by which we can determine a feminine identity
that moves us away from the western patriarchal model.

When we think about reclaiming, the first elements that probably
come to mind are the ceremonies, the dances and songs, or the languages. Yet there are many subtle facets of our cultures that can also
be reclaimed, such as the philosophies or the values that stand behind
the ceremonies. In this section, I will look at ways we can reclaim our
identities and culture through a framework of relationships, as it seems
to me that so much of our world is defined by the relationships we
create. I also think that Native women have successfully reinstated ways
of relating. Diane Hill, a Mohawk educator and healer, acknowledges
women's roles and responsibilities: "Women are teachers of how to
build relationships. We are the holders of this knowledge. We teach
people about the relationships that they have with each other and
with all things within Creation — but, particularly, with the earth,
moon and water."

Our aunties and grannies have always kept an eye on how we are
managing our relationships. Now, in the healing and recovery of our
nations, Aboriginal women return to these traditions of relationship,
and as they do, they shape and define the meaning of Aboriginal
womanhood.

## CHAPTER TEN

# OUR HUMAN RELATIONS

❖

## WORLDVIEW WITH CHILDREN AT THE CENTRE

INDIGENOUS NATIONS MAY DIFFER vastly from one to the other, but they all share a similar approach when it comes to children. Children sit at the core of every traditional Native society; they are the heart of our nations. Maria Campbell (Cree/Métis) has explained the traditional social organization of her people through the diagram replicated here:

DIAGRAM 3: SOCIAL ORGANIZATION

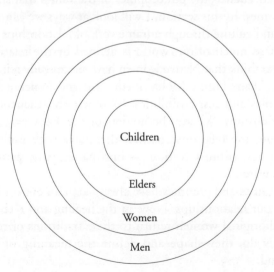

Children

Elders

Women

Men

In this worldview, children are at the centre of the community. The elders sit next to the children, as it is their job to teach the spiritual, social and cultural lifeways of the nation. The women sit next to the elders and the men sit on the outside. From these points they perform their respective economic and social roles, as protectors and providers of the two most important circles in our community.

Aboriginal children are precious to us because they represent the future. They are not considered possessions of the biological parents; rather, they are understood to be gifts on loan from the Creator. Because of this, everyone in the community has a connection to the children, and everyone has an obligation to work for their well-being. Each one of us has a responsibility to them.

The seventeenth-century Jesuit missionaries of New France were struck by this distinct Aboriginal approach to children, stating that "the savages love their children extraordinarily."[1] From their perspective, Native people over-indulged their children; they loved them "excessively" and raised them without discipline. The missionaries failed to recognize that Aboriginal people disciplined their children through more subtle methods, such as storytelling or teasing. The Huron and Iroquois, for their part, described the French mothers as "porcupines" because of their stern attitudes towards their young. They were appalled by the rigid disciplinary methods and the corporal punishment they witnessed among the settlers; practices that were common to seventeenth-century European childrearing.[2] European children of that time were considered "chattels of the patriarch," whereas Aboriginal children were accorded a great deal of autonomy and freedom. The contrasts were great, as this first meeting of European mothers and Indigenous mothers took place in an era where child labour was common in Europe and Europeans believed that children needed strict discipline, underscored by punishment.[3]

The autonomy accorded to Aboriginal children caused a lot of trouble for the Jesuits and other early missionaries in their efforts to get the children to remain in school. In his history of residential schools, J.R. Miller points out the contrasts between Native educational processes and missionary teaching practices. He describes how the Huron children who lived in New France responded to their first encounter with western educational practices:

These experimental classes near Quebec adhered as closely as circumstances allowed to the Jesuits' curriculum, pedagogical techniques (including a competitive atmosphere created by public prize-giving and exhibitions, a heavy emphasis on recitations, and examinations), strict discipline, and intensive proselytizing. Very quickly the Indian children responded with resistance and evasion to this harsh and unfamiliar regime. They either refused to cooperate or ran away, or both. The Jesuit teachers found that residential schooling was incompatible with what they had denounced earlier as the Indians' belief "that they ought by right of birth, to enjoy the liberty of wild ass colts, rendering no homage to anyone whomsoever, except when they like."[4]

What "the missionaries failed to appreciate" Miller concludes, was "that their rigorous pedagogy was not compatible with the three Ls of traditional Native education": looking, listening and learning. Native children were well-schooled in these ways. They knew the ways of their people because they observed and participated in the adult world on a day-to-day basis. They were not separated from the ongoing affairs of the community or nation.

Even today, we have leaders who are working with the knowledge they acquired at the feet of elders who took them to council meetings, spiritual gatherings and national political forums. At a recent elders' gathering in Ontario, Tom Porter spoke of attending Mohawk Grand Council meetings as a child, and from that early age, learning tremendously from his role as a translator.[5] Wit'suwet'en Hereditary Chief Theresa Tait remembers attending meetings with her grandparents at the time when the British Columbia Chiefs were beginning to unite and mobilize against Trudeau's "White Paper."[6] Ivy Chaske was four years old when she attended community meetings about the relocation of her community. Chaske points out that elders did not consider it unfitting for her to be a participant in these meetings. In her experience, children were not excluded from key community functions.

We have held onto many of these practices. You can attend most Native gatherings and find children in the room, if not close by. Contemporary Native women like Ida LaBillois-Montour continue to educate their children in the traditional way. As a mother who has always been active with organizations in Montreal, the province of Quebec and nationally, LaBillois-Montour recalls taking her two-year-old daughter to many meetings which were translated into English and French. Her daughter passed the time by playing with the French/English translation equipment at her feet. When her daughter was older, she was able to speak both languages and would translate the meetings for LaBillois-Montour. As the president of the Quebec Native Women's Association, Michèle Audette must often travel. Although it is difficult, she tries to bring her two young sons along with her on business trips. In my work with Native social and political organizations, I have worked in offices where older children were filing or colouring at the board room table and younger children showed up in the lunch room with their childcare workers. I have done consulting jobs and facilitated meetings for First Nations communities while breastfeeding a baby. I am not suggesting that it is easy or even possible to get certain types of work done with children around, particularly in the unsupportive environments we often find ourselves in. I offer this information as an example of how our communities have maintained something of a sense that there is room for children in our "adult" environments.

In spite of having held onto this value, Aboriginal women and men still have work to do in order to rightfully reclaim the significance of children in our communities. This work is urgent — not only because Aboriginal children have been (and are yet) assaulted, but because the focus on children and the respect that our societies gave to children was so severely damaged with colonization. Maria Campbell describes the role that colonization played in destroying the social organization that placed children at the heart of our nations. She refers to the concentric circles with children at the centre (Diagram 3):

> When the colonizers started to break that circle down, one of the things that the missionaries saw was that the women were so strong. They couldn't quite understand what was happening, but they knew that if they moved the children out of the centre of the community, and removed them from the women and elders, they would win.

Removing the children was another effective way to conquer Native peoples — ripping the heart out of our communities, which was done first by forcibly placing our children in residential schools and later in foster homes through the child welfare system.[7] In the 1960s, thousands of children across Canada were "scooped" and put into foster homes or adopted, often by families out of the country. As Maria Campbell says, "In our stories this is known as 'the time of the black car.'"

Native women are now reclaiming the centrality of children in their lives and in the life of their communities. For many, caring for children is the first truth. The caring for children, in fact, should take precedence over our efforts to reclaim ceremony. Maria Campbell comments that the first step in rebuilding the nation is creating safety for the children:

> If we are going to talk about homeland and coming home, we have to provide a place that is warm, where our children are safe and our grandchildren are safe. For me, that is where it starts. Never mind getting a drum and having a drumming ceremony. First, come home and make porridge for the babies; the drumming and ceremonies will follow.

Melanie Corbiere practices the value of caring for children in the educational work that she does with young women. She told me about a new mother who had frequently missed the women's circle that Corbiere facilitates. The young woman felt bad about her absenteeism; she felt that she was remiss because she had not participated in the spiritual practices of the circle. Corbiere explained to the young woman that her first responsibility was to her child: "You are not shirking your spiritual responsibilities. That child is your spiritual responsibility. That's what children are."

Children are the heart of the community, and are precious spirits over whom we must watch. Ivy Chaske emphasizes the sacredness of children. When I conducted my interview with her at her office, my baby girl was in attendance because she was still too young to be away from me for any length of time. Towards the end of our interview, Ivy looked at my baby playing around her feet and said, "To me, there is no doubt in my mind that this child came from the spirit world. When I see babies and children, that's where they came from. How can you not be kind to them?" She talked about how we have lost some of that sense in our communities and, like Maria Campbell and Melanie Corbiere, pointed out that it is not the outer manifestation of tradition but the value of the sacredness of life that is important. She acknowledges that this has been lost to many of our families:

> I know some of the most dysfunctional, disrespectful families, who all have their Indian names, and they have all done their ceremonies, but there is no respect for the spirit of the children. No acknowledgement that they just came from the spirit world. They just don't have that. We have lost that.

What needs to be reclaimed, then, is the sacredness and central position of children in our lives and in the lives of our nations. This will, in turn, have a profound effect on our understanding of ourselves as women, and how we are positioned in our societies. In reclaiming the sacredness of children and putting them at the centre of our communities, we empower ourselves in a number of other senses. We begin to understand ourselves as people with a sense of purpose, with responsibilities and with a connection to creation that runs through the generations. Many Native women have stressed to me that children are the responsibility of both the men and the women of the community, but that we have distinct ways of realizing our responsibilities to them.

Katie Rich, former president of the Innu Nation, told me that she started working in politics after having witnessed children suffering in her home community of Davis Inlet. I will share some of her story here:

> It was one of those cold days in February. I went to the local store here and there was a couple that wanted me to take their groceries home. I brought the groceries to the house, and when I went into the house, the whole thing really shook me, because I saw children, five or six of them, huddled together around the stove (range). They had opened the oven door, and they were trying to heat themselves with that. There was no heat in the house.
>
> That really struck me, and that's when I decided to get involved

in the community. I kept thinking about those children. I didn't know any of them. I just saw them huddled together with no pants or anything, and I said: *This is not normal. Our kids don't have to live like this.* Because I had gone through the same thing, and I had seen my brothers and sisters like that before.

Rich's drive has been reaffirmed again and again through the suffering she has seen among the children in Davis Inlet. In 1991, the house next to her own had a fatal fire, in which six children died. It stands as a reminder and motivator to Rich in her political work, as do the high profile problems of children sniffing gas in the community. Many women have told me similar stories about how they take their motivation out of a sense of responsibility to the children.

When we begin to understand the significance of our children, we also begin to understand ourselves as women. We can then see how significant women are in the circle of human relations, and this understanding extends through every aspect of our lives.

## LIFEGIVERS

*Women are powerful because they birth the whole world.*
— Shirley Bear (Mingwon/Maliseet)[8]

As lifegivers, women bring the children into the world, and for this they have traditionally commanded a great deal of respect. As Barbra Nahwegahbow puts it: "They talk about women and the ability to give life; that it is like the Creator. The Creator gives life, and women are like that. They give life. You can't get much better than that, really!" If we can reclaim the traditional notion of woman as lifegiver, we can reclaim a vital sense of our power. Whether we eventually give birth or not is not important; it is the power of the symbol of lifegiver that is significant.

How do women reclaim the power of lifegiving? Many of us begin to look for the significance of birth, creative energy and lifegiving as it appears in our ceremonies. Ojibway midwife Carol Couchie interprets the sweat lodge ceremony as a metaphor of birth. The dome-shaped lodge has often been equated with the womb of mother earth.[9] During the ceremony, a fire is lit outside the lodge, and the grandfathers and grandmothers (rocks ) are placed in that fire. Couchie interprets these as the genes of the ancestors. The fire/heat represents male energy and enters the womb/lodge, which represents female energy through the rocks. After this symbolic act of procreation, the people inside the sweat lodge go through a period of growth. Like new life, their growth takes place in a hot, dark, wet, and female place. When they crawl out, it is as though they are being born. The line of cedar that trails out of the sweat lodge is like an umbilical cord; it is the lifeline. The firekeeper watches from outside in the same way a midwife attends a birth. It is her or his job to make sure that everything is safe, to care for the life line, and to allow the birth process to happen.

Couchie also relates the Sun Dance to birth metaphors: "One of the things that men try to do in the Sun Dance lodge is tear their flesh. This can be compared to the same way a woman will tear her flesh giving birth. The Sun Dance ceremony allows a man to give to the community with total physical exertion. Anyone who has given birth will understand this." Today women participate in the Sun Dance, but they have not always done so. Traditionally, it was understood that women already had what the men were seeking.

The many teachings around menstruation can also affirm about our power as lifegivers and women. Our way of typically dealing with menstruation at present is to acknowledge and adhere to menstrual taboos. We know enough not to use traditional medicines or to participate in certain ceremonies while "on our time." This is but the first stage of reclaiming traditions around menstruation, but it is helpful, because, at the very least, it acknowledges the power of a woman. It acknowledges that she has the ability to cleanse and prepare herself to be the intermediary between spirit life and life on earth. Yet we must go on and reclaim more than taboos, with their current emphasis on what we can't do.

Many women are beginning to pick up and implement those traditions which speak to us more about our power (that is, what we can do; what we are capable of). Puberty rites related to the "first moon" of girls are now taking place in many communities. They are being pulled out of the past to shape the women of the future. Elder

Kathleen Green explains the tradition that many women are now building on:

> A long time ago our people made moon lodges for young girls that were on their time that first time. And every month for one whole year they would go into that moon lodge, every time they had their moon. They would receive teachings: this is where they would hear the sex education and the parenting skills and the basic life skills. How to take care of themselves and to respect themselves as women.

Green acknowledges that few of us have the time or the opportunity to go in to a moon lodge every month, so she and others have adapted this menstrual tradition through reinstating the berry fast. In this practice, pubescent girls are expected to abstain from berries or berry products for one year, during which time they meet periodically with older women ("aunties" and "grannies") who instruct them about basic life skills they will need as adults (including sex education). Girls who pass through these ceremonies have a better chance at understanding the sacredness and power of womanhood and how it is related to their lifegiving ability.[10]

Most contemporary women have not had the opportunity to have such teachings as young girls, and so many discover the power of themselves and how it relates to menstruation when they are already adults. Diane Eaglespeaker told me a story about how menstrual taboos helped her to think about her power as a woman. She was at her first Sun Dance when she began to menstruate and consequently had to leave the ceremony and go up on a hill to fast and dance by herself. She felt upset at not being able to continue with the Dancers below until her mother came to explain to her that she was as strong as any of the others, carrying on as she did. Eaglespeaker remembers thinking, *This is what being a woman is all about. No matter what the adversity, we keep going!* Her mother nurtured her at this time by teaching her traditional methods of burying menstrual pads and encouraging her to take care of herself. This experience, says Eaglespeaker, left her feeling good about her womanhood.

Eaglespeaker demonstrates the need to reinstate teachings and practices that work alongside our menstrual taboos. Women are beginning to look for alternatives to the simple "You can't come into this ceremony, because you are on your time." We need to know, then, what *can* we do? Where *can* we go? What do we need to learn, and what is our work at this time? Myra Laramee, a Cree/Métis teacher recalls that, traditionally, every time there was a ceremony, a moon lodge went up. This is where menstruating women would go, and they would have particular work to do. Laramee explains that the menstruating women were to pray that any of the negativity that might want to come and hurt or harm anyone be filtered back through their blood and sent back to Mother Earth to be neutralized. Laramee has reinstated these teachings and practices in her own work. She creates a space for menstruating women at ceremonies so they, too, can do their work. She says to these women, "Now ladies, those of you who are bleeding for this ceremony, I want you to come and join me. So that we can protect the ceremony, that we can pray about the ceremony, and that we can do the job that we were originally intended to do when ceremonies are going on." This approach takes the reclaiming a step deeper — it allows menstruating women to explore and appreciate their power. It also protects against any conscious or unconscious feelings that menstruation and menstruating women are somehow problematic. The notion that menstruation is evil, a curse, or, at best, a nuisance is so deeply ingrained in the dominant consciousness that we need the physical and philosophical spaces that allow us to truly reclaim Indigenous understandings of menstruation.

Women do not always have to engage in ceremonial aspects of menstruation. Some simply acknowledge it as a time for rest, and they slow down in their lives accordingly. Some people don't cook at this time. This is related to the taboos but is also a recognition that menstruation is a time for rest, seclusion and introspection. It is also a time for women to be together, and so there is room to explore how women can reclaim these aspects of menstrual tradition. However we implement traditions in this area, reclaiming our womanhood involves recognizing menstruation as a power time, a special time and a time that is particular to women.

Another symbol related to the woman's ability to produce and nurture life is the skirt. Many Aboriginal cultures understand the skirt to represent the hoop of life.[11] Ruth Morin (Cree) learned the importance of the skirt when she met a female elder on a plane. The elder gently tugged at the knee of her pants and said, "This stands in the way of your power. Because when you wear a dress, your power and your female energy can connect with the earth in a much easier manner." Up until that point, Morin did not know about this. Today, she understands the significance of women wearing skirts:

> The skirt itself represents the hoop of life. And so, as a woman, you need to walk like a woman, you need to sit like a woman, you need to conduct yourself as a woman, and part of that is being recognized, not only on this earth, but also in the spirit world, as a woman.

"I took it as a message," she says of this encounter, then laughs, "so I have not worn pants since that day!"

Laverne Gervais-Contois has also mentioned how the teaching around the skirt was a revelation to her feminine identity. Gervais-Contois once attended a teaching by Vera Martin on the role of the woman in Ojibway culture. At one point in the session, Martin stood up and slightly bent her knees so that her skirt touched the floor to create a circle around her. "This is my tipi," Martin told the women in attendance. Gervais-Contois, an addictions counsellor, was struck by this image, thinking, *"It's true. This is her. This is her world, her tipi. You have to respect the tipi. If you walk in a different way, or start drinking or staggering, then you are away from your tipi."*

When Vera Martin told me about the skirt-as-tipi, I felt not only a great sense of responsibility but also a great sense of what I can only describe as mother love. In our interview, Vera reiterated the teachings I had heard from Ruth Morin: "You wear this dress because the energy from Mother Earth needs to always be there ... That is the teaching of the tipi. The kindness and caring and understanding and acceptance. All those things. Love. The tipi and the skirt is me, this body, that is me. How beautiful we are. How loved we are by the Creator to give us this work that is so beautiful. Bringing life into the world."

There are extensive teachings about the tipi, that, for example, involve how the poles represent different strengths and values and what they mean when they come together to make a home. I do not have those teachings and so cannot discuss them here, but next time I hear them, I know they will be even more significant to me in terms of my womanhood. What I do know, though, is that the teaching around the tipi/skirt speaks to the pure physical, creative and spiritual energy of woman as lifegiver, and it speaks to her responsibilities as one who must nurture life once it has been produced. The power of woman to nurture is embraced spiritually in our cultures. The importance of children is also recognized. These two elements create a powerful infrastructure that informs our way of interpreting our cultures and women's roles within it.

## THE ABORIGINAL IDEOLOGY
## OF MOTHERHOOD

*I grew up with a sense of women's responsibility for all the people. It's not just women's responsibility to the children — we have a responsibility to all of the people. We have to. We are the lifegivers. We are the life force of the nation. Our responsibility is to everyone; male and female, young or old, because we are that place from which life itself emanates. And there is nothing greater than that.*

— Ivy Chaske (Dakota)

In this quote, Ivy Chaske identifies the Aboriginal ideology of motherhood. Aboriginal women have a claim to authority through this ideology, for we not only birth the people, we have been given a lifetime responsibility to nurture the people. Many Aboriginal women have already reclaimed this ideology and see it as their innate spiritual right. These rights are, as Andrea Chrisjohn points out, already ours:

We don't need to convince anybody of our rights, or try to control society. It's about who we are: lifegiver, nurturer. Nobody can take those rights away from us, and nobody can give them back to us. We are born with those rights, but it is up to us to make them strong: to look at them in a really healthy, positive way, as a woman.

Understanding these rights in the positive sometimes means having to unlearn what western society has taught us about motherhood.

When women like Chrisjohn talk about mothering, they are worlds away from the western ideology that condemns the mother to the role of family servant without any decision-making power. In their view of mothering, women know they have a responsibility to everyone in the community and are given the authority to exercise that responsibility.

In Aboriginal ideology, producing life and raising children are understood as the creation of a people, a nation and a future. The Iroquois recognize this authority both informally and formally, as exemplified by their traditional political system. In this system, older women (clan mothers) are seen as the most suitable members to choose the upcoming chiefs by virtue of the fact that they have watched all the children closely from their earliest years. They have overseen the growth of the future community members, and thus can make well-informed decisions about who should carry which responsibilities.

According to Andrea Chrisjohn, women define the well-being of the nation because of the role they play in teaching the young:

> We produce life. Because of the fact that we are mothers, as a whole, we are responsible for the community. We have a community responsibility to ensure that these young ones are all taught the same responsibilities to the overall community and nation.

Diane Hill concurs that societal change often comes through women, "because we are the ones who bring forth life." Hill says, "In raising the next generation, we are responsible for providing people, especially our children, with the teachings that will enhance respect, peace and co-existence for all of us."

Western ideology has separated women and mothers from decision-making power and from participating in the governance of community and nation. Marilou Awiakta (Cherokee) has written about the dangers of excluding women from power and governance, stating that we must ensure that "the gender capable of bearing life is not separated from the power to sustain it."[12] When we internalize this understanding, we unlearn western ideology and can begin to see that it is not right that we are often excluded from the major decisions that are made in our families, communities and nations. Many

Aboriginal women have had their decision-making authority taken away from them. If we can reclaim the Aboriginal ideology of motherhood, we can reclaim the power to make important decisions and restore balance to our communities. We have traces of this skill and authority among us that we can build on. Mohawk herbalist Jan Longboat commented, "You know, most Mohawk women today don't have trouble making choices and decisions. They are good decision-makers." She believes that this arises out of Iroquois tradition where the women have always had important decisions to make.

In the Aboriginal ideology of motherhood, all women have the right to make decisions on behalf of the children, the community and the nation. The Aboriginal ideology of motherhood is not dependent on whether, as individuals, we produce children biologically. Women can be mothers in different ways. I have heard many stories of magnificent "mothers" who have adopted children as well as adults and provided them with the guidance and love that they needed. Vera Martin speaks of Mother Thomas, a seventh degree Midewiwin (medicine) woman who adopted her. At the time, Martin was already herself a (biological) grandmother, but she benefited for many years from the "mothering" of this older woman. Maggie Paul talks about Grandmother Lupé, an Indigenous grandmother from Mexico, known as the "President" of her community and called upon internationally to help with the healing of our nations and creation. Neither of these women had biological children of their own. They are thought of as mother and grandmother in the figurative sense, and their role is the same as that of any mother: to teach, nurture and heal all people, not just their own.

Other magnificent mothers are those women who do not have biological children of their own but take on the role of aunties. They do not consider this to be at odds with how they understand themselves or with how they work within an Aboriginal ideology of motherhood. In the Aboriginal world, mother, auntie and grannie are fluid and interchangeable roles, not biologically defined identities. Sylvia Maracle points out that her traditional teachings support this type of fluidity. In our interview, she reflected on what she was taught:

> The teaching never said in order for me to be an auntie, in order
> for me to nurture, that I have to have children, because, as you

know, I don't. I have a certificate that says I adopted my sisters, and in the longhouse I am both a mother and a grandmother. Never did I learn that this was biology based. I learned that it was human based, it was spiritual based, it was family, but never in that sense of "Oh, it has to be me." The teaching is about relationships.

Maracle's office wall is covered with pictures of children to whom she is known as auntie. She plays an active role in guiding and directing children, some of whom are blood relatives and some of whom are not. Her reclaiming of identity has involved learning to be an auntie in a traditional sense, and she points out that that this is something that came long after her siblings had children. When I asked her about Emma LaRocque's challenge, that we find new concepts or words that might help us get away from the loaded concepts of "mother" and "nurturing" (as they have been so gravely distorted by western thought), she shrugged and said, "Maybe auntie would be a better word."

The difference between a literal understanding of motherhood and an Indigenous ideology of motherhood is exemplified in Wanda Whitebird's experience. Whitebird was conditioned for biological motherhood in the western tradition, whose ideology emphasized being a "good wife." This "training" failed her, as it left her with no sense of authority or decision-making power. Whitebird points out that it left her totally unprepared to be a mother: "I had not learned how to be a mother. I had not learned how to be a human being!" Her experience as a young mother proved unsustainable — she could not support her children let alone herself. Years later, after having reclaimed her Native identity, Whitebird became a mother to an adopted son who, she claims, "made me realize what a mother is." Her reclaiming of Native identity also taught her the value of children and the responsibility of women to care for them, whether or not they are biological mothers: "That's really what they mean about being aunties and grandmas. We don't have to birth the children. We don't own them. Children are gifts. They don't belong to us. They are here, and we look after them; we nurture them."

Sometimes women choose not to have biological children so they can better fulfil their roles as aunties or grannies or serve the community.

Barbra Nahwegahbow plays the role of auntie to particular children but also, through her work as a longtime community leader and activist, services the Aboriginal healing and recovery movement:

> I've approached my work as somebody who really wants to see the community heal and recover ... I think there is certainly a large amount of caring in that; you know, that nurturing part as well. I haven't had any children, by choice, really. I sort of feel like I had a big family to look after.

## BALANCE OF THE FEMALE AND MALE

*For me the creator God is both totally male, and totally female. It is within that totality, that completeness that God is ... We as created human beings are both male and female. We have both qualities within us but one predominates. Men can be nurturing and affirming as well as women can. Men have by and large lost that quality of nurturing and affirmation by the violence in the world that they have to live in, and the images that they are constantly presented with. If we want to heal as men and women we have to bring the image of the Goddess back into our hearts and our minds, and our souls. The Goddess represents gentleness, affirmation, life. She also represents woman/eternal woman.*

— Art Solomon (Ojibway)[13]

At the core of Aboriginal cosmology, there is an understanding that the world is comprised of the female and the male. It is important that the relationship between female and male, in all its manifestations, is balanced. The restoring of balance between the female and male individuals, energies and properties of our universe is critical to our well-being as women as well as to our well-being as a people.

As Sylvia Maracle points out, there are two halves of the medicine wheel — male and female. Every human being enters the world on one or the other side of this wheel, but each one of us is also given the qualities of the other half. We all carry the duality of creation, but most people sit in a place where they are either predominantly male or predominantly female. As females, we are said to have natural abilities to create and nurture, and males are said to have natural abilities to protect and provide. This, of course, raises all sorts of alarm bells by feminists and other progressive groups that have been working to get away from the way patriarchy has turned these qualities into tools of oppression. This is a struggle that must take place in a (western) world that sees no value in creating and nurturing and only knows how to protect and provide by being dominant and controlling. Yet if we conceptualize these qualities outside of the patriarchal framework, they can become empowering. In the Aboriginal worldview, creation is powerful, and the protector is there to support the creative process. The principle for these two sides of the wheel is balance and harmony, not dominance, and, as Art Solomon points out, we must learn to work with the quality that is not our predominant quality. Our life work is to seek peace with that other side within ourselves and where it exists externally. Two-spirited (homosexual) people must find their balance by making peace with both sides.

Symbols of female and male balance can be found everywhere in the Aboriginal world. We have brother sun and grandmother moon; father sky and mother earth. We talk frequently about the significance, the properties and the energies of water (equated with the female) and fire (equated with the male). We know that both water and fire are critical to our survival and that the balance between these properties must be respected, as each has the ability to consume the other. A traditional marriage, according to Myra Laramee, was understood as two paths moving along in the same direction: "There can't possibly be one path, as in *we two become as one*... It was never intended for us to walk or interfere with each other. That is why there is fire and there is water. Hence men and women." Laramee, a partner in a two-spirited marriage, does not see this to be heterosexist or at odds with her reality, as the peace between fire and water still needs to take place, both within her person and within her marriage.

The essence of creation is thus dependent on the relationship between fire and water. Wanda Whitebird offers some of the most fundamental examples:

> If you go down seven layers beneath the earth, there's fire. But what's on top is a bunch of water. Because the world is made up of seventy-five percent water. So are we. As a human being, if we

don't have water, we are going to die. But if you don't have body heat, you are going to die too. You can't live without either one.

New life is dependent on the marriage of these properties, as Ojibway midwife Carol Couchie points out: "Maybe women can have babies without having sex, but they still need that male energy (the fire)." All of these teachings remind us of the sacredness of life and creation itself. When it comes to fire and water, male and female, Whitebird emphasizes, "It is about living in harmony. It's not about what one can do better than the other."

Our ceremonies help us to remember the need for balance between the male and female. Some Aboriginal ceremonies are gender specific, and most mixed ceremonies involve gender divided tasks and responsibilities. So many of our ceremonies include fire and water, and in these ceremonies we usually require men to tend the fire and women to keep the water. In reclaiming the ceremonies, we can reclaim our traditional respect and balance with one another. Gertie Beaucage has talked about how the Midewiwin Society of the Ojibway reminded her of the need for female-male balance:

> I maintained for a long time that men were very expendable. Getting a better understanding of the male-female balance has raised their level of importance, instead of just being glib about their position in the world! [laughs]
>
> Midewiwin offers a very real understanding that creation doesn't continue without male-female balance. There is nothing that you can do that is completely female, nor completely male. Even in the way that the Midewiwin society operates, the teaching lodge, the sweat lodge — I mean, the men can bend as many poles as they want; if the women are not there to tie the poles together, they will not have a lodge. It's a very simple but very profound teaching tool, that each of them plays a role, and they can't complete their work without each other.

Many Native ceremonies teach that everyone has responsibilities by virtue of their gender and that all responsibilities are valued. When we work through these responsibilities, we are contributing to restoring and maintaining the balance of the universe.

Native arts also remind us of the need for male-female balance. Catherine Martin points to Mi'kmaq basket making as a demonstration of this. Once finished, Mi'kmaq baskets are a symbol of the harmony and beauty that is achieved through female-male co-operation:

> Most of the basket makers had a partner, a friend for life. Without their husband, they couldn't make their own baskets, because in basket making you have this role. The women weave. The men cut the wood. The men prepare the wood. The women split the wood. The women weave. The men put the hoops on and the women put the decorations on. Without each other, you can't make the best basket. The woman and man team made those baskets. When one was widowed, you always saw a change in what they produced.

> When you look at how a basket is made, you see how a woman and a man work together with love, as together they make the basket.

In many of our "performing" arts, there are distinct roles for males and females. Some of these roles are complementary and represent balance between male and female. Others symbolize the distinct relationships that men and women have with creation. If you look at a pow wow, you will notice the "traditional" women dancers barely lift their feet off the ground. This is because of the relationship they have with the earth, as women. I learned this from Ojibway actor Sandra Laronde, who said, "I would love to have that connection to the earth. You can tell when dancers have that, and when they don't." The distinct roles are also evident in our music, which often involves separate songs or roles for men and women. At pow wows or other gatherings, women and men generally do not sing together. We often have women's groups and men's groups, and the most common arrangement for men and women singing together is where the women stand and sing in a separate circle around the men who are playing the "big drum." In this case, the separate circles represent the different roles, but also the balance between the two.

There is a reason for these distinct roles, and many women will advocate learning about the teachings behind these gender divides in our art and ceremony. Better understanding of these teachings can be empowering for women. The teaching behind the big drum is one example. Myra Laramee explains how parts of the teaching are overlooked:

> One of the things that is not taught anymore is the reason women don't need to sit at the drum. The big drum was originally given to men to learn about their relationships with women. The drum is the essence of women's spirit. The heartbeat of Mother Earth. How many times have you heard that? But the part that doesn't get taught holistically is that when a man takes a sounder in his hand, and he starts that beat in motion, he is giving life to that womanspirit, and he is calling on that womanspirit to come and teach him how to be a man.
>
> One of the things that is not taught, either, by men anymore is that that drumstick is never to be raised higher than the shoulder. The minute that you raise that drumstick higher than the shoulder means that you can lift your hand to a woman in that manner.
>
> I have seen men sitting at that thing, and they are making that drum bounce off the floor. They do that to their wives too. They make their wives bounce off the floor.

Wanda Whitebird makes the point that we need to differentiate between teachings that are supportive and those that are practised in ways that are disempowering to women. The teaching of the big drum can be detrimental to women if taught in the wrong way:

> If we look at the teaching that woman is the drum, and we need that balance of life, where the men sit at the drum, and the drum represents woman, and the women stand behind the men — if you could still do all that with respect, then I can understand it. But if men use it as an excuse not to be with women, then I think that's sick.

In some of our art and ceremony, these distinct gender roles are shifting, and this is cause for some controversy. The shift usually entails women participating in ceremonies that have traditionally been reserved for men. Some traditional female thinkers worry that this shift will upset the balance of the female and male energies of the universe. For example, Ivy Chaske has been asked by some of her elders to tell women that they are not supposed to go into the sweat lodge. Chaske explains that women do not need to "sweat" because they have a natural ability to cleanse themselves (through menstruation). She states that we risk forgetting about our natural abilities if we are cleansing by going into the sweat lodge. In the sweat, we begin to replenish ourselves with male energy, rather than connecting to the female energy that is all around us all the time. "When we go into those lodges," Chaske points out, "we are denying female energy."

Other women see the shift in ceremonial or artistic roles as the natural reflection of changes we are experiencing in our societies. Diane Eaglespeaker, a Blood Sun Dancer, agrees that traditionally women didn't go into the sweat lodge and that they didn't Sun Dance. She participates in both practices now, which she sees as congruent with the shifting roles that women have taken on. Women now do work that was traditionally done by men, such as bringing in provisions (money) to sustain the family, and with these changing roles, they take on new roles in the ceremonies.

Yet, even though women now commonly go into the sweat lodge, there are still many areas that are slow to change — the big drum being one example. Many women sing and play hand drums, but to sit around the big drum is still taboo. It is not clear to me why one tradition would change and another remain firm, but the lesson I take from all of it is that we have to uncover the gender teachings behind the practices before we can make our decisions. I agree with Sandra Laronde's comment that "just because something is traditional doesn't mean we have to agree with it." Sitting at the big drum is something Laronde does not do, because she doesn't know enough about the tradition: "I'm just going to wait on that because I don't know enough about it yet."

Contemporary Native ceremony and art need to teach about the male and female in terms of balance. If they are practised and taught with this in mind, they will help to maintain balance in our lives, communities and nations. This sense of balance works for men as well as for women. For example, some women advocate that we must learn about both fire and water, male and female, so that we can respect and appreciate the responsibilities of the other gender. Full moon ceremonies are usually only attended by women, but Wanda Whitebird believes that there is a place for men at these ceremonies, where they could learn to honour the moon:

> The full moon ceremony is to honour our grandmother moon. We recognize that as a ceremony that honours Anishinabekwe (Ojibway/Native women). It doesn't mean that men can't be there. It would be good if men were there, because men should learn what women know. The reasons why men and women are segregated at this point is because of the abuses men and women have both suffered at the hands of each other. They feel safer with the same sex around. And so it is a healing process. At the beginning, there was always a man at my full moon ceremonies, but the women didn't feel comfortable. And I'm a firm believer in what has to be done for the individual to feel comfortable.

We all need to learn about the other side of our medicine wheel in order to make peace with it and seek that balance. This is a complex task for modern day Aboriginal people, as we are working within a mainstream patriarchal society, riddled with elements of, as Myra Laramee would say, a "Euro-Christian hangover" and with many gender conflicts that we have developed as a result of our recent and dark history. Reclaiming and restoring male and female balance means we need to find ways to work with one another and to work with all of our abilities, male and female, for the better of the collective. As we find peace and balance within our human relations, we need to also seek balance in our relationship with creation.

## CHAPTER ELEVEN

# RELATING TO CREATION

❖

*There is a type of corn that has the kernels covering the tip, a short-eared corn, and the centre kernel is used as a medicine for the baby if the mother dies. This must have been from the old days, when there was probably a higher rate of maternal mortality. They grind up one kernel, mix it with water, and give it to the baby to remind the baby that it still has a mother. In the Indian world, you are never an orphan. You always have your mother the Earth and your grandmother the Moon, and all your relations in the community. So it helps. It doesn't make up for it, but it helps.*

— Katsi Cook (Mohawk)[1]

OUR RELATIONSHIP WITH CREATION involves connecting with all that exists around us: plants, animals, land, water, sun, moon and the sky world. Because the land is our Mother Earth, and the moon is our Grandmother, Native women have a special relationship with these parts of creation. To many Native women, reclaiming a relationship to land is as important as recreating Indigenous social and human relations, because the land is something through which we define ourselves, and it is essential in our creation. Aboriginal women do not see the land as a wild material resource that needs to be developed, possessed, or controlled; rather, the land is a relative with whom we have a special relationship.

This understanding has withstood five centuries of colonization, but many of us no longer have an immediate relationship with the land. Women who have lost their sense of connection to land or territory can find themselves in crisis. Educator Helen Thundercloud recognizes this problem. She addresses it in her healing work by taking people back "to their first hurt": homelessness. Thundercloud works with the knowledge that many Aboriginal people feel deprived of a home. Our people may have been removed from their traditional territory or frequently relocated because the land was coveted by Euro-Canadians. Many Aboriginal people were removed from the land of their childhood and placed in residential schools or foster homes. In the United States in the 1950s, there was an urban relocation program that moved people off their traditional territories, and in Canada this happened informally, as people have had to leave the land to find employment in urban centres. Many Aboriginal women leave their home communities and move to urban centres to escape violence and abuse. Helen Thundercloud understands this dispossession: "We are a land-based people, and as colonized people we've had no home. And because we have had no home, there are a lot of other problems that are attendant to that." The dispossession of land and homeland factors heavily into identity problems for Native peoples, and the struggle towards a healthy sense of identity is linked to reclaiming that space.

Native women talk about how they revisit their relationship with the land as part of a positive identity formation. Haunani-Kay Trask is the director of the Institute of Hawaiian Studies. In her book, *From a Native Daughter: Colonialism and Sovereignty in Hawaii*, she writes: "To know my history, I had to put away my books and return to the land."[2] Sylvia Maracle describes our deep relationship with the land that is so vital to understanding our origins:

> We have been taught by the Elders and Traditional People that one cannot answer the question, "Who am I?" until one knows where s/he comes from ... You have to go out and be with your first teacher, your mother, the earth. You have to take off those other clothes, those other glasses that you put on to present your-self to the "other" world, and see what it is that we had.[3]

Sometimes women feel a need to reclaim a particular geographical space in order to define their personal identity. Janice Acoose has written about making a return visit to her family homelands. The return to *place* as well as to people is significant in directing her struggle against the part of her person that was "heavily indoctrinated by the power of white european canada's many christian patriarchal institu-tions." She says that she did not feel "adequately prepared to continue working as an Indigenous educator and activist" because she had been disconnected from her relations. The visit to her home communities helped her recapture her sense of self, as her identity is grounded in the place and the people where she comes from. After fasting and participating in a ceremony in her home territory, Acoose reflects, "I began clearly to understand the importance of reconnecting to the collective consciousness of both my maternal and paternal ancestors, to strengthening and empowering all Indigenous families, communities and nations."[4] Place, therefore, is significant in that it allows one to connect with one's ancestors.

Janet Campbell Hale is a Coeur d'Alene from Idaho. She spent her youth moving frequently around the western United States with her mother. Her reclaiming of self involved returning to the reservation where she had lived on and off until the age of ten. On one trip, she took her adult daughter with her because meeting her ancestors would help her daughter learn about her own identity:

> For an Indian, home is the place where your tribe began. (For some, for my tribe, that place is also where the tribe continued to live after the land was made a reservation.) Home is a place where your people began and maybe where your family began and where your family still is.[5]

Michèle Audette, an Innu who lives in Montreal, has told me of her plans to return to the land of her ancestors. She feels the absence: "Je me sens pas solide" (I don't feel grounded). Audette also sees it as her duty to foster the relationship between the land and her children, who have thus far been raised in an urban setting; to re-establish the relationship with the physical territory they once knew. In the interim her sons can learn from her brother who currently lives close to the land.

## WOMAN AS LAND

*Starting to connect with Mother Earth as a woman, I think that's pretty important. Because she's that mother for all of us, men and women. That's a pretty important ally.*

— Barbra Nahwegahbow (Ojibway)

We often hear the term Mother Earth, but what does it mean? When our women reclaim and realize an Aboriginal understanding of the concept, they find strength and enlightenment. This realization is key to understanding our identity and femininity.

Native women know that a connection to the land can provide a connection to a sense of the female. When I interviewed Elder Shawani Campbell Star, I asked her, "Was there a time in your life when you came to some kind of consciousness about being a woman?" She said she had always had a sense of being female because of being raised in a natural environment in rural Guyana: "I was intensely connected to that natural world. And I believe that is an experience of the feminine, looking back." Although Campbell Star qualifies that being connected to the environment in this way is the privilege of any natural human being, her connection helped define the female for her, because "the giving-ness of the earth was always there."

A number of women say that their personal realization of the earth as female was a turning point in their lives. In her early years of searching for her identity, Ojibway Elder Edna Manitowabi was told by several elders to "go home to her mother." Says Manitowabi, "At first I thought they meant my biological mother, but she died when I was twenty-one. Then I thought maybe they wanted me to go back to my reserve ... It was when I started to ask myself questions about woman, that's when I realized I had to find it from earth." She explains how this was a transfomative experience:

> When I connected to the Earth, it was like a mirror, like seeing myself. And when I saw a crane or a bulldozer digging into the Earth, it was like a form of rape. I just felt like that machine was scarring me. I began to realize that Earth is Woman and what happens to woman happens also to her. And she's feeling that.
>
> As a woman comes into her own spirit she finds Spirit within her and she begins to stand up. I'm just coming to that. It's like I talked about all along, but it's only now that I've really come to understand it.[6]

For Nena Lacaille-Johnson, her realization of the earth as mother was a life changing experience. While on a camping trip on Vancouver Island, she had a near-death experience in which she found herself looking down on the coastline from above. This vision inspired a tremendous sense of love for the earth as mother, and Lacaille-Johnson made the decision to return to the earth and continue living. This vision also changed her sense of femininity, as she could see the strength and power of the earth mother. It removed her sense of vulnerability as a woman. She remembers coming back to the camp and having a new perspective on her female travel companion who had been playing the role of the "helpless female" on the trip. Lacaille-Johnson explains: "I was always coming to her rescue. If she tripped over something, I would have to help her ... When I came back, I remember watching her and thinking I wasn't going to play that role. Something had changed in me about my own femininity. I could be more empathetic to her, but I wasn't going to be rescuing her anymore." Lacaille-Johnson's sense of female/male roles shifted as a result of her new understanding related to the power of earth mother and woman. She was able to see that women don't have to rely on men, and that women don't have to become men to be self-reliant.

Maria Campbell's connection with the earth is strategic in allowing her to maintain her strength in a particularly female way:

> I live in the country, and the river runs by my house. I can see it from my kitchen window. That river is a strong feminine image for me, because she is the veins for the earth. I can feel her power. I can hear her at night.

> I see eagles in the river valley. There are four nests of them in the hills by the river. I see sometimes fifteen of them, and sometimes only three or four. I see them feeding their young. I hear the kiyotes howl at night, and right now the mothers are teaching their babies how to howl. For all of them, like me, the river is important.

Reclaiming a connection with the earth's waters can be a particularly powerful experience for Native women. It is a feminine force that Sylvia Maracle respects and understands:

> The thing that strikes me about the water is that it will take the shape of any of the vessels that we put it in. If it's a bowl for ceremony, it doesn't matter if it's a rock or a pottery bowl, a wooden bowl or a copper bowl.

The other thing to remember about the water is that it is the strongest force on the earth … Even the wind can't do what the water can do, in terms of determining the process of life. And we know that water comes first before life itself. We know it has responsibilities to cleanse us, to quench us, to nourish our thirst; that it is also responsible to allow us to sit beside it to find peace.

But whether it's that single drop, or the largest body of water, it represents the female element. That is our role in terms of tradition; we have the capacity as women to take those shapes, but also to make those shapes. We recognize that we don't have the kind of power where you bang your fist on the table, but that we have the power of the water — that sort of every day going against something that ultimately changes the shape of the thing.

These images offer valuable teachings about a woman's abilities; they suggest that women have the power of the force of life itself. Women learn that they are adaptable, and that they are able to direct and withstand long processes of change. At the same time, teachings about water instill a sense of responsibility among women because of their capacity to provide and sustain life. As I have pointed out earlier, women are usually deemed responsible for taking care of the water in ceremonies and otherwise. Myra Laramee explains that this reflects the key role of women in creating and maintaining relationships:

The water is so important to what we do with each other. It is what connects us. When we are in that circle and that woman gets up and passes the water, she is doing more than passing the water, she is creating that spiritual umbilical cord, and without her to do that, we just sit as separate entities. The minute that she passes that water from soul to soul, you are attached to that central spiritual connection. And you can drink from it.

The teachings about water can help women see themselves as key players in any community and can give them a sense of the responsibility they have in facilitating relationships.

The image of Mother Earth, Grandmother Moon and the waters speak of lifegiving cycles, and these teachings are as old as we are as peoples. The earth produces and nourishes and the moon regulates.

In turn, the waters of the earth are vital in that they bring on and sustain life. All of this understanding helps with female body image, and with the feminine cycles that women go through. When an Aboriginal woman begins to see her body in relation to Mother Earth, it brings a sense of sacredness. Like Mother Earth, the female body is to be celebrated in all its cycles.

Ceremonies help us to celebrate ourselves and our connection to the creative forces of the universe. Aboriginal women are reclaiming their relationship to the moon through ceremony as a means of recapturing a sense of their femininity. In Ontario, many Aboriginal women have begun to revive full moon ceremonies. This relationship to the moon is not New Age fad: it goes a long way back. Jan Longboat remembers her grandmother telling her that it is important to celebrate the moon, because the moon is female energy.

Other communities are bringing back teachings and ceremonies that help young girls understand their power in relation to the earth as mother. In Ontario, Edna Manitowabi conducts berry fast ceremonies for young girls entering puberty. She reminds us all of the importance of recognizing the entry into womanhood:

> Celebrate that young girl who has just become a woman. That's a gift we are given! Celebrate that first flow, that is like the earth, when she's flowing in the springtime. It's the same thing. That's who we are as women. We all flow. We all bleed, and that's how we bring forth life. That's how we mould and shape life. That first blessing that was given to women is that you open the door and water issues forth. You are able to take that life into your arms, take her to your breast. Celebrate that miracle!

A recognition of the earth cycles in relation to female cycles can also help women who are ending their menstruation. Maria Campbell's reclamation of traditional understandings about the moon have helped her through menopause. Aligning herself with nature has allowed her to understand more about her own body. As Campbell points out, this is an understanding she had to reclaim:

> When I started my menstrual cycle, I didn't pay attention to those teachings, because who talked about the moon when they talked about menstruation in the 1950s? But as I got older and I

went back to the old ways, I started to pay attention to my body and how the moon affected me. Once I understood that, then I could work with her and it helped me go through my change and all of those women things. I never really had a bad time because I understood how the moon affected me, and I was able to teach that to my daughters. I think it made a difference for them. In Cree, the moon is Kookoomnow — Grandmother. How can she hurt us if we work with her?

Cree Elder Kathleen Green's menopause was characterized by cold sweats, hot flashes and plenty of crying. She went to see an Elder who talked about the moon and the waters of the earth and about the different types of waves in the ocean: "When that tidal wave comes in, that is when your feelings really get out of control. And when the tidal wave leaves, that is when you are calm." The cycles of the earth and her waters and the regulating powers of the moon can be affirming to those distinctly female physical and spiritual parts of us that also know about transformation, creation and change.

Finally, the Aboriginal female association with the earth can help us to better understand how we have been affected by western patriarchy, and in so doing, can assist in our recovery process. Edna Manitowabi demonstrated this to me through a story about her arrival at menopause. This time coincided with the end of her marriage, leaving her with a sense of being "uncelebrated" and "all used up." She was able to shift out of this thinking after having reflected on an insight that was relayed to her by a Cree Elder, in a conversation about how the earth has been misused:

> You know, over there in Europe, they refer to her as old. The "old world." And here they refer to her as the "new world" … We have to try to keep her young here. Because over there they aged her, they aged her over there, and they used her up … Even in some places over there … she can't give life anymore. They are starving. And they are fighting. So over here, we have to make sure that we celebrate her. And keep her young.

From this story, Manitowabi began to understand the sacrifices she had made in her life, as a woman. She had participated in the kind of unbalanced relationship that western society expects of Mother Earth and of its women. The end result is that when one is no longer able to give it all, one is "uncelebrated" and perceived as "all used up." Through this equation, Manitowabi was able to articulate her vision of the often unbalanced nature of female-male relationships in mainstream society. "You give because you care," says Manitowabi, "but the sacrifices I made as an integral part of my being, as an Aboriginal woman, were taken by my partner as an expectation that did not require reciprocal sacrifices. Everything was to benefit his spiritual growth, not mine. I gave him my power until I felt 'all used up,' desecrated. This behaviour created imbalance in our relationships." She explains:

> The "old world," Christopher Columbus and all the colonies brought a sense of patriarchy to this "new world" and inflicted it on us, the Indigenous people. Our men learned how to oppress us, and our women have learned to accept it. In our original teachings, men celebrated "mother life." They honoured and respected women, acting reciprocally as oshkabewis, helpers. There was a recognition that we all have an integral part to play in forming and developing relationships.

Manitowabi realizes that, like the earth, she has a responsibility to nurture and sustain. Yet she sees how this responsibility can get easily twisted out of shape by the takers of an unbalanced society. She remarks, "I guess that is something that we learned from the western worldview: that the women are the givers and men take." She concludes: "It's the earth who gives life, who does that nurturing. And there's a difference between giving and nurturing. I think that's what we have to get back to. To find that." Her personal response has been to make an effort to nurture herself. This has led to a feeling of being rejuvenated and focused in her life.

The western conceptualization of the earth in terms of property ownership is markedly different from Indigenous relationships with Mother Earth. When we think about this, we can begin to be more critical about where we fit in as women in our societies and how it affects our relationships. Sandra Laronde sees a parallel between women and earth, drawing attention to how this has been negatively construed in the western experience:

How women are treated is how the earth is treated. Even the way we talk about the earth — raping the land — we use the same words when we talk about the abuse and violence against women. You can see the parallels and a lot of disrespect for Mother Earth. Territorial. This is my land. My woman.

Indigenous people know that no one can own the earth, and, likewise, no one can own people. Aboriginal women can see that they can never be the property of a man, and that they are not there to be dominated, controlled or domesticated in the western way.

The visions, philosophies and traditions that have been presented in this chapter come from our ancestors, yet they are practical tools for our survival in the twenty-first century. How do Native women successfully use these tools in their modern lives? How can we learn from those who have reclaimed balance in their quest for identity?

*V*

# CONSTRUCT

❖

# CONSTRUCT

❖

THERE COMES A POINT in the definition of Aboriginal womanhood where we must make sense of how ancestral traditions can fit into our modern lives. This is the "re-cognitive" part of our *recognition of being*, the part where we actively construct modern Native female identities. Some women I have spoken to have referred to this process as "re-inventing myself," and they stress that this is an ongoing activity that lasts a lifetime. When we engage in this process collectively, we engage in the ongoing process of reinventing or reconstructing Native womanhood, which begins with the self. We must first wrestle with the question of "Who am I?" and then work through how that fits with our family, our community and our nation as they presently exist and as we would like them to be. This is a common model for change in our societies, founded on an Aboriginal understanding of relationships. I will work through this circle to explain how Native women reconstruct themselves, and in so doing, how they define themselves within the family, community, nation and all of creation.

DIAGRAM 4: RELATIONSHIPS

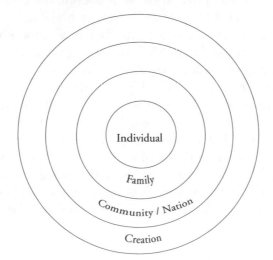

## CHAPTER TWELVE

# THE INDIVIDUAL

❖

A KEY PLACE TO BEGIN reconstructing self is with the understanding that we are all sacred beings. Many Aboriginal women understand and recognize that all life is sacred, that life is granted to people, plants and animals by the Great Mystery, and that we have an immediate connection to every part of creation because we all come from the same sacred place. When a woman understands this, she can understand and build on the sacredness of her own life. The sense of sacredness is timeless, and there are therefore many ways that we can work it into our modern lives. As women, it can directly influence how we think of our bodies and what we do with them.

## THE FEMALE BODY

Through the story of her youth, Edna Manitowabi demonstrates the changes that can take place when we reinstitute the understanding of woman as a sacred lifegiver and when we begin to live with the knowledge that children are sacred gifts from the Creator. After having experienced alienation during her first few pregnancies, Manitowabi was reminded by the elders that there is no shame in a pregnancy, because pregnancy involves bringing new life into the world. This teaching refutes the Christian tradition that was instilled in Manitowabi at residential school: that any child born "out of wedlock" arrives shrouded in "sin." Manitowabi's early pregnancies were dominated by feelings of "You're easy, you brought it on yourself." When she received the Aboriginal teachings about the sacredness of life and the woman's role as lifegiver, she was able to appreciate her role as a woman and to more effectively mother her children. She recalls: "It wasn't until I started to learn from those old women and those old men about the sacredness of life that I began to honour and respect and celebrate that new life. I wanted to be a good mother. I wanted my children to have a good life."

Manitowabi's pregnancies took place in the 1960s, but her story is relevant to young people today because we continue to grapple with the issue of "sin" vs. "sacredness" in our contemporary bodies. Aboriginal teens may not carry the same sense of shame around pregnancy as they once did, but there are still many who punish themselves (and are punished) through careless treatment or abuse of the body. Women might engage in unsafe or unwanted sex, eat poorly or abuse ourselves through dysfunctional eating patterns, alcohol abuse, smoking, or other things that are unhealthy for us. All of us, young and old, have work to do around remembering and reconstructing the sacredness of our bodies. One way we can do this is to think of the female body in relation to its lifegiving ability.

Mohawk herbalist Jan Longboat has always thought of health in terms of revering the sacredness of the body. She told me that her mother taught her respect for the female body by speaking about its role in creation: "Mother always used to talk about preparation. Preparation of the body to give life. And I started to think about that at puberty, really. She was very conscious about keeping healthy to give life." This thinking inspires healthy eating, something which Longboat contends was more prevalent among women when they were more aware of their role in creation. For Longboat, the female body is "gifted" because of the ability to give life, and this gift must be handled with the utmost care. Carol Couchie talks about care for the body in relation to the woman's responsibility to look after the water. Looking after the water means keeping your own body clean and respected.

Reconstructing the sacredness of our bodies can also be useful in addressing the prevalence of teen pregnancy in our communities. Our high teen pregnancy rates may be due to our acceptance of pregnancy, our reverence for the sacred, and the place of children in our societies. It is also true that, traditionally, Aboriginal girls often began to have children during their adolescence. But we must re-examine these traditions and reconstruct the values behind them so that they fit our modern lives. Our economic and social structures don't support adolescent pregnancy as they once did, but we can still work with the value that made pregnancy a cause for celebration. To do so, we must ask ourselves, *What does it mean when we say life is sacred?*

In our conversation about teen pregnancy, Sylvia Maracle said it best: "Life is sacred isn't a mantra to go out and have sex!" Maracle's comment was lighthearted, but she went on to explain the serious nature of bringing life into the world, according to Iroquois tradition. There was at one time a two-year period of preparation before a couple would try to conceive a child. One only entered into this process after establishing a partnership that was suitable for raising children. This time period would start with the couple making an offering of tobacco at one of the (Iroquois) seasonal ceremonies, such as mid-winter, strawberry, green corn, or harvest. So for example, "In mid-winter, you put down your tobacco. You say, 'Okay. We are going to make this commitment now, to bring new life into the world.' And so one mid-winter goes by, and by the time the second mid-winter has passed, two years have gone by. *Twenty–six moons.*" During the course of these two years, a couple has many things to consider. Maracle differentiates this kind of preparation from "cute discussions about how to decorate the baby's room," because it grounds one in the reality of the life changes that will be necessary, and in the long-term nature of the commitment:

> You offer your tobacco and you wait. You start to learn with other people's children. You start to learn patience. You give things up; you sacrifice things as a couple because now you can't just run out to the coffee house at ten o'clock, because they smoke there, and you can't drag the baby in it.
>
> You learn to communicate. You learn some songs. You talk about names. You know what the clan is, and you talk about how the child is going to be raised.

The couple must also ask themselves "Who is going to support this child?" This involves thinking about the extended family relationships that they will build upon or create. Traditional support mechanisms involve giving tobacco to aunties and uncles as a means of asking them to take some responsibility for the child. Maracle comments, "Selecting those people is not an easy task, because they are not necessarily going to be your high school buddies, or whatever. You have got to be as creative and as imaginative about where that child is going to walk as possible. And so that is another reason why they say you offer your tobacco and you wait all this time."

According to the tradition, *life is sacred* also involves developing a relationship with spirit, so that you are prepared to call the new life when it is time. Aboriginal people will often say that we choose our parents when we come from the spirit world. Maracle points out that the two-year contemplation period enables parents to "create the relationship so that the spirit you call knows who the parents are." This involves learning to be honest about who we are, both with ourselves and with others.

Whether they follow these teachings literally or not, teens (and older people) can benefit from thinking about the sacredness of life according to Aboriginal thought. It might encourage young women to take better care of themselves, to think about their sexual activity, to use birth control, to consider their relationships or to respect themselves and others. The sacred nature of a woman's body can be particularly useful in helping Aboriginal girls with some of the issues they commonly face. Diane Eaglespeaker, a Blood who works with Aboriginal youth in the city of Calgary, speaks to her students about honouring the body by considering their actions and by protecting themselves by using birth control. She tells them that part of honouring the body means that one does not put everything on display, as in the case of youth who sport extremely tight or revealing clothing. Eagle-speaker addresses them with questions: "Why do you feel that you have to promote your body this way? Are you a 7-Eleven? Everything is cheap?" Her teasing calls attention to the incongruity of putting their sacredness out for sale or public consumption.

Ojibway Grandmother Vera Martin helps young girls understand the sacredness of their bodies through the teachings she offers during a berry fast. As I have explained earlier, in this practice, pubescent girls are expected to abstain from eating berries or berry products for one year. During this time, they receive teachings about womanhood from periodic meetings with older women who are acting in the traditional capacity of aunties or grannies. Martin talks to the girls about "what they put into their bodies," emphasizing that they must take care of what goes into their space because it is a sacred space. The fasting helps the girls to think about what they are eating; for example, they must examine food products like juice or ice cream to ensure that they do not contain berries. Martin encourages them to carefully consider *everything* that they will put into their bodies as women, "including the sex organ."

The berry fast is becoming more popular among Ojibway, Cree and Iroquois peoples, and there are similar types of puberty rites being practised in other nations. Although not as popularly known as it was traditionally, the Siksika have a feast to honour a girl coming into womanhood (following her first period). The feast is only attended by women, and, as with the berry fasting, older women use this time to talk to girls about values like honesty and to teach them the need to nurture, honour and respect their bodies. All of these practices help young girls deal with the many issues that they will face as teenagers growing up in modern times. Vera Martin's discussion about what girls put into their bodies may help to offset unhealthy promiscuity or careless intercourse. Ruth Morin is the Chief Executive Officer of Nechi Training, Research and Health Promotion Institute. She explains that the berry fast teaches self-discipline. This is symbolized in the initial ceremony, where the girls are repeatedly offered berries which they must refuse:

> The rite of passage is really key in helping us teach our daughters about the power of woman, and about behaviour. About self-discipline. About learning how to say "No," and about how to make choices. If we do the ceremonies right, I think they have potential for prevention of HIV and AIDS and other sexually transmitted diseases as well as unplanned pregnancies, and different issues like that ... I think that these rites can be a traditional means of prevention programming.

As with the body, sex and sexuality can be positively constructed when understood through the realm of the sacred. Cherokee writer Marilou Awiakta has articulated how far we have strayed from this understanding:

> Thinking of sex as an "it" and women as sex objects is one of the grooves most deeply carved in the western mind. This groove of

the national mind of America will not accept the concept of sex as part of the sacred generative power of the universe — and of woman as a bearer of this life force. The life force cannot be owned as property, used and consumed — or merchandised.[1]

The old teachings about sex "as part of the sacred generative power of the universe" are perhaps even more important today, where, as Myra Laramee has observed, "So much of the world is based on whether you get it or you don't!" The obsession and commodification of sex, and the way in which women are used in this transaction, can be countered by Aboriginal women when they rework the sense of the sacredness of the experience.

There is a vast continuum of views about the place for sex in our lives. Some women advocate celibacy prior to marriage. Others have expressed that there is a place for consensual sex with various partners for the pure physical enjoyment. Our differing views come, in part, out of tribal traditions where some nations valued celibacy and others endorsed multiple partners throughout a lifetime. Yet most would agree that sex is natural, enjoyable, and something that belongs equally to women and men. When we see it as a sacred gift that we are given, we are likely to give it more value, and to allow ourselves to be open to the pleasure of that gift. As Myra Laramee has commented about sex in the old days, "Nothing was taken for granted!"

People who are working in the Aboriginal healing movement have expressed that we need to find ways to separate sex, intimacy and love. Because of our history, this is an especially pressing need. Traditionally, our families had the responsibility to teach intimacy,[2] but residential schools took children from their families where love and intimacy were taught and turned them out at the other end with literally no teachings about sex and how it relates to intimacy and love. I was really taken when Shirley Williams told me "I was starved for love" upon leaving residential school. Rita Joe's experiences of love, sex and intimacy after leaving residential school also demonstrate that students were ill-prepared to manage their needs in these areas:

In Halifax I had contact with boys other than my brothers for the first time. When boys said something to me or looked at me, I would be surprised by their flirting. We hadn't been allowed to go near the boys at school. The most we did was throw notes at them that said, "I love you." Real contact with boys went to my head and I had sad experiences and sad realizations. Growing up, I had not experienced many expressions of love. Now, here were people who seemed to want me. I became a willing partner in what I thought were expressions of love.[3]

For a full century, Native children were removed from biological parents and placed in residential schools where they often learned negative behaviours related to sex, intimacy and love. Many learned their dysfunction in foster homes where they were abused. We are seeing the effects of this history pass down through the generations, where Aboriginal people who are the age of Rita Joe's grandchildren are still becoming "willing partners" in what they believe to be expressions of love. Many of our families have no means to teach intimacy and love because they were not party to these lessons themselves.

We are moving through recovery from this history of sexual abuse, incest and family violence, and our communities are working to find ways to understand and create intimacy and love without sex. Calvin Morrisseau, an Ojibway author who works in child welfare, writes:

> Men, in particular, must know and respect the tremendous responsibility they have in teaching our children about intimacy. We must demonstrate through our actions the importance of treating all of God's creations with gentleness and respect. In that way, we will teach our daughters and our sons the importance and sacredness of womanhood. They will see that intimacy means showing affection freely and unconditionally.[4]

Aboriginal women must work with our girls to create an understanding that there is a place for sex, a place for intimacy and a place for love in their lives, and that they have choices to make about how it all takes place. Sylvia Maracle advocates that we teach girls about sex, and let them know how to create intimacy and love so that their bodies do not become sites of unfulfilled need or confusion. She teaches about the complexity of these experiences by using the medicine wheel that speaks to our physical, emotional, mental and spiritual needs. Some of the traditional ways have been lost, but Maracle asks, "What if all the aunties woke up across the country and said, 'I am just going to do one workshop and six or ten or twelve of our young women will come, and we will have a fifty percent success rate.' Think of the odds, over a few years of doing that! And when those young girls are ready to take our place as aunties, they can say 'Something really twigged in my mind when my auntie told me this.'"

Ruth Morin recognizes the need for these kinds of teachings: "We don't have built-in ways to pass along the teachings about sex." She explains that understanding the sacred nature of sex can help to offset some of the abuses we have encountered in the past:

> Viewing ourselves with a sense of sacredness is vital. How do you handle date rape, for instance, if you view yourself as a sacred being? How would you view one who has tampered with that sacredness? Would you tend to view a single abusive act of this nature differently than a molestation that takes place over several years? Viewing oneself as a sacred being has implications for healing. It has implications for prevention as well, for sacred beings do not act in this manner toward other sacred beings.

Reclaiming a sense of sacredness of the body can be helpful for Aboriginal women who wish to construct healthy lives. The greater meaning of our lives can also be enhanced when we reclaim our sacredness, because we then begin to see ourselves as beings with a sense of purpose.

## SENSE OF PURPOSE

When we conceptualize our connection to the sacredness of all creation we can begin to see that, as individuals, each one of us has a purpose or a reason for being. Our purpose is something that we bring with us from the spirit world. Valerie King-Green explained this to me:

> They say that you've agreed to a purpose before you came. You knew what you were going to be doing. So you have to continue on or you're dishonouring what you said you were going to do, and you are dishonouring life. This is what you told the Creator you wanted to do and learn.

Women who are working in the Aboriginal healing movement know that rediscovering a sense of purpose is critical for the well-being of our individuals as well as our nations. Diane Hill emphasizes how important it is to reconnect with our purpose:

> The answers related to who we are, how we are connected to life, and why our spirits have entered this life are already inside us. So we just have to be taught how to open ourselves and to look inside for the purpose of remembering. We just need to remember who we are.

> When we were born, we knew the reason for why we came. But, for many of us, remembering is difficult because our true selves are covered over by the memories and feelings associated with the painful experiences in our lives. The spiritual task before us requires us to work our way back through all of those experiences to uncover our true selves by remembering who we are and what our gifts are.

Hill uses this knowledge in her healing work with Aboriginal women. Women can build this sacred sense of purpose into their lives, and work with it to validate and guide their life experiences and life work. Our purpose is almost always tied into what we do for the community, as Barbra Nahwegahbow has experienced:

> Art Solomon talked about the gifts that we are given by the Creator, and how you need to use them for the good of the community. So that's something else I think about a lot. Because he said, "You know, when you are standing in front of the Creator and s/he says, "What have you done with the gifts I gave you?" I want to be able to say, "Well, I did this, and this and this ..." [laughs]

> I think, just as a Native person who was given certain gifts and certain responsibilities, I really feel it's my obligation to use those for the good of the community. That's what I have tried to do, in the twenty-five years that I've been working.

When I interviewed Art Solomon about Aboriginal youth suicide in 1993, he told me repeatedly, "There is a purpose and a meaning for every life." Solomon's teachings encourage us to see the value of our individual gifts and to work with what we have been given for the well-being of ourselves and our communities.

Often a woman's sense of purpose is validated when she receives her Indian name. Ruth Morin says that our spirit (Indian) names are a guide for us. Our names tell us where we came from and where we are going, and what we need to do. When Valerie King-Green received the name "Gigidoninikwe" (She Who Speaks the Truth), she felt encouraged to continue to speak up where she sees injustice. King-Green remembers being punished and feeling like a "scapegoat" while growing up because of her outspokenness: "If I felt it was right in my heart, I would say something, no matter who it was. I always thought I was strange or weird because nobody else would do it." She continues to be outspoken. She laughs and says, "I'm still that way, but my name keeps me strong now. And I know I am doing it in a good way, and it's coming from my heart, not to hurt anybody."

Our clans also solidify our sense of purpose. Edna Manitowabi remembers going back to her home community of Wikwemikong (on Manitoulin Island in Ontario) after having been active in the Native spiritual revival movement of the 1970s. At that time her father told her that she was of the bear clan, and he explained the characteristics of the bear. Among the Ojibway, the bear is a healer, one who protects the community and the people. Manitowabi appreciates that her father gave her this gift. "In telling me that, he told me who I am. That I am a bear, and what the bear does. What the bear symbolizes. The bear and the teachings told me to centre myself, and helped me to find my direction in life. There was a sense of clarity and mission."

As we learn to validate the purpose of each individual, we can build communities that are inclusive. Ojibway Elder Lillian McGregor learned from her parents that "everybody is given something to do on this earth, some way to use their hands, or feet, or their head." McGregor remembers that her parents never condemned anybody, and this has helped her to recognize the value of all human life and to honour differences. Jeannette Armstrong's community understood that each member had a purpose, and that each person had her/his own gifts to bring. This ensured that those who are perceived as "different" were treated respectfully:

Traditionally, our community said, "There is a reason for that person to be. We don't know what that is. Maybe in fifty years we might know. That person is unique and we are really lucky to have her/him." Every once in a while a unique person is born. And they bring magnificent, tremendous gifts. You don't know what direction that is going to take, in terms of how they interact with other people, or how they look, or what they think, or how their intellect works. There are some real good stories based on that stuff.

Reconstructing a sense of the sacred and a sense of purpose into our lives and communities will validate our existence as individuals and will teach us to value the lives of others. It is important, as Myra Laramee says, to choose our own path: "One of the teachings that I follow in my life is the humility to see yourself as a sacred part of creation. When I consider that, I think that there is no option in that teaching to walk ahead or behind someone. You have your own path."

Our family relationships provide a good place for us to begin implementing this sense of purpose and balance.

## CHAPTER THIRTEEN

# FAMILY

❖

*A Native woman gives her child unconditional love as she receives it
from Mother Earth. She teaches her child a reverence of and a profound
respect for all creation, because everyone in creation participates in a
manner than perpetuates and strengthens life. Father sun teaches
woman that life grows in the web of creation. In raising her child, a
Native woman teaches that responsibility lies in nurturing and renew-
ing the relationship with all creation.*

— Betty Bastien (Siksika)[1]

THE ABORIGINAL FAMILY HAS ENDURED a lot of trauma through colonization. The introduction of patriarchy and the systemic removal
of our children have obscured the place of Aboriginal women and
children. We now have elders who are abused or neglected and men
with no sense of family responsibility. But in spite of these losses, many
Aboriginal family traditions are still in place, and our women are able
to call on these traditions as they do their work towards reconstructing
the Aboriginal families of the twenty-first century and beyond. In so
doing, they also rework the understanding of themselves as women
within the family structure.

One of the traditions that contemporary Aboriginal women can
call on is the notion of female-male balance. In this tradition, the
raising of children is not the responsibility of women alone. The
western model has taught us that children fall under the sole authority
of the father, who delegates the caregiving to the mother. Our aunties
remind us that childcare was traditionally understood to be the responsibility of the community, which included men, women and elders.
Lee Maracle describes how this works: "Men and women together
provide for and protect the children. It gets distributed between uncles,
aunts and parents. It's not the mother or the father that is responsible

for the children, but the family collective. So everybody plays a role in that." Drawing on this tradition, Aboriginal women can rethink the function of the family, learn to see it as more of a collective and look at how men and women can work together in a more balanced way.

A balance of responsibilities is possible during pregnancy. Because of our ability as lifegivers, women will always have a particular biological role in the early stages of childrearing. Yet while we are carrying, birthing and nursing the children, our men can assume responsibilities that support us as well as involve their participation in these early stages. Art Solomon taught men that it is their responsibility to support a pregnant woman and create the most comfortable environment for her to do the work of bringing new life into the world. Tom Porter describes the traditional responsibilities of Mohawk men during pregnancy:

> It must be understood that when a woman is pregnant, her husband is also pregnant. Whatever health and mental precautions are observed by pregnant women, the father is also obligated to observe as well. This is the traditional Mohawk or Iroquois understanding.[2]

Porter writes that men should not consume anything that "changes the natural state of mind," that parents should not argue and that men need to abstain from hunting during this time. He states that it is the men's duty to *"en ha te nikon riioste* (be very kind and patient during this nine-month period)."[3]

These traditions instil responsibility in Native men who are expecting to be fathers. Although it may no longer be relevant for many men to observe things like hunting taboos, we can translate most of these traditions to suit our contemporary lifestyles. In her work with Aboriginal teens, Sylvia Maracle advises the young parents to abstain from watching violent movies or engaging in violent behaviour, not to stay out late at night, drink, or engage in any other type of behaviour that would be difficult or unfitting for either the father or his pregnant partner. These expectations are drawn from our spiritual understanding that what either the male or the female parent ingests will be taken in by the unborn. These teachings connect the father to the child and encourage him to make the practical changes in his lifestyle that will be necessary to undertake an active parenting role.

Jan Longboat learned from her grandmother that the traditional parenting role of the man was to be a "helper" to the woman:

> I used to listen to my grandma, who was a midwife. She always said our belief was that it was the responsibility of the man to be in calling distance to the woman ... It wasn't that the man had to be right beside her all the time, but within calling distance of need. That was the concept of being in the supportive role to women.

She remembers her father "always being there" for her mother, of being "a total helper." Her parents had established both respect and balance in their childrearing responsibilities :

> My mother always said that when each child was born they spent two years right with them. So during the night, if the child woke up and my mother was sleeping, my dad would put the breast to the baby. He was still fulfilling his role of helping, but it was only my mother who could nurse that child. I thought that was so respectful, for a man to do that. The baby was right there, always with them, until the next one came along. So that was how he helped. And even though my mother would cook the food, my father always fed the children. He always made sure that we were fed. So that was sort of the working together, and I guess that's what I mean by total helper. Helping a woman.

Jan connects these teachings to her son's generation. In contemporary young families, the specific roles of men and women are still intact, and the role of helper still applies when a child is born:

> A few years ago, my son and his partner had a child. When this child was born, he wanted so much to be a part of the child. He soon realized that he could not perform all the things that child needed; that the mother had a role in nursing the child, and that he had a role in supporting the mother. He had never thought of that. It became so profound; he became very aware of men's roles and women's roles.

Young Native men can be instilled with pride and a sense of responsibility to the family when they learn to respect the exclusive ability of a woman to birth and nurse a child and when they see and respect the part they play as the helper.

Cree Elder Kathleen Green teaches young couples that childrearing is the responsibility of both men and women. She bases her teachings of male-female responsibility for children from the old ways that were taught to her by her father. Green recalls her father instructing her brothers, "When you start having children, it is a fifty-fifty responsibility." She laughs, remembering, "One of the things he used to tell them was, 'When you start having children, you are going to feel good making those kids, so you look after them!'" She applies these principles in her day-to-day work. For example, she once overheard a young couple arguing over who would get out of bed to care for their crying infant. The mother said, "Oh it's your turn to feed the baby." Then the father said, "Oh it's your turn to change the baby." Then the mother said, "It's your turn to get up." Green went and stood by the door and said, "Mary, Roger, listen. Both of you felt good making that baby. Now both of you get up. Roger, you didn't tell Mary, 'It's your turn to make the baby.' And Mary, you didn't tell Roger, 'It's your turn to make a baby. So both of you get up and take care of that baby.' Both of them got up. One of them picked up the baby, changed the baby, and the other one went and made the bottle." Green continues, "I said, 'Never be lazy to get up and look after your children. It's a fifty-fifty responsibility.'" According to Green, "That's one of the teachings that I received. And that's what I teach."

Not only is the man a helper, he is also the protector. This role can be easily understood in the modern context when we look at his participation in childrearing. He has to protect that sacred space so that the child can be nurtured and the mother provided with what she needs. In traditional ways, the man's responsibility was to care and provide for the family. Ojibway Grandmother Vera Martin has talked about the role of men in terms of the sun: the man is "the sun and all of those things that the sun does." When I asked her "What is the role of the men in reconstructing the nations?" she replied:

> The man needs to learn about his job. His job is to take care.
> Like the sun, he always goes away, but he always comes back. He

is always coming back faithfully, no matter what. You and I can't see him, can't feel him, but we know he brings that light and that warmth and all of those things. He is always working with mother: winter, spring, summer and fall, he does that work that he does. He protects. He goes and circles.

From this teaching, we can see how the man can "protect and provide" in a way that is about helping and bringing warmth, as opposed to being controlling or dominating.

Aboriginal women must now come to terms with family structures where there is often no male presence. For many women, alternative extended families provide care and assistance. Nena Lacaille-Johnson, for example, raised her children in the 1980s without a male partner. She and a number of other single Aboriginal mothers created an extended family system by living together, "sharing the house, sharing the expenses and sharing the parenting." Lacaille-Johnson eventually bought a farm which she ran with a number of other women and their children. Occasionally, they needed help from men nearby: "The men would come every once in awhile. The warriors would come up from Akwesasne and put a fence up for me; help out. But it was basically a farm for the women and kids."

Traditional family systems can be reworked to situate women at the centre of an extended family and allow them to assume the authority they have earned by virtue of their gender and age. This process requires active and considered "construction work." Men can be called upon from within the extended family or community system to help. Uncles and grandfathers, biological or not, have a place in working with mothers and their children. They can fulfil the role of helper and bring men's teachings to single-mother households or those of two-spirited Aboriginal partnerships.

Extended families, biological or other, can provide support and a sense of purpose for older women by returning them to their traditional place of authority. Aboriginal grannies today are able to call upon and model the self-determination of Aboriginal grannies of our past. As members of the extended family, they are called upon for their leadership and guidance. Lee Maracle, a mother of four and grandmother of four, contends that contemporary Native women need to find ways to make the old ways fit into our lives. She has had to rework traditional understandings of female authority to make sense of her role as a grandmother. She walked me through this process:

> Everything that is brought into the wigwam belongs to the wife. That is the saying. That is what we are left with. Well, what does that mean in a modern context? What does that mean to me?

> It means that I am supposed to manage all of this, as one of the heads of my family. Well, who is the head of my family? As a female, how did we pick these women to head up our families? How did we delegate who did what, and whose gifts were what? We don't have these systems anymore.

> We have to have the opportunity, the time, and the capacity to develop those systems, in the way that they were intended to be. I think the will of the women is there, but the opportunity and the capacity is not.

In spite of the missing pieces, Maracle has "worked out in modern terms" the authority and respective responsibilities of the members in her extended family, particularly as they relate to raising of the grandchildren. Following on Sto:lo tradition, the women in Maracle's family are understood to have authority over matters of the household (such as relationships, childrearing and family well-being). When there are problems, Maracle (as grandmother) forms the "hub of the wheel."

Maria Campbell has grown into her traditional grandmother role over the years. Following her father's death, Campbell's brothers and sisters began coming to her for counsel. She claims that this has changed somewhat from the days of her grandmother's decision-making authority: "Now they make their own decisions, but they will come and talk them out with me." Like her grandmother before her, Campbell's decisions are trusted because they are based on what is going to be the best for the nieces, nephews and grandchildren, the future generations of her family. Campbell reflects that this is one of the pleasures of becoming an older woman.

Some contemporary women begin to assume the authority of grandmother as head of the family even while their mothers and grandmothers are still alive. Theresa Tait and her female cousins have begun to explore traditional models whereby they take on the responsibility to mediate extended family affairs. While Theresa and her cousins are still in their thirties and forties, they feel a need to play the role of traditional grandparents and aunties because so many people in the current elder population have been lost, assimilated or are otherwise unable to fulfil their duties as heads of the family. Tait and her cousins recognize that the absence of a traditional grandmother results in family and community breakdown. She maintains that there must be someone in place "to ensure that there is safety with children and that there is a family support mechanism set up."

Tait sees a need to exercise grandmother's authority, for example, in the administration of community justice and disputes. They would like to establish a justice system that puts healing before punishment and incorporates the role of grandmother and the extended family. This system would recognize that the person in trouble "is the responsibility of our house, our system and our extended family. So we have to take him into our house, and we have to find out what the problem is. Find a mediator, and take him through the process of healing, if that is necessary." Tait acknowledges that "in our communities today, we have got dysfunction in every family. There are none of us equipped to do all the things that are required for a person to heal themselves." In the alternative justice system they envision, money and resources would be allocated to help "the house" or extended family take care of its members. In the true spirit of the Aboriginal family collective, the grandmother's authority is recognized and respected. She carries heavy responsibilities, but she is not left to carry these alone.

However they construct their families, contemporary Native women continue to value their role in influencing the future through the responsibilities and the authority they carry as the mothers, aunties and grannies of the nations. Many Aboriginal women understand very clearly that they hold the power of the future in their hands. Mohawk healer Diane Hill has commented on the importance of this understanding as it relates to motherhood:

> Women must pay attention to how they can help their children
> contribute to the well-being of the nation. We must help our

children to spiritually connect with their purpose in life. By observing them, we can often tell who the next medicine person, seer, chief, or builder between cultures will be. As mothers, we can help our children to understand themselves, their gifts, and how these gifts can be used to help not just people, but the entire creation.

Our responsibility is to bring those people up so they will further enhance peace and co-existence amongst us.

Peace and co-existence come with identity, purpose and balance; purpose and balance are paramount to healthy family structures. One of the greatest responsibilities we women have is building and maintaining these values and characteristics in our families. As mothers, aunties and grannies, our influence over the family determines the well-being of the community, the nation and the web of creation.

CHAPTER FOURTEEN

# COMMUNITY AND NATION

❖

*Our people will not heal and rise toward becoming self-governing and strong people both in spirit and vision until the women rise and give direction and support to our leaders. That time is now; the women are actively participating in insuring the empowerment of their people.*

— Nongom Ikkwe (Native Women of
South East Region, Manitoba)[1]

ABORIGINAL WOMEN ARE OFTEN credited as the instigators of the labour force behind community development processes. The Royal Commission on Aboriginal Peoples, an extensive five volumes of research published in 1996, brought into public view that "in community after community, the leadership is being demonstrated by Aboriginal women."[2] Many women I spoke with remarked on this phenomenon, indicating that it was testament to the strength of our women. We develop these skills and strength from all of our roles — as mothers, as activists, as community leaders.

Native women will often say that their motivation for engaging in community development comes from a sense of responsibility to the children and the need to preserve justice. They work with a consciousness of how their decisions in the family and the community will influence the people seven generations into the future. Because their motivation is so fundamental, Aboriginal women know to call upon each other to "make things happen" when they see injustice in our communities or when they want to fill a community need. In our interview, Katie Rich described an event that took place in 1993 when she was the Chief of Davis Inlet [Labrador]. She had been sitting in the court that periodically visited the community and was alarmed at the rapid-fire manner in which the system dealt with the people being charged: "The defense lawyer came with the court circuit and he didn't have time to see his clients. Five minutes, that's all he had with each client ... I was seeing people sent to jail from left to right, and I thought *This is not right. Something needs to be done here.*" After consideration, Rich came to the conclusion, *"I need to call on the women."* The end result was that Rich and about thirty other women kicked the judge out of the community and scared away the RCMP in the process. When I asked Rich why she had called the women of the community to action, she replied, "Well, I think women are the ones that can make things happen. Like all mothers, I did it for the children. I'm sure that is how the other women looked at it when I asked them to help out in what I was doing."

Another way that Aboriginal women become involved in community development is through the enactment of our age-old responsibilities to create and nurture. Native women recognize and value the skills behind nurturing, many of which were learned when they were mothers. Nora Bothwell, formerly the Chief of Alderville First Nation [Ontario] suggests that "Native women traditionally were the teachers. I believe that they have to be the initiators and motivators as well. Women have the quality that they can do a hundred things at once. You have to when you have kids and have to run a household on a limited budget. Women can push."[3]

These are also skills that make someone valuable as an employee. When Dorris Peters was applying for a job as a prison guard, she was asked, "What makes you think you would make a good guard?" Her reply was, "I have seven children of my own, and I have five foster children. I have guarded them all their lives. I have been a foster mother for twenty-five years. I think that is why I would make a good guard." It appears that Peters was right. During the course of her career as a prison guard, she peacefully quelled a riot and effectively nurtured a number of Native women into a more positive sense of well-being.

Marlene Brant Castellano provides another example of transferring mothering skills to the workforce. She spent ten years at home raising her four sons, and this helped to prepare her for her career as an educator. She has been the chair of the Department of Native Studies at Trent University in Peterborough and the co-director of Research for the Royal Commission on Aboriginal Peoples. In both of these positions,

Brant Castellano actively fostered relationships in the work environment in the manner of a Mohawk woman nurturing family, community and nation. The result was a caring work environment where people understood and practised interdependence. This worked well for Brant Castellano, who was always at risk of taking on too much work: "I always had this sort of maternal response, of 'Well, if it needs to be done, I'll volunteer to take it on.'" Fortunately, the family that Brant Castellano had created in the workplace practised that traditional responsibility of protecting and caring for mother: employees would recognize when she needed help and offer to do the necessary work.

At one time I worked for the Chiefs of Ontario under the direction of Andrea Chrisjohn. I asked her how she saw her role as executive director. She explained it in terms of how a clan mother would work with the clan:

> It goes back to the clan system. All you have to do is take those same principles and apply them. There are specific roles and responsibilities that are required of each member in the clan system. You take on your responsibility. The wolf doesn't say to the bear, "Now listen, this is something that you need to be doing." The bears know what their responsibilities are, whether it's through their chiefs or their clan mothers or the faith keepers.

> We have people here who have great expertise in terms of writing, in terms of their knowledge of health, social and economic issues. As each of them knows their clan responsibilities, they know exactly what is required of them. You give them that responsibility, and you just bring them back together and you share it.

Many Native female administrators are like effective mothers because they create the conditions for growth and self-determination in the workplace. Ida LaBillois-Montour, a Mi'kmaw who has been the executive director of the Montreal Friendship Centre for the past twelve years, has successfully demonstrated this:

> I have a staff of forty, and I try every day to help them make decisions. Yes, I am the boss here. The place needs a boss. But I don't make decisions for them. I never tell them that their solution is right or wrong, because that is not the way to teach. I have to

teach them that they have to take action and responsibility for the decisions they are going to make to solve that problem. And that is how I teach them, every day.

Aboriginal women also incorporate a division of labour that reflects traditional division of responsibilities. Not only can women manage differently because they are more attentive to relationships in their work, but they also bring strength to our communities and organizations through innovative approaches that re-establish balanced gendered responsibilities. One example is the way the Barrie Native Friendship Centre (Ontario) is managed. Lee Maracle holds the position of internal affairs director and works co-operatively with a male counterpart who is the external affairs director. Maracle manages the "internal social relations within the community," including staff and Friendship Centre member relations and operations. Her male counterpart works with the "outside" bodies, such as funders, the government, and affiliate organizations. The finance director, also a woman, manages the distribution of wealth (funding) within the community that makes up the centre. When there is flexibility to make decisions about "wealth distribution" (for example, where monies go within the centre), the women working on the "inside" (internal affairs and finance) have the authority to make those decisions. This system corresponds with what Maracle describes as a traditional economic system — the men bring resources into the community and the women manage those resources as well as the internal social relations. This system "works comfortably" for the community that is the Barrie Native Friendship Centre, likely because the players have consciously reconstructed a system based on the principles of balance.

Many Aboriginal women are cautious of the institutionalization of gendered responsibilities, however. There is a very strong potential that such a division will create ghettos of female labour in which women carry many responsibilities but are not accorded any authority. Lee Maracle is clear that the work-without-authority dynamic is typical of the interplay between Aboriginal female community work and the Aboriginal men who hold political or decision-making power. She points to the emptiness of the frequently quoted expression "Women are the backbone of the nation." In our current political climate, this expression doesn't ring true:

We have become the builders without power — and we have built every organization on this continent. We have gone out and waged every struggle. We have gone out and we have petitioned, we have demonstrated, we have done everything! But we don't have the authority and the framework for directing action.

Despite the efforts of women to create alternative systems that incorporate balance, women still do not have authority in the political sphere of nation and community. The consequence of carrying weight with no authority, Maracle says, is that "eventually our backs will snap." Because "if women aren't managing the centre, then the backbone becomes a weight — the ability to carry weight."

To correct this imbalance, Lee Maracle advocates reclaiming the traditional educational process that will teach women how to direct the affairs of the community and nation. In doing so, we must keep in mind Sylvia Maracle's assertion that "traditionally, if a woman was a good hunter, she was allowed to hunt. If a man was a good seamstress, he was allowed to sew. It's just so that we learn to use the natural abilities of people." Both Sylvia Maracle and Jeannette Armstrong agree and stress that the ultimate goal is to allow everyone in the community to use their natural abilities towards the well-being of the collective. If this means that, collectively, women are more effectively able to manage and men are collectively better at negotiating, there may be ways of institutionally recognizing those gifts to accommodate the men who really know how to manage the village and the women who excel at negotiating. We have spent so many years working within patriarchal systems that it will take considerable reconstruction work to collectively shift into a place where we can be sure that women and men can achieve balance through a division of responsibilities. Yet many Aboriginal women see potential in the idea, providing that it works the way it once did. They caution that male and female structures within our institutions should not impede an individual from practising what they do well.

Several women have pointed out that gender-divided responsibilities have to be considered within clan responsibilities. Clans offer balance, structure and order to a society. In a modern-day reconstruction of roles it can be tricky to work out how clan responsibilities work with gendered responsibilities. The structure of clans may place women in what could be considered men's work, and vice versa. As a Mohawk and a member of the Wolf Clan, Sylvia Maracle is responsible for what might be known as external affairs. She explores how this would work in a gendered system where women are managing internal community affairs. "Am I responsible for external affairs that take me to New York State, to Ontario, to Quebec, to the world? Or am I only responsible for New York and Ontario and the guys are responsible for the rest of North America and the world?" Likewise, men who are part of the Bear Clan in some nations might be responsible for healing, a responsibility often taken on by women. In the end, it involves a careful constructing of roles so that everyone in the community has a part, that each part is valued (whether male or female, bear or wolf), and that we are respected as individuals with various gifts.

Native people are also attempting to reconstruct balance by working through some of these ideas in our governance structures — the place where Native women have lost the most power over the years. Reserve communities continue to operate under the *Indian Act* political system, in which a chief and council are given the authority to make decisions about their community. Of the six hundred and thirty-three Chiefs in Canada, only eighty-seven are female.[4] This pattern has, in part, evolved from some tribal traditions where the men worked as the chiefs and the negotiators. However, it is largely due to the imposed Euro-Canadian political system that only validates the voices of men by handing them exclusive authority over the governance of our nations (as I discussed in Section II: "The Colonization of Native Womanhood").

Nonetheless, women are able to create places for themselves within the current political system and can reclaim their traditional female political authority. Andrea Chrisjohn (Onya:ta'ka) thinks of the *Indian Act* political system as a temporary and unsatisfactory measure, but she has managed to find a way to make her traditions work within that system. During her twelve-year term as the executive director of the Chiefs of Ontario, she enacted the traditional Iroquois political female role of overseeing the work of the chiefs. She explains how she used to work co-operatively with the Ontario Regional Chief:

I know that each time I attended a session, I ensured that I heard what was being said, and I watched. I watched people's reactions, and reactions of the audience. I would go back to the Regional Chief and say, "This is one thing that you need to be clear on."

I think a woman has a better reading. Again, it goes back to the fact of having watched your children. There are so many things that are so much the same that you see in adults. For me, it is difficult for a woman trying to sit here and sit there at the same time. I don't see women being chiefs. I see women really giving the direction, and ensuring that our partners carry those instructions out.

This being said, Iroquois women like Chrisjohn will continue to advocate for more female chiefs because they understand the stage we are at in our development. They understand the need for gender equity. Inuit women, for example, took on this challenge during the developmental stages of Nunavut. In 1997 a proposal was put forward to institute a political structure that would support a male and female seat from each riding. This initiative represents the equity standpoint of Inuit women and also recognizes that women deal with difficult issues of relationship and family that are not being addressed in the male-dominated political spectrum. Monica Ittusardjuat is an Inuk advocate for the gendered system:

We should ensure that the women's voice is heard because we deal with a lot of social problems. We deal with pain and anger and emotions that men generally don't deal with ... We have a high suicide rate and unemployment rate. People are going through cultural grief, and it has to be dealt with. The thing is, it is easy for the men to talk about pollution or water delivery or garbage pick-up, things that are tangible, but with feelings and emotions, they don't talk much.

Unfortunately, the proposed system did not receive the support it needed through plebiscite. According to Ittusardjuat, "the general feeling was that if women are to be elected or voted into office, they should be voted for their abilities and skills, just like everywhere else."

Ittusardjuat and other advocates feel this was a missed opportunity to re-instate a female political voice in their evolving system of governance.

Aboriginal women have made other attempts to make inroads into the political system where opportunities have presented themselves. During the 1980s, the Native Women's Association of Canada worked on developing a "motherhood discourse" that would provide women with political authority by virtue of their traditional roles as teachers, nurturers, and mothers of the nation. In this way, they sought to move away from the legal rights struggle and to take up what many understood as the supreme rights we are born with — those rights that are given to us by the Creator as females. Jo-Anne Fiske argues that this may have been possible at the community level in some cases (such as with the Carrier), but that the discourse failed when the Native Women's Association of Canada was excluded from the 1992 constitutional talks.[5]

Other political activists have organized at the provincial level to establish women's councils as one way to gain political recognition. Yet Michèle Audette, president of the Quebec Native Women's Association (QNWA), cautions that councils and secretariats are of little use unless they are given real political power. She advocates having authority that is clearly delineated in writing, having power that is officially recognized and having seats at the table when decisions are being made. She sees the need for having protection in "black and white," such as in the creation of laws that would protect women. The QNWA has expressed their need to have meaningful input at the national and the provincial level, following on the recent establishment of gender equality secretariats at both the Chiefs of Quebec and the Assembly of First Nations. The QNWA congratulated the chiefs on their attempts to deal with gender inequity but quickly followed with an appeal that the recommendations of such secretariats effect real policy development. These secretariats are at present just beginning to review issues of gender inequality among our peoples, but will they provide Native women with real political authority, and make way for change? Tired of hearing apologies for not being invited to the table when decisions are being made, Audette took it upon herself to go to Ottawa, where she addressed the National Chief of the Assembly of First Nations.

The forthright manner of Audette, a young female leader, inspired me to think that young Native women are learning to speak out more about their need for political representation. In our interview, Audette made me laugh when she recalled the delivery of her message to Grand Chief Fontaine. She said: "Écoutez, Monsieur: Félicitations pour votre 'equality gender.' On est fière de vous. Mais s'il vous plaît, respectez tout le travail qui a été fait par nos femmes, nos ancêtres, depuis des centaines d'années que ces femmes là revendiquent l'égalité." (Listen, Sir: Congratulations for your "gender equality." We are proud of you. But please, respect all the work that has been done by our women, by our ancestors, for the hundreds of years that women have been reclaiming equality.) Audette recognizes that there has been little respect and recognition for the tremendous responsibilities undertaken by the women, including popular education, social justice, and the social welfare of the community. She is clear that such responsibility must be recognized with corresponding authority.

Lee Maracle suggests that we can do immediate things to bring back balance in the governance of our nations. It might be as simple as recognizing the need for two chiefs, for a male and a female leader. As an example, she points to the 1997 elections of the Assembly of First Nations (AFN), in which Phil Fontaine narrowly beat Wendy Grant-John to obtain the position of National Chief. Maracle comments, "She need not have lost. All he had to do was put out a chair for her, and say 'Okay, we need two Grand Chiefs.' We had a dual system before and we can have a dual system again." Maracle does not think of the AFN as the defining body for our governance, but she identifies this as an opportunity where we could put the old systems of male and female balance back into our governing structures.

It is clear that we have a lot of careful thinking to do about how we want to reconstruct our position of authority in our respective nations given our current marginalized position in Aboriginal politics. The equity stand may be the best approach, and it may be that women's governing bodies need to address social issues because women have more experience in this area. In the future, however, many Aboriginal women hope to reach a stage where they can reconstruct our age-old supreme authorities back into the management of our communities and nations.

However we do this, women envision that we must create human communities that value balance and the input of all individuals. The clan system reminds us that everyone has a place and a responsibility. I like the way Wit'suwet:en Hereditary Chief Theresa Tait explained their traditional society to me:

> We live in this pond, and we have divided ourselves up as to how we are going to live in this pond. So there are the frog beaver clan and the big frog and the wolf that go and drink from the pond. There is the fireweed. There are five clans that live in this pond, and the pond might be small or it might be very big. If you talk about reserves, the pond is the reserve. But if you talk in the traditional sense, then the pond is much larger. My pond gets larger, because I now have extended family here and there, who are welcome to come and drink at this pond, and vice versa.

Tait points out that colonization has fractured our pond and its structure is no longer clear. As women, we have to work on cleaning it up through healing our families, clans, communities and nations, but only through collaborative effort will we be able to achieve that sparkling, crystal-clear state of being as peoples.

## CHAPTER FIFTEEN

# CREATION

❖

*I get my strength from going up into the mountains, or going out for
ten days and just being with nature. I pray when I take something
from the earth and I give something back. I respect nature, and I care
for everything that the Creator provides for us. That is my spirituality.*
— Theresa Tait (Wit'suwet'en)

WOMEN AND MEN BOTH have responsibilities to honour and support
all of creation, and these responsibilities apply as fully today as they
did when we first received our instructions.[1] We must reconstruct the
way we carry out these instructions as many of us have forgotten how
to honour creation or have grown distant from creation through our
urban lifestyles.

As women, we are closely connected to creation: our waters are
regulated by the moon and we travel through similar cycles and sea-
sons as we bring forth and nurture life. As Shawani Campbell Star
has pointed out, we have the potential to be "intensely connected to
the web of life." We also have an innate understanding that the creative life force itself is female, as Ivy Chaske explains:

> Women are part of that great mystery, that power of creation.
> Creator is a very recent term that has come out of contact. People
> talk about the Great Mystery. If you break down the word, it
> talks about the sacred mystery, but it also encompasses the cre-
> ative life force on this earth, and everything that has that life
> force has some of that power. It's more than just creation of
> things and beings. It's life force, and the power that comes with
> that life force.

Ivy's understanding of the life force corresponds with Myra Laramee's
description of "womanspirit," that force which is made up of "all

those universal energies that come together." Womanspirit stands behind how we are all connected together. Our connection to this creative life force may be maintained today by fulfilling some of the particular female responsibilities that we were given.

We know that we have a responsibility to look after the water. How can we do this in our modern lives? Ivy Chaske, a Dakota living in Toronto, was reminded of this responsibility when elders posed the question to her: "If there are fifty to sixty thousand Indians living in the city of Toronto, how come the lake is so sick?" The women's responsibility of taking care of the water is as valid in downtown Toronto as it is in the bush. We may not stop pollution in one day, but we can recognize and nurture our spiritual connection without much difficulty: "It doesn't matter if there are three million other people in the city. When you are standing at that shore, and you are facing that water, there is just you and the water," Chaske says. This is a practice that many women take the opportunity to do when they are near water — they put down their tobacco and say their prayers. Connecting and identifying with the water helps us to think about our relationship with it — about what we might be doing to unconsciously pollute it and what we can do to cleanse it.

Native women also fulfil their responsibility to the earth by working with children and teaching them respect for the environment. Nena Lacaille-Johnson, for example, left Toronto and moved out to the country. Her dream was to have a farm and raise horses in a place where she could help her children and others develop their relationship with the earth. She recalls, "I started thinking about how I could help kids get back in touch with creation. I knew I was doing it for my own children, but here were all these other children as well!" Michèle Audette contends that, as educators, Native women can help the younger generations re-establish their familiarity with the land. Like many urban mothers, she makes an effort to provide the time and space for her sons to develop a relationship with the land. Beverly Hungry Wolf encourages mothers not only to teach their children about environmental concerns but also to alert their communities. She asks women to speak out about the damage that is being done to the environment, asserting that we should be particularly motivated because of our close relationship with Mother Earth: "As givers of life, we can reclaim our special closeness to nature and the Earth Mother any time we want it! Think about this, then speak out your feelings. You have an obligation to think about this; you have a right to be heard."[2]

Alerting our communities also means alerting our men. Because of our close connection to creation, we can take on the role of reminding our men of their duties to protect the environment. There are many opportunities for men to pick up this duty through environmental activity, from protesting against environmental crimes to ensuring that our future developments are sustainable. Sylvia Maracle agrees that women have to speak out on these issues:

> There is a point at which the woman has to say, "The children, our family, our communities, our nations are in trouble. There is great threat." And in terms of the natural world, that is easy to point to. Whether it is logging or mining or hydro-electric diversion, or pollution, or whatever. Then it is up to the guys to say, "Okay, what do you want us to do about it?" and "How do we go about doing that?"

Maracle adds, "I think that women have an increasing role to talk about resource development, so that everyone understand it really is for future generations. That we don't just want to consume and not replenish." This is what Maracle refers to as our "tremendous responsibility to remind each other and our men that we exist at the goodwill of creation." Whether we do this as mothers or as board members of resource-driven corporations, the end result will be greater balance between environmental concerns and economic development.

In the end, we must act.

# VI

# ACT

❖

# ACT

❖

WHEN I ASKED GERTIE BEAUCAGE about the role of women, she reflected on the process she went through as a young woman seeking answers about our place in the world. She came to understand that Native women define themselves through responsibilities. Native female identity is tied into the questions "What is it that you have to do?" and "What is it that you are capable of doing?" These questions tie into the original questions that shape the identity journey for both Native women and men. When we have considered *"Who am I?" "Where have I been?"* and *"Where am I going?"* we must determine *"What are my responsibilities?"* The "Who am I?" is therefore inseparable from the "What is it I must do?" Each understanding feeds the other to construct an identity.

Andrea Chrisjohn believes that Native female responsibility can be part of a process of self-determination that moves from the individual right out through the nations:

> It's easy enough to say that there has to be more respect given to women. That first respect they have to give themselves. Know who you are, what your responsibility is, and assume it! Understand your role and how clearly that is attached to your nation.

Because of our responsibilities to self, family, community and nation, we are required to act. I would like to conclude my journey around the resist-reclaim-construct-act medicine wheel with a few examples of how women are exercising their responsibilities.

## Chapter Sixteen

# NURTURING SELF

❖

*I think sometimes we don't slow down enough. I mean the women have a lot of work to do, but we need to go into the silence. We need to be able to stop for a minute and focus on ourselves; to have that time for ourselves as a woman. We are so focused on our children, our spouses, our jobs, that we don't stop long enough anymore to focus on our own gifts.*

— Jan Longboat (Mohawk)

SEVERAL OF THE WOMEN I interviewed for this book talked about the importance of nurturing themselves. This is a responsibility that many of us are slow to learn because of societal pressures on women to be self-sacrificing. Acting on responsibility to family or nation doesn't mean that we deny our own needs or undermine our responsibility to take care of ourselves. As Ojibway Elder Edna Manitowabi has pointed out, there is a distinction to be made between "giving it all away" and "nurturing." Like Mother Earth, we have a responsibility to regenerate and replenish ourselves and to allow others to assist us in that process.

Women who work as healers speak of the necessity for self-love. In their interviews, both Gertie Beaucage and Helen Thundercloud gave me examples of the relationship between self-love and a person's overall well-being. Self-love is especially important as a protection against abuse. Thundercloud, who left her husband after he hit her once, says: "Once you love yourself enough, you will never allow anyone to hit you. That was the fortunate thing about growing up with my grandmother. She taught me that this space around you is sacred. The only way that anyone can touch it is in a loving way, and at that, with your permission."

According to Gertie Beaucage, interference with love for self and the ability to self-nurture sets the conditions for sexual abuse. Teaching all children to love themselves, she says, fosters a positive identity:

> One of the long-term methods that abusers use is to tell the victim that nobody else loves them but him. What he essentially does is he isolates the child from every other source of support, including the child's own self-esteem. You need to be able to love yourself and believe in yourself. You need to believe that you are valuable, worthwhile, capable — all those things that define us as human beings.

The need to regain a love for self is critical for Native women. Our collective history of colonization has fostered internalized racism and self-hate, which we also apply to our spouses and other family members. Verbal abuse in the form of racist slurs often come from husbands. Many women have had to live with comments like "You're no good. That white woman I had last night was better than you," or "You are just a squaw." When a woman leaves an abusive marriage she must learn to love and celebrate herself. This is not an easy thing to do after coming through a marriage where a sense of her self-worth has been stripped away. After having suffered low self-worth through the course of her first marriage, Valerie King-Green reclaimed her sense of self through recovery: "I guess what I've learned is to begin to nurture myself. To help myself feel good about Valerie. I feel I have come full circle; coming to a place where I realize that I have to start with me. I'm the one that is lifting myself up. I'm the one that is celebrating myself."

An essential component for all women in their journey towards self-acceptance is "down" time (to use a modern term) — taking time for themselves to replenish their energies. Like Mother Earth who needs to rest under a white blanket every winter, many women know that they need periods of silence in order to continue their work. Perhaps we are lucky in that we come from traditions where menstruation is understood to be a time for rest, seclusion and contemplation. Today, we may not be able to go and sit in a menstrual hut for several days, but many women do make an effort to be less active during their "moon time." Whether during the menstrual cycle or otherwise,

Native women know they must make conscious efforts to create the silence that they need. Ruth Morin laughs about the first time she instigated this in her family. She closed herself in a room and put a sign on the door which read, Please Do Not Interrupt. I Am Utilizing This Time To Achieve A Goal. Morin explains, "We need to draw our own lines, and not always get eaten up by the demands that are there. We must have our own balance too, because of the demands and the pressures to be everything to everybody."

Positive energy is another important component that is essential in nurturing ourselves. Ruth Morin talks about what learning her spirit name has meant to her. Her Cree name translates in the English language to "One Who Walks on a Path of Light." For Morin, honouring her name has involved learning how to steer away from people, places or things that will have a negative influence on her — what she calls "the darkness." For Aboriginal people who have been raised in an alcohol and drug culture this understanding is critical. It means beginning to think about what you are putting into your body, who you hang out with, and what physical spaces you place yourself in. For women, this is critical learning. Diane Eaglespeaker teaches that "you don't have to have alcohol or drugs in your household. You don't have to have anger there. You don't have to have arguing, bickering, name-calling. *This is your sacred place.*" So many of us don't understand this, she says. When she tells people that children can grow up in homes where these things very rarely happen, many women respond, "You're kidding!" Eaglespeaker always replies, "No, I am not kidding. If someone is going to scream and yell in my home, they may go outside and do it. Not in here."

Native women who have developed a strong sense of themselves also have also developed a strong sense of who they will allow into their tipis. Lee Maracle and her family make deliberate choices about who they invite into their home. They also know they are each responsible — men and women — for maintaining a healthy and balanced family structure:

> As we move out into the world, we establish relationships with other people that augment that, not detract from it. We all have that agreement with ourselves: that we are not going to invite people into our homes that are going to distract, or detract, or

corrode or threaten those existing relationships. The men know the role they play in that. It's very clear.

The ability to draw boundaries for the people we let into our homes can help us protect ourselves from abusive men or others who may cause us trouble.

Nurturing self is an act of self-love that helps build a positive identity. As women reclaim and reconstruct their identities, they are better able to move out into the world and nurture others as well as nurture their own visions of the future.

## CHAPTER SEVENTEEN

# NURTURING THE FUTURE

❖

*I've seen real community development happen in Indian country in the last two decades as the healing movement is starting, like I've never seen before. Our women made this investment in our people, and so our whole* modus operandi *isn't from this negative perspective; this perspective of a downtrodden, desperate, marginalized, poor people. We may still be poor, we may still be marginalized, but we are not so desperate and downtrodden in the sense of recognizing who we are. These young ones we are raising are going to be phenomenal. I believe you'll see a generation of leadership that will be what we saw seven generations ago — before all the alcoholism, the lack of self-reliance, the welfare introductions, the control of the military and then Indian Affairs.*

— Sylvia Maracle (Mohawk)

IN SPITE OF BEING ONE of the most marginalized groups in North American society, Native women continue to hold onto a sense of their power to make change. They can appreciate the outcomes of their actions of the past and continue to look for ways to nurture the future.

As the community members responsible for overseeing community well-being, Native women of all Indigenous nations have the responsibility to speak up about the way things are being run. We have a responsibility to create a healthy future by speaking to the injustices of the present. Sylvia Maracle demonstrates that women can do this in any aspect of their lives: through paid employment, as volunteers, as mothers, aunties, grandmothers or as community activists:

> The fact that I am a Mohawk woman means to me that I have license to make changes in the world. I have my instructions

from the beginning of time to look at the world we live in, to challenge and encourage people to return to our roots. Some of my great aunties, who are still alive, don't bat an eye in telling someone they know or someone they don't know, "This is what has to be done." I grew up that way, and now I get paid to do it.[1]

Finding our voice is not always easy. Many women have experienced a period in their lives when they have had no voice. Many have been through marriages in which their husbands did not value or listen to anything they said or told them directly to "shut up." At the community level, we may have tried to voice our needs and concerns, but our recommendations and directions were given no value. These experiences validate our need to find our voices so that we can speak up and speak out and name these oppressive experiences.

This is especially true for young women. Elder Shawani Campbell Star encourages young women to develop the skill and the courage to speak up: "It's not that women don't notice when an oppression happens. But what does it take to get up and say, 'This is what I am seeing, and it is not okay'? That's what I want to see more of." In her work she tells young women to "listen for the principle of justice and speak to it."

Sometimes this means talking about things that are not welcome. This has been Katie Rich's experience. She speaks out about the poor standard of living in her community of Davis Inlet, Labrador. When she first began looking at these issues, she remembers being surprised that community members would talk so openly about their oppression. She now realizes how important it is to voice oppression:

> People are saying that we should be ashamed of how people are living. Well, that is the way it is here in the community. That is the way we live. At one point, for example, in a three-bedroom house, we counted twenty-seven people. And guess who ends up sleeping on the floor? The children. So those kinds of things we have to talk about.

When she was president of the Innu Nation, Rich applied this principle. She maintains that, as a political figure, "the only thing I know is to tell the truth, and to tell how things are in the community."

Reclaiming the authority that we once held can provide the courage and the motivation to speak up and speak out. We can start to do this when we begin thinking about our responsibility to the future. Lila Tabobondung, who has worked in community development both on and off reserve, believes that we "can't just sit there and not do anything" about injustices when they are happening. She recognizes women's traditional responsibility to do this: "It's going to have to be the women who are going to have to start talking. There are a lot of women who have been holding back and who have the responsibility to speak up because it is our children's future that is at stake here."

The traditional responsibility to speak is integral to Carrier culture and has been embedded in their "ideology of motherhood." This ideology embraces all aspects of the social structure and compels women to be active at all levels. This (anonymous) Carrier woman describes how she understands community responsibility:

> You can't stop right there at home. You need to get out there and speak up for your family. Who else is going to do it? You need to go out and get those men jobs. You need to make things happen when the men don't do nothing for the water and the sewer. That's women's business, to speak up for the families.
>
> It's all the same thing, really. You have to have the respect of the people. You have to look after them if you want to be a leader. That's what I do. I've been chief. I've been president [of a voluntary association] and I'm clan leader. It's the same thing. You speak out for your people and you lead them, make things right for them. You don't sit back and say nothing.[2]

In the Carrier tradition, "to refrain from social action can be construed as negligence."[3] This responsibility is also evident in the tradition of the Wit'suwet'en. Hereditary Chief Theresa Tait is aware that, traditionally, women were allowed to speak out and moreover that they had duties to do so. But she has had to fight hard to reclaim this position, because patriarchal practices that silence women have crept into both the elected and the traditional political structures of her nation. Tait has experienced this first hand. During a treaty negotiation she was questioning, she was told, "Women are not allowed to speak." She is respectful of the traditional protocols around who can speak when and where, but she also knows that women have the right to voice their concerns. Tait draws upon her position as hereditary Chief to voice her positions: "I always force myself to speak. And I always force myself using my traditional name, using my language." Tait gives us an example of how we can reclaim traditional structures that validate the voices of women in decision making and governance.

Older women are also speaking up and speaking out. We know that in our earlier societies, women's ability to speak up only got better with age. Marlene Brant Castellano points to the traditional Mohawk reverence for the words of older women, stating: "The tradition is that when you get to be a mature mother and an auntie, you are looked to for advice — but by the time you get to be a grannie, people listen up!" Vera Martin agrees that it is good to get older. For Martin, being older doesn't mean just sitting around waiting for your kids to call: "The old way was, the grandmothers used to sit around and gab. They were the bosses. The grandmothers would call you on your behaviour, including the leaders." She and her peers are working on reclaiming their traditional political authority. Maria Campbell has also experienced the authority of age. She has always been outspoken, but she finds that people are more inclined to listen to what she has to say now. She recognizes that the edge disappears from more youthful outspokenness, and becomes more subdued in older age:

> Older women are more gentle — tougher, but more gentle. I always think about it as the difference between red thunder and black thunder. The red thunders are the young ones that just crack all over the place, and you have to watch them. Black thunders are the ones that just sort of roll around. My grannie used to say, "Listen to them. They are taking their babies for a walk."

The future of our families, communities, nations and planet depend on us finding our voices, nurturing ourselves and reclaiming our authority and power. Women are instilled with the responsibility to speak out about injustice and they must act in positive ways to address those things in need of direction.

# HELPING THE MEN

*Those Indian men did not learn sexism from the traditional teachings. They learned it from women teachers who were subservient to male principals, they learned it from the white boss on the job, so I don't blame Indian men.*

*Traditionally our men were builders, hunters and shaman, but when they moved into cities, they were without work, they were isolated and filled with self-hate. I saw it in my family. As long as our men are drunk and dying in doorways, as long as our children are kidnapped and adopted out of our communities, we will remain an "endangered species."*

— Ramona Bennett (Puyallup)[4]

Nurturing doesn't stop at ourselves. We also need to encourage men to heal, recover and reclaim. We have many strong and powerful men in our communities, but we also have those among us who engage in alcohol and drug abuse or perpetrate sexual abuse or domestic violence. Some assume the patriarchal dominance that they have been granted by mainstream politics and religion, and some suffer hard lives on the street. Native women acknowledge the suffering of Native men, interpreting those who engage in dysfunctional behaviour as products of colonization. Many Native women have been able to continue their traditional responsibilities of creation and nurturing, but many men's responsibilities have been greatly obscured by the colonial process. It is more difficult for men than it is for women to define their responsibilities in the contemporary setting and reclaim their dignity and sense of purpose. Sylvia Maracle describes how colonization has driven men away from their roles as providers and protectors. In her analysis, men's responsibility to provide and protect has become increasingly strained as a result of change in governance. Our communities moved away from the land where men could hunt and provide into a more urban, industrialized society where men had to "find jobs" to provide. And of course, racist barriers kept Native men out of jobs. The introduction of the social welfare system intensified a dependency that Native men had never experienced before. These are things that pushed the men further away from their roles.

The concept of protection has changed, too. In a contemporary society, how can Native men protect people against racism, sexism or homophobia when they are part and parcel of that process? Furthermore, protection has really become a paramilitary sense in North America. It's done by police services. So Native men's roles of providing and protecting their communities and nations were replaced by the rules, regulations and legislation that governments created. It became harder and harder for the man to realize his role in the evolving culture.

As their aunties, sisters and grannies, it is our duty to support Native men through their recovery. It is important, as Valerie King-Green explains, to help them find their roles again: "One of our roles is to pray a lot for the men, because this is the time period when they are going to be really weak. They don't know what their role is, and we have to pray for them to gain that strength." In our work to reclaim ourselves as Native women we must strive to remember balance and seek ways to honour men as well as women.

Our recovery should never involve competition with men or a sense of superiority to men. In fact, we need to recognize the sacred qualities of men as we do in the women. Laverne Gervais-Contois raised this point: "I hear a lot about the sacredness of my role as a woman today, but I don't hear a lot about the sacredness of man. So I really feel that we have to start talking and having these teachings out there about the sacredness of man. What does it mean?" I agree with Gervais-Contois. We need to think about how to define the sacredness of man in an *Aboriginal* way which engenders balance. We need to recover from the western tradition of God the Father — a type of sacredness used to justify and maintain male dominance. Although I did not explore the question of "the sacredness of man" (which I think deserves a book unto its own) with the women I interviewed, they were very clear that the sacredness of woman does not imply that women are in any way better than men. We sit together in the web of life, not in a hierarchical structure that places one gender (male or female) in a position of superiority and dominance. The well-being of our world is dependent on this male-female balance.

Native women stress that our efforts to recover as women must work in conjunction with the recovery of men. For this reason, many Native women's organizations offer men's social or health programming.

Simona Arnatsiaq, co-ordinator of the Women's Program for the Qiqiktani Inuit Association, works with a "community wellness" focus. She explains, "If you want a woman to be well, you have to make sure that her husband (who may be an alcoholic or a wife abuser) heals." At the same time, Native women must let men lead their own recovery process. We want to be careful that our support does not "aid and abet" them in their dysfunction, but that it helps them look at past and present dysfunction. Valerie King-Green has said that our support entails "being honest with them, but not shaming them." Although we can be understanding as to the origins of dysfunctional behaviour, "helping the men" does not mean making excuses for abuse. Nor does it mean that we sacrifice our own well-being, ignore or excuse injustice, or fail to address violence or male-female imbalance that is a reality in our communities. Professor Emma LaRocque has demonstrated that an uncritical approach to "healing" can be extremely dangerous to the victim and can perpetuate violence, fear and intimidation. She draws on the example of the increasingly popular "healing" practices that attempt to reintegrate sexual abusers back into their home communities through "healing circles" that often include the victim. LaRocque makes the important observation that the "healing" of these offenders is implicitly more important than the well-being of the victim, and that the emphasis on "forgiveness adds stress and guilt to victims of sexual assault, something that victims can do without."[5]

How can we prevent dysfunction in the future? We start with ourselves and we start with our families. One of the most fundamental ways that we can ensure healthy men of the future is to think about how we are raising our boy children. It is our responsibility as women to create caring human beings who know and practise self-determination. We need to teach them, as Laverne Gervais-Contois points out, to have "that sense of protectiveness and taking care of their children." We need to pay particular attention to their (often neglected) emotional and spiritual development, so that they learn that these are valid parts of their being. Diane Hill tries to help her son pay attention to the intuitive senses that Euro-Western society generally denies in men. She says, "We talk about spirit. I have him practise by telling me about his dreams and what he senses about people. So, he is learning about how to listen to the inner voice." Hill also tries to create a safe environment in her home so that her son can feel free to cry or express emotion. There are too few opportunities for male children to express sadness or pain, something which Hill sees as part of the "oppression that affects men."

Sylvia Maracle told me a story to help demonstrate the need to instill a sense of self-determination in our little men. Here it is in its entirety:

> The eagle gets ready to have children. Eagle makes a very conscious choice about a mate. You know, it is not like she went out for a dance on Saturday night, and she gets pregnant. She makes a very conscious choice that she is going to have it, and she mates. In the case of the eagle, when she mates, she expects it to be a lifetime commitment. She is not destroyed if it isn't, but she goes into it saying, "I want to make this commitment."

> Eagles go through a cycle of living together before they have their little ones. He works as hard as she does at getting the nest ready. The nest is made of really big logs, they start out as big around as your arm, and bigger. They bring them ... smaller and smaller and smaller until you have just the little wee ends of the stems of leaves, where the twig is. Then they groom each other to get that nest ready, and that's when they put all their down in. So you start with this log nest this big that goes down to a softest down.

> When those eggs are coming ... he contributes that whole time. They share that responsibility. And then the little ones come.

> The little ones struggle to be born. They are not very strong, and that eagle egg is a little bit stronger than most eggs. And so they really struggle to get out. She doesn't get overanxious and say, "Oh I am going to do this, I am going to do that." She learns patience right away, because she wants those little ones to learn that patience and that strength.

> So the eagles have their young, and they take turns with them. If he's not there, believe it or not, eagles will help other eagles. They don't kill the babies, but usually they are both there.

> So now they are growing, and she's feeding them. She's teaching them stuff, and there comes a point when she decides it's big

enough, that she makes a conscious decision about how she's going to equip them to live. And that's how the old people talk about it. She makes a conscious choice that she's going to teach him or her how to live.

So what she first does, is she blows away all the down in the nest. So you have them little soft twigs, and he's a little bigger now. And then a few days will go by, and she'll take those out. And then the bigger sticks, and this will happen over a period of weeks, until finally there is just those big logs that they first put down there, and that little guy, he could fall down through the nest if he isn't careful. But she's teaching him self-reliance; she's promoting his independence. And she's saying there's a time when you have to get out of my home.

After telling me this story, she concluded,

I don't think that Native women are doing that any more. I don't think we are raising our young men in the same way we raise our young women. I don't think we are equipping them to live, to be independent, to be self-reliant, and to leave her house. And to leave her house doesn't mean I go and find a woman and I move into her house, and she does all those things for me that my mom did.

Like Maracle, many Native women will stress that our little men need to regain their strength, dignity and sense of purpose by learning how to "get out of the house" once again. This means weaning themselves from any unbalanced dependence on women, and learning how to fly on their own. Native women do not need to do it all for their men. As Myra Laramee told her five sons, "You will want the woman that you walk with, not need her."

By being strong female role models, our boys will be able to learn about the many capabilities and responsibilities of Aboriginal women. Likewise, their presence in our lives will teach us many things about the responsibilities and the potential of the Aboriginal men of the future. Michèle Audette, the mother of two young sons, values the learning that comes from sharing her life with her boys:

Je me dis c'est pas pour rien qu'on m'a donné des garçons. C'est un défi d'apprend à essayer de comprendre ce qu'ils vivent, puis essayer de leur démontrer ce que je vis, mais qu'au bout de compte, nos objectifs, ils sont commun. Pour mieux être. (I say to myself that it isn't for nothing that I was given sons. It is a challenge to learn and try to understand what they live, and to show them what I live, but that after all, our objectives are the same. For improved well-being.)

# RAISING THE GRANDMOTHERS
# OF THE NEXT GENERATION

*I look at what I have done in forty years, and I feel sad because I only have forty more years to do the rest of the things I want to do! So what I have to do is instill a sense of responsibility in my daughters, and what I can't do, they have to do. My daughter, the very oldest one has a very strong sense of responsibility and commitment to the community. She already has it.*

— Ida LaBillois-Montour (Mi'kmaw)

Educating both boys and girl is equally important. Native women educate young women and girls so they can carry on building the nations of the future. Some women are doing this type of educational work as aunties and grannies. They work with traditional teachings and ceremonies to help girls learn self-worth and self-respect. As I have demonstrated in the previous section, older women take the opportunity to use traditional ceremonies like the berry fasts to help our girls become the strong women that we want them to be in the future.

Self-determination is an important characteristic we want to instill in our girls. In our interview, Gertie Beaucage explained how this was part of her upbringing. In her family, there was no attempt at controlling children; rather, the important part was to try and get them to understand the consequences of their actions:

If I decided that I wanted something, or I wanted to do something, I was never asking permission. The notion in our family was that, if you believe that something is important to you, a necessity, it was your responsibility to say what it was, and to figure out how you wanted to do it.

I remember being young and hearing someone say, "And what will happen after?" [laughs] That was always a very important part of the plan — was to figure out what was going to happen after. And to be prepared to live with it. I don't know too many women in my family who complained about what happened after. It wasn't encouraged.

Vera Martin defines self-determination as respect: "For me, respect is allowing people to make their own decisions, being able to make choices and accepting the consequences." In her role as Grandmother, she is "helping young girls work through the consequences." This kind of teaching is important for young girls, as it allows them to begin to see their potential as self-determining individuals, rather than powerless members of society. It teaches them that they have to be responsible for the choices they make, and that mistakes are part of the learning process. While these lessons do not overlook or ignore the many real obstacles which Native girls will face, they encourage girls to see that there are ways to resist and make change. Native women play an important part in this teaching. They pass these lessons on through traditional parenting or mothering roles that involve giving a child the space to define her autonomy and to take responsibility for herself.

When we see how easily we give up our power, we begin to reclaim our self-determination. Girls often learn that others can do things better than they can or that there are things that are not possible for them to do. Jeannette Armstrong pointed to our physical strength as an example of this. Women in her family have always done physical work alongside the men. While her grandmother was managing the ranch, Armstrong and her sisters spent their youth doing the physical labour with the boys and the men. Over the years, women have learned to allow men to do things, even physically, that we have traditionally been able to do. As Armstrong points out, we have learned to ask men to do things for us that we are capable of doing ourselves:

> We have abdicated our own power in a lot of situations. It's the woman in the castle game, you know, where everybody waits on

her. They give her privilege and a pedestal place in order to gain
her favour now and then. You know, it is the same thing as a
prostitute. For me it is not really a good thing for women to do
to themselves. If they are going to really look at who they are and
reclaim their power, they have to understand that they are physically
capable, mentally capable and emotionally capable to do anything
and everything. And doing it.

In addition to teaching girls physical and emotional independence,
it is also important to contextualize the loss of independence and
self-determination. Native female educators stress the importance of
engendering a critical consciousness about colonization and how it
has affected women. Shawani Campbell Star encourages us to use
whatever educational opportunities are available to help our people
understand and contextualize our past. Campbell Star values the
work Aboriginal female educators are doing in urban Aboriginal organizations. She understands the importance of taking it one step at
a time:

> I think everything is a progression. Taking women from a street
> level, for instance — whatever is done to make them feel plugged
> in and proud is what has to happen. And in some cases, that is
> making a shawl, learning a song, things like that. I think that's
> fine. But down the line, hopefully there will be opportunities for
> women to understand the roots of their colonization and what
> happened from it.

Many educators build this consciousness-raising into the work that
they do. Gertie Beaucage, for example, works with young girls who
are beginning to explore relationships: "One of the things I try to be
clear about is the history and the impact of colonization ... to be
very clear about the historical relationship of the settlers with the
original people of this land. I am very frank about the kind of racism
and sexism that's attached to adolescent male-female relationships."
Beaucage wants Native girls to understand how their sexuality has
been contextualized and defined by our colonial history, and how
this affects the way they conduct themselves, sexually and otherwise.

In her healing work with women, Helen Thundercloud encourages
women to develop an awareness of the fact that "we ain't white." This

means rejecting white stereotypes as well as Native stereotypes. She suggests that Native women living in poverty need to recognize their particular situations in order to resist their oppression. The key to this, however, is to acknowledge that the ideal is not embodied in utopian stereotypes of white culture:

> Sometimes women are in such a fragile situation that they want to pretend that they've had a "normal" life. And that means a pretend picket fence, pretend food at the table, and toothbrushes of our own. But all we had was a vague sense of loss that we were not, could not ever be Dick and Jane, with a dog named Spot.

> You know, we all wanted to be Dick and Jane. It is one of the tragic results of a systemic educational system. Well, we ain't white, right? And therefore this is the primary thing that we have to acknowledge. We ain't white. We are special. And in what way are we special?

Thundercloud also helps young women deconstruct the white ideal. One of their exercises is to examine the magazine rack at the corner store and look at the way women are presented. She makes them think about this and asks them, "Why is this not you?" Often the last thing the girls recognize is that the women are not women of their colour:

> There is a real problem for all females in our society about body image, but with our young people, it becomes a bigger problem because the sexism inherent in those magazines is intertwined with racism as well. After we do some work, they begin to recognize that. We've got to start seeing the society, the media, all that shit out there, that's the enemy for our people. It doesn't represent us, and it keeps us oppressed. And once we recognize that, we've got our first tool to start working against it. And then we start creating our own materials.

Young women need to see how they are written out of the white ideal and how their identities have been negatively constructed through our historical experience.

This book is filled with the stories, the strength and the teachings of the grandmothers that have guided the women I interviewed. As I neared completing the interviews, I began to wonder what stories the granddaughters of the twenty-first century would relate about *their* grandmothers. We must pass on the stories, the strength and the teachings of our experience.

As teachers, healers and nurturers, the women who make up this book are actively influencing the girls and young women of our communities today. They use formal and non-formal education processes and serve as role models in their capacities as caregivers and relatives, through their work for organizations, and as teachers, professors, healers, community workers and leaders. Native women are preparing the grandmothers of the future by teaching about Aboriginal history/herstory. Our future generations will have a stronger answer to the question "Where am I coming from?" As Marlene Brant Castellano says, "Part of my responsibility to these little ones is to help them know their heritage, where they have come from, and to help them learn about the value of relationships, and how that applies to whatever place they find themselves."

In addition to relating age-old traditional knowledge, we can also relate the history of our personal experiences. People of the current generations have witnessed dark times as well as the rebirth of the nations. When I asked Laverne Gervais-Contois what stories she will have to tell the next generations, she began by saying:

> Probably the stories I am going to tell them are about my involvement. About women, and how they dealt with life in general. About coming away from a dysfunctional background, where I saw someone get shot, where I saw someone get knifed, and I saw my grandmother being raped. The stories I am going talk about are the ones that are saying, "Hey, *that shouldn't have happened.*"
>
> I am going to tell about going back into the Native community. I grew up hating brown eyes. Going to face those brown eyes and trying to feel comfortable and fit in are the stories I am going to tell.

The women who are found in the pages of this book can tell stories about residential schools, internalized racism, participation in resistance movements, recovery from alcohol abuse and relearning how to build healthy families. Gervais-Contois and countless other Aboriginal women will also tell our grandchildren stories about the love, sense of community, family and esteem that they have experienced though their involvement in the Aboriginal healing movement. They will tell both the warrior stories and the love stories of our century, stories that will help us to shape a better future and reclaim our identities as strong and powerful women.

# VII

# PAUSE /
# REFLECT

❖

# PAUSE /
# REFLECT

❖

THE JOURNEY AROUND THE MEDICINE WHEEL of resist-reclaim-construct-act eventually brings us to a place where we must pause and reflect. It is a place where we can think about what we have learned and begin to ask new questions that can guide us around the wheel again.

I have gained many invaluable insights from the journey that has produced this book, and I have many new questions. I feel as though I have uncovered but a small corner of the vibrant knowledge of our women, and there are some days when I feel that I really don't know much about Native womanhood at all. When I stop to reflect on my learning, however, I can appreciate what I have learned and am able to think about how it might fit into my life and the lives of others.

An important part of my journey has been to find ways that help me make sense of tradition in a contemporary context. This helps me to resist that "vanishing Indian" narrative, that somehow I no longer exist as an Aboriginal person because I don't have the same lifestyle of a Cree/Métis woman who lived 150 years ago. As I pause upon completing this book, I reflect on how our teachings about Native womanhood fit into every aspect of our lives as we are living them in the twenty-first century, and how they can help us build healthy communities for the future. I can provide a few examples here, but I encourage the reader to look for her or his own.[1]

I think that the teaching about woman as lifegiver and Mother Earth is very applicable to where we stand in the present, and it can heavily influence where we are going. The bottom line for me is that we live in a time of widespread violence and ecological destruction. On the whole, we seem to have lost our reverence for the sacredness of life, along with the respect that is due to those that create and nurture it. Sometimes I feel rather hopeless about all of this, but then those basic teachings about Mother Earth help me to feel confident that there is power and potential for those who work from a place of creativity and love. Lifegiver teachings validate the work that is done in that spirit, because no matter what happens, Mother Earth continues to nurture, continues to create, continues to heal. Out of love, she brings life, joy, beauty and renewal.

I think we can fit this simple teaching into every corner of our daily lives, whether we spend our time as parents or as business women; whether we drive a bus, write books or work in a daycare. We can begin by asking key questions: *What is the source of my motivation? How do I define my day to day relationships? What am I creating and how does it affect the seventh generation?* As Native women, we learn that, like Mother Earth, we are the embodiment of transformation and change, and when we understand this we can begin to appreciate the responsibility that comes with this power. We begin to see how it has always been possible to effect change from a standpoint of creativity, love and nurturing. We can begin to see how we figure prominently into change.

No doubt this sense of power and responsibility can be daunting, but we can call upon that significant (yet often neglected) reminder from our first Mother for reassurance: that our ability and our responsibility to nurture is only as strong as the care that we receive. In other words, if we don't take care of mother (be it Mother Earth, or the human mothers), she can't take care of us. In a world where women struggle with the sense that they have to "do it all," the lifegiver teaching can encourage us to take the time to look after ourselves without feeling guilty or apologetic about it (as women are wont to do). The lifegiver teaching further reminds us that we need to build a community of helpers who know how to help us without controlling us. It may encourage us to recognize the magnificent and arduous work of our bodies, such as at the time of our monthly cleansing, during the course of pregnancy or nursing, or at menopause, and to use our support networks during those times. We can learn to really appreciate the partner who will say "You are a nursing mother, so I will cook while you have a bath." We may feel more inclined to accept the friend's offer to baby-sit, or to honour the employer who recognizes that we are sometimes tired because of our numerous responsibilities (including the particular work of our female bodies).

Perhaps knowing ourselves as lifegivers will give us the courage to tell the guy who is harassing us on the street to "Show some respect!" We may draw upon the lifegiver teaching to fortify ourselves against violent language that calls down our bodies, to help us recover from sexual abuse, and to resist the exploitative images of women that jump out of the newspaper box at us every day. Maybe it will help us get rid of the feeling that we don't deserve good things or that we are being "selfish" in taking care of our needs. Whatever the case, learning the lifegiver teachings that come from Mother Earth can encourage us to honour ourselves as women and to expect that others will do the same.

The skirt as our tipi is another teaching that is helpful to me in my reflections about personal balance. It reminds me to ask, "Am I leaning too far in one direction?" For example, I might be paying too much attention to my mental state while neglecting my emotional, physical or spiritual well-being. Maybe I am throwing my centre off balance by filling up with alcohol. How does that affect my home, my family or the environment that I am creating around me? The tipi further inspires me to think about what kind of boundaries I am setting, so I can say, *This is as far as I can go without upsetting the balance*, or *Perhaps I should refrain from having more children*, or *That job will demand too much of me*.

I think the tipi can be particularly helpful to women and girls when they are establishing relationships, because it encourages them to ask, *Who do I let into the circle?* and *How do we maintain the balance once we are there?* These are important questions. Do we set boundaries about the people we let into our lives? Do we consider that space to be sacred? Our tipis are said to be the classrooms of our children, so we have to think further about how we can pass on a sense of balance. What do the future generations learn about the role of mother while they are in that circle? Is she creating an environment where they feel secure and loved, and where they are witness to the nurturing that she receives? And who are the men in the tipi? Is Daddy like the sun: a presence that we can always count on; the one who brings warmth, security and comfort the moment that he returns to the tipi? Does he facilitate growth and do we know what we can expect of him? If a male partner is not in the picture, who and where are the uncles that might fill in, and what are they teaching about the sacred role of men, about respect for life, about being a helper?

So many women today are stressed because they are trying to do paid work, look after children and do all of the domestic chores as well. The tipi reminds us that the household is about balance. This means creating interdependent communities, as they once were, where everyone pitches in and does what it takes to ensure survival (mental, physical, emotional and spiritual). Most modern Native women need the stimulation, the growth and the income that comes from working outside the family home. And men too, whether they are working in paid labour or not, need to know how to change a diaper as well as change the oil; they need to know how to wash the dishes as well as wash the car (as the former need more frequent attention). We need to build environments where childcare is respected for the work that it is; where we nurture the nurturers (including Grandma, the underpaid daycare worker or the teacher who takes time out for rest and learning). It means creating a workforce that gives some lee-way to men and women who wish to make time for their children or to care for their aging parents. It means validating the ones that nurture, rather than dismissing them as "not working" or "not contributing to society."

It will not be easy to fulfil the teachings as I have suggested here, but change begins with a vision. I am hopeful that if we draw our circles out of that vision, we might begin to reconnect with values of interdependence, creativity and nurturing and move away from our reliance on a world that places an unhealthy emphasis on material successes as they have been defined by the dominant society. Balanced tipis that are homes to healthy gender relations will further teach our children how to nurture and protect life and will encourage the future generations to once again honour the sacredness of all creation.

The skirt as tipi is a direct reminder that we need to have a connection to Mother Earth in order to feel balanced, and this is as pertinent today as it was 500 years ago. As an urban Native person, it reminds me that I have to seek out the time and space to nurture my relationship with the natural world, and that I have a responsibility to share those opportunities with others. I have heard Jan Longboat talk about the need to "relearn the language of the universe," which I believe is especially important at this time of environmental destruction. Some Native women have access to people who know the plant medicines or to those ones who can teach about hunting the traditional way. Those of us in urban centres can work with what is accessible, such as gardening, learning from the birds or listening to the trees. Children are remarkably receptive to the wonder of creation, and it is our duty to help them build on those natural relationships. We can encourage them to recognize when we are wasting heat, water or food. We can remind them to give thanks, and we can teach them that you never take something without first giving. The future of our natural world is dependent on what the children learn about these relationships and how they manage them.

On an individual level, I am leaving this book with a stronger sense of myself as a Native woman and an educator. Learning about the strength and authority of Native womanhood has helped me to be more courageous. When I feel vulnerable, I call on those powerful granny stories and think about responding with that same combination of kindness and the "no-nonsense approach" that I have recorded in these pages. As an educator, I have learned that it is my duty to speak up about injustice, and as a Native woman who knows her responsibilities, I feel I have a right to be heard.

In my capacity as a Native woman, an educator, and the author of this work, I hope to have contributed to a dialogue that will help others find respect and balance in all of their relations. I give thanks for the learning and for the opportunity to be part of the vision. Meegwetch.

# CONCLUDING DIALOGUE

KIM ANDERSON

&

BONITA LAWRENCE

❖

# CONCLUDING DIALOGUE

## Kim Anderson & Bonita Lawrence

❖

IN KEEPING WITH THE IDEA that knowledge is collective, and that in building knowledge "one speaks only as another voice in an ongoing cycle of conversation,"[1] I decided that a dialogue with a peer would make a good conclusion to this book. My conversation with Bonita is an example of the kind of dialogue that I hope the book will inspire. I don't want this book to be taken as a pronouncement of what a Native woman is, but as food for thought in the ongoing work of defining ourselves as Native women.

Every reader will find different things to challenge in this book, and every reader will take inspiration in the different gems that she/he discovers in the course of reading it. I chose to speak with my friend Bonita Lawrence in this dialogue because I had a suspicion that she might challenge me on some of the assumptions I have made! Bonita offers an example of how we can understand this text and how we can apply this to our own experiences.

Our dialogue was open and conversational. It took place in August of 1999. In its entirety, it lasted about two days! I have, of course, edited the dialogue and organized it into the way it is presented here.

By way of introduction Bonita describes herself as a mixed-race person of Mi'kmaq and European heritage, who grew up off-territory and only began learning about traditions later in life. She is an auntie, does traditional singing, and recently became an assistant professor in the Institute of Women's Studies at Queen's University.

BL: Well, to begin with, I liked a lot of the examples that you give which suggest that embracing the traditions means giving ourselves space as women to take care of ourselves, and that we don't have to feel guilty or apologetic about it. I'd gotten an impression from the first Elder I worked with that following traditional ways simply meant giving of ourselves endlessly for the needs of our people. So I would do that until I was ready to drop, was so stressed and worn out. And then sometimes I'd just want to back away from that and say "I just need to look after myself" — but feeling guilty, like it's a selfish "white" thing to do. I like how you challenge this way of thinking — especially that analogy about how the European approach has been to treat Mother Earth like something to use up — and that this was how women have been treated as well. I like the idea that caring for ourselves is part of caring for the earth — but not in a "new age" sense— in a sense that we are an important resource which needs to be called upon respectfully.

KA: Feeling apologetic is deeply engrained in the consciousness of women, I think.

BL: Or not taking care of yourself. I think it comes at all levels — like who the hell has the time to look after themselves! [laughs]

KA: Well these things aren't exactly easy. I am not saying, "Oh, I have got it all sewn up," because I am not very healthy myself! With sickness, stress, and all that. And I haven't set it up so I get many breaks from my children, and then when I do I always feel guilty.

I am writing because I want to say, "This is what we should strive for: to take care of ourselves, create our borders and not let negative people into our tipis." But all of this is the vision. It doesn't mean we have to beat up on ourselves if we don't do it, but to understand that there is something to strive for. We are not here to judge ourselves or anybody else. There are ways of seeking balance.

I am saying that there is a vision for society. Well it sounds kind of utopic, having this world where nurturing is valued, where there is a reverence for life, et cetera. I don't have the answers, but I think we need to start thinking about some of these teachings in a way that is meaningful to us. Like the skirt, for example. How can I think in terms of creating a circle and linking my energy closer to Mother Earth? How can I make boundaries for myself and my family and see that as my responsibility? It's not a privilege, but a responsibility. And once I begin to see that, then I don't feel that I don't deserve to have some rest. I don' t deserve to have a partner who is going to look after me. (Not by controlling me, but being my helper.)

BL: I like the way the book is not suggesting a knee-jerk way of taking in the traditions — it's a very different process the women are talking about. For example, one of the women talks about how you don't have to go to the teaching circles when you have a young child. Your job is that child. Or Maria Campbell says, "Don't worry about buying the drum, and having the drumming ceremony — go home and feed your kids some porridge and make sure they have a warm kitchen." There is a tendency now to follow the teachings so literally. To take them at face value. Do we have to follow traditions by rote? Or are they about a way of living that we can apply to our lives as they are? I am a little torn, in that there is a strength in the things we are taught, and in getting together for ceremonies, for example. It is important to learn about, say, women being responsible for the water or the berries — there are certain teachings that come with that that are important. But when you're living a life that doesn't have much room for attending teaching circles or ceremonies, or when the others in your family don't like to attend them — then maybe it is more important to spend the time with your friends or family and build your family's strength together as you are. That's important for me, since my family is of mixed heritage and not many of them have been involved in the Native community. Maybe it's more important for me to be involved with my family than to keep going to learning circles without them. I like this book because it encourages that approach if you need it. It doesn't say these are THE traditions and you have to do it THIS way. Your book says that you can take the traditions and apply them where you are, or where your family is.

I think a lot of the trouble I have had with learning about our culture has come from feeling that I'm not "allowed" to question traditions. For example, my reaction to the thought of sitting on a plane and having an Elder tug at my pants and tell me I should be wearing a skirt — that would anger me. What does that Elder know about our family history, the hard labour of the women in my family who have had to be the men and support us all, my angers growing up about being objectified sexually, being physically and sexually abused. In my family, our lives have been fairly devoid of male helpers or male protection. And you do your best to find balance despite this. How does wearing a skirt help do this, given the kind of lives so many of us lead?

KA: I think there is always freedom to question the teachings. I don't think anybody denies that, and I think that you have to double-think things. That is part of an Aboriginal pedagogy: double thinking, double listening. You don't just listen to the teaching once and go home with your instructions and apply the teaching by rote. Maybe the teachings will tell you something different the next time.

BL: I resist the idea that it involves being ordered around. Don't think. Do this. Do that. That is not necessarily how we have to take it.

KA: It also depends on how it is taught. Are we being given the whole picture? Simply wearing a skirt is not what it is all about. To me, wearing a skirt is about creating boundaries. It is about making sure that you create your boundaries and a healthy space for yourself, and that others learn to respect that.

It is the same thing with the menstruation teachings that often result in a woman being told: "You go sit over there." Let's make sure that when these traditions are involved that we speak up and tell people what the tradition means. Western notions of bleeding being "bad" or "dirty" creep into the way we practise our menstrual taboos. So we need to remind people that our "moon time" is really about our power, and then find ways to practise the taboos in a way that symbolizes power, rather than exclusion.

I had a thought about this when I went to Anishnawbe Health (Toronto) a couple of weeks ago to see a traditional healer. First of all, I was going to see a male healer. I would have preferred to see a woman but this was the person who was available for the job that had to be done. I went in and a young male helper to the healer came up to me in the lobby and sort of blurted out "Oh, you're not on your time, by the way, are you?" I knew he was asking the question because menstruating women aren't supposed to be around the medicines — but the question is kind of embarrassing and invasive when asked in such a public way, by a man, and without any context to it. I knew that they would likely ask this question, and because I have been empowered through the process of writing this book it didn't hit me that bad. But it is hard not to feel uncomfortable with this type of questioning because most of us have grown up to think of menstruation as shameful, a curse or an embarrassment. It was just another example of how we need to be more clear with the teachings around menstrual taboos, and find better ways of relaying them.

BL: One thing I was thinking about was that if I oppose the teaching, am I just being "too white"? I really tried to adopt THE traditions wholeheartedly — like wearing a skirt and following menstrual taboos at first. I remember I went to my first singing workshop at Anishnawbe Health. They did this whole set of physical exercises connecting our bodies, our breath and our voices. Then they had us sing the AIM song. I had never sang the AIM song before. We were sitting, back to back feeling the other women's energy and our own, and singing it under our breath, and then gradually we sang it louder and louder, and finally we were standing up, and we were just like howling it out with such power! What a thrill. It was kind of a nationalist pride. I walked out of there, like a traditional female dancer, swaying in my skirt down the street. I felt very proud to be in a skirt as a Native woman. That's what all that symbolized, and it was really exciting. So I really tried to observe all the practices. And some of it was my determination that this was going to be who I was, and this was what you had to adopt.

It all worked fine until the day that we were supposed to sing at a feast, and lo and behold, I was on my period. And another woman in our singing group was on her period as well. So instead of going into the room and joining the circle, we stood in the doorway to sing. The rest of the singers were in a circle in the middle of the room, and we were standing in the doorway, singing with them. Now already that felt kind of weird. Then we sat outside the feast room, on the floor in the stairwell the rest of the time. I remember the woman I was with didn't see this as a problem. She instructed me, kind of importantly, "Now the women have to bring us food." I felt like saying, "You're being a fool to think this is an empowering thing for us to do, as women, to be sitting here in the stairwell outside the feast. And why is it women have to bring us the food — so there's another bloody job for the women to do? Why the hell can't the men bring us the food?"

Nobody could see us there, or talk to us. When people were leaving and came out into the stairwell, one guy said to me, "I didn't see you inside. How are you doing?" and he started talking to me. I couldn't say anything. "Why didn't you come in?" he asked. I thought, *"He doesn't know I am on my period. There is nothing traditional or sacred about us being out here in the stairwell on our period. To them, we just didn't want to join them. And whatever happened in there, we were not part of it."* And this worried me. Because I've already learned the hard way, on two different occasions in my life — if I use the considerable power I've been given as a woman to support ways of living which disempower me, then I will leave myself powerless to resist real danger, abuse and violence if it comes my way, as it has in the past. I've learned this the hard way — it's that "double learning" — in my gut as well as my mind, that I can't deny. So ever since then, the menstrual taboos as they are practised right now have struck me as ... unsafe. And yet I understand how the power of giving life that it represents is so important to honour.

KA: I was really taken when you told me, "We have to create alternatives, not just exclusion." What do we do with the tradition of menstruating women not joining the circle? The questions we need to ask are "Where do they go?" and "What do they do?" We need to create space for them. We need to find ways to say "These women go over here, and these women go over here. And the women who are menstruating have their particular teachings, they have their particular prayers and songs, they have their particular type of work they are doing." I think that we need to research and recreate. Maybe that knowledge doesn't exist in all cultures anymore, but maybe we can borrow from our sister nations where it does exist. We can go to somebody like Myra Laramee and give tobacco and ask, "What are some of the things that women do when they are menstruating. How can we build that into our ceremonies?" I think it is important not to take the teachings in the facile way that we sometimes apply them.

BL: Especially when you find that every single time there's a ceremony you want to attend, you're on your period! Last winter, with one exception, every woman's sweat that was held in the Toronto region was on the same week of my period. For the entire winter, November until April, I couldn't sweat. It was hard, too, because it was a really difficult winter for me. A lot of hard things happened that winter. I really needed those sweats.

I was also wondering: what about the wounded Elders? I mean, the ones who do harm to people who trust them? This affects how we reclaim our traditions. It can be really hard, dealing with that.

KA: One of the things I learned from interviewing Laverne Gervais-Contois and Maria Campbell is that we take a risk when we put our Elders on a pedestal. It sounds very trite but it is true. Maria Campbell and other women have pointed out that some of the ways that we treat Elders comes from the village priest days. We are used to dealing with priests in that kind of a power dynamic. And so we treat Elders that way — we give them that power and a lot of them are taking it. Maria Campbell said, "What is this business of Elders having people running around, getting them tea and stuff?" I recognize the incredibly draining work Elders do and I know that we need to assist them in this work, but when I see some of this stuff happening I think about Maria Campbell saying to me, "Sorry, but that reminds me of the priest coming to visit."

BL: And taking the best of the food! [laughs]

KA: I think we do it to ourselves too. We have learned to put people on the pedestal, and we do this especially with the Elders. But our system doesn't have to work like the one with the priest, where we think he is closer to the big guy because he is further up the ladder. We can remind ourselves that our teachers are people too, with all the wounds that so many of us carry. And I think we have to have the same forgiveness for them that we do for anybody else.

I think that hierarchical thinking really is going back to the village priest. Being a ward of the state type of thing, instead of being a self-determining individual. Now, I think there was traditionally a lot more respect given to Elders and older people and parents. You did have reverence for those people, and you listened, and there are teachings about obedience to your parents.

BL: But that is a deep teaching. There are things, for example, that I feel if I were to do, I would be betraying my mother. There are things I don't listen to. There is that difference between the deep obedience and the deep learning and the shallow — the "I have to listen to you because you are on a pedestal."

I think a slavish kind of obedience is a function of unfamiliarity too. When you come into a community as an adult, you learn the stereotype about "the wise Elder," which is then combined with the authority of the village priest. In our communities people are insecure about their knowledge of "tradition." So how do we evaluate the words of Elders when coming into a community as an adult and not knowing how to question teachings and authority in a deep way?

KA: Well, one of the things that I have gained as a result of writing this book is the confidence to be able to question things. Because now I feel like I can kind of separate the wheat from the chaff. I feel like I can approach tradition from a critical perspective, especially when it comes to gender, and I feel more confident questioning some of the teachings.

For instance, Emma LaRocque told me about being in this Elder-youth workshop where a male Elder stated, "Man is the lawmaker, and woman was created to serve man." And then this man said, "No one here can question this. If you do, I will walk out." As Emma pointed out, "What is a decolonizing youth supposed to do with this statement?" Well, this is an extreme example, but I am ready now to say to that Elder "Excuse me, I beg to differ, and let me explain, according to my knowledge, how it really did work."

So just having a smattering of our historical traditions and knowledge has at least given me ways to take things apart and look at them and to challenge unbalanced use of tradition.

BL: That's important. In a sense, it doesn't answer the issue about what to do when your trust has been violated by an Elder — but it can give us the tools to place our trust more carefully. It means we don't have to throw out the baby with the bathwater. It just means that we have to think about this a little more. I am always torn between the literalist approach and the generalist approach. For example, you have to respect the traditions of where you are at in the moment. If you are at a pow wow and they strongly believe that menstruating women will affect the drum, then you shouldn't dance. But on the other hand, if you are at a Native woman's shelter for abused women and the women are on their period and they need some healing, should they be denied access to the circle around the fire? I mean, there's a danger of the "anything goes" kind of thing, but in that framework where the women are abused and they need to heal, having access to the fire seems the most important thing.

KA: Well, these are the debates around changing tradition and around how much license we can take. Do we work with particular traditions? Do we work on a Pan-Indian approach? I think these are things that are really complex and a big part of our development right now.

BL: The other concern I have is that in reclaiming the traditions, we are also rebuilding our nations, and the rebuilding the nations part can be interpreted in a patriarchal way. It is subtle. For example, we often talk about traditional things in ways that leave out women.

This is one thing I like about some of the "third world feminism," as they call it. Women who have been through colonial movements in other places have seen how anti-colonial movements appropriate notions of the woman representing the nation while at the same time placing stringent controls on the women as part of gaining control of the national destiny. And that is something that I wrestle with now when I think of reclaiming the Native traditions. In urban settings, for example, teaching circles often admonish the woman. What she can wear. How she has to sit. When she can drum. What instruments she can use to drum. Whether she can drum at all. If she can sing. Some people say the woman should sing in the man's voice — that women should sing low. Other traditions say, "No, the women have to have the high voice." You can't be singing at your comfortable voice level: you have to be learning that high, high thing. To back up the big drum. There are all these prescriptions and dictations about every aspect of *the roles and responsibilities of women.* And partly because I am not a man, I don't hear much about the responsibilities of men. Is that really being taught to the men?

I worry about this urban traditionalism, and when I hear this constant emphasis on the responsibilities of women, it bugs me. How many responsibilities are most Native women already saddled with? Especially single mothers with the lowest income and the largest families. Native women know more about responsibility than any other group in this whole society! [laughs] And yet all the urban teachings keep going on about the "roles and responsibilities" of Native women, in ways that I think are about creating this image of womanhood which gives us pride in our nations. And that is problematic.

There is the sense that women are representing the nation. Everyone is really investing in what Native womanhood should look like and act like, in ways that they are not doing with Native manhood. And that is, I think, because in anti-colonial movements, women are so suited to represent the nation because we have been the mothers and the caretakers of the culture. The easiest way on a superficial level to feel like a people is to control the women. Before you do any of the work about really helping the nation, the first and easiest step is to dictate how the women should be. Then you are a people. Because you have these women who symbolize your nation. So there can be very patriarchal forces invested in acquiring power for the nation, through determining what the woman can do.

KA: I think the "mother of the nation" ideology is being used in a number of different ways in our communities, but it is a bit different than how it is used with other peoples. Joanne Fiske writes about how the image of motherhood has been co-opted and adopted by men in various nationalist movements — for example, in South Africa with Winnie Mandela — but she says that Native men haven't done this because they don't have the same type of religious background that equates male honour to female purity.[2] So the "mother of the nation" thing in Aboriginal politics has also been called upon by Native women, like the Native Women's Association of Canada. And also, women were considered the mothers of the nation in the truest sense in our recent histories. But they may not be anymore. Maybe it is now being applied in that controlling way, as you suggest.

BL: I think that Indigenous peoples all over the world — in Africa, even in Europe — were all mother-based originally. Any land-based culture is a mother-centred culture. It is how far you have gone from it that's important to consider. And we have faced colonization here. We can't simply go out and recover our traditions as if they haven't been affected. And as Emma LaRocque says — were our traditions always automatically positive?

My sense is that, while the "mother of the nation" ideology is sometimes used in an empowering way, there is also an investment in the image of Native woman as representing our culture going on too. A lot of men are learning respect for themselves as men through learning to genuinely respect and honour women. But then there are others too who are only getting the message part way — who have an image in the back of their minds about that "traditional Indian woman" who exemplifies the nation (and who they can tell what to do in order to feel powerful as an Indian man). I remember I used to see those old American Indian Movement posters featuring Buffy Sainte-Marie when she was young — it's as if she was this "beautiful Indian chick" who symbolized the heart of the AIM struggle. That was pretty crude — but its those kinds of things I'm talking about — it's hard to pin down in words.

KA: I think there is a lot of lip service out there to "Our women are the backbone of our nation." You know, you always hear "Honour the women" and "The children are our future," and so on.

BL: I think that the constant focus on women comes from that tendency to symbolize the woman as the nation. So everyone is obsessed on the woman; not because the woman is getting all the benefits and privileges in the society, but because we are intent on rebuilding the nation, and it is easy to talk in terms of the woman, instead of in terms of the man.

KA: But there is something real in that too. Traditionally the women were the teachers and were the ones raising the children and passing on the culture.

BL: I don't deny that the women's strength in the traditions is not real. But I do think that a lot of the emphasis in the urban organizations is wrongheaded. And the reason they are not talking about the roles and responsibilities of men is that it is much easier to chastise and discipline women. [laughs] And it is much easier to invest in that image of woman as being "theirs" — part and parcel of the rebirth of their nation.

There are some other contradictions that I run into about traditional womanhood. What about all our young women having children at the age of seventeen? I mean, university, for all its colonialistic logic, gives you time to think and space to play in your life a bit, to try the world on a bit. I found it empowering. If I had had children, I would never have gone to university. I am the first in my family to go. In my family, we had to choose university or motherhood. You can't have both when you come from a poor background with limited options. You can do both if you wait until you are in your thirties, and you are really, really savvy, and you manage to write those papers with the three kids, which so many Native women do.

Kim, you have been able to have children and work because of the support from your family, which comes from men having already achieved a certain comfort in their lives. You can write this book because of the space that you have created for yourself and that others have helped you to create.

KA: And the path that was already laid out for me.

BL: And I can sit here doing this interview because of the freedom of being the fifth kid, who did not have to spend a lot of their youth helping support the family as my siblings all did. I was able to find the space to go to university because I was the youngest.

Now I don't want to tip over into that feminist framework which simply says that "having kids holds women back." I think feminism is too one-sided that way — they quite happily look at only one side of the picture — empowering the woman economically, which often means not having children. I think the feminist movement has too easily accepted the idea that because you need a certain degree of economic control over your life in a capitalist society, that having children can weaken you in that respect. I like the way that Native women are trying to find the path where family is not sacrificed to achieve personal goals, where the men and women are supporting one another, so that you don't have to find your power as a single woman to have a voice in society. But I am wary of what happens when a lot of our young women have children and are not careful about who comes into the tipi. They don't have the economic background to have family support. So it really means that that generation is not going to go to universities. They are not going to be the policy makers. We live in a secular society where you have to have a certain clout as well. It helps that we have had so many women in the urban organizations with leadership roles, but they are all people who have, by certain circumstances, managed to find themselves there.

KA: Well, motherhood can't be empowering if you don't have the supports that go with it. And as you always remind me, a big piece of it is the function of poverty.

BL: I also wanted to ask you about this thing of "women need to have babies for the nation." That is kind of putting the nation above the individual, the collectivity above the individual, and I think the well-being of the individual and the collective are connected.

KA: I think historically it comes out of sheer survival needs. Maybe that is why the Huron women would instruct their men to go out and kidnap a couple of people from the English! They said "We're tired of birthing the nation! Go out and kidnap a couple of those people over there!" [laughter]

An Elder once said to me, "Well, some women choose not to have children and that is wrong because that is our responsibility." To me that is not a good place to be. There was probably traditionally a fair amount of pressure on women to have children, because of sheer survival, right? It was literally survival of the nation or the clan —

you had to have the babies. But we have to move on from that, because we don't have a population problem here (although some would differ).

BL: What we need is guidance for our youth!

KA: Absolutely. And so if you want to talk about women being mothers of the nation, then there is a really significant role for people like you and the other women I have spoken to who don't have children. Those women are doing their work too. You are doing your work as a university professor in a situation where there are very few Native women and very few poor women. You are carving out that space for them. So I think you have to consider carefully what your responsibility is as a mother of the nation. How do you fulfil that responsibility? It doesn't necessarily mean you are going to birth as many babies as you can. Because there are lots of Indian kids and youth out there who don't have the support, the space or the guidance. I think that we have to think a bit more critically about that, and also think about how we work with tradition and how it changes. How our needs change. And how we use the values.

BL: I was wondering, working on this project, what are some of the things that you see about feminism? What do you think about feminism generally?

KA: First of all, I don't know very much about feminism. I have done very little reading and have had very little exposure to what is happening out there in Women's Studies classes. I don't know enough to critique it because I am not up on what is happening.

I think Indian women resist feminism for a number of reasons. There is the fact that many women working within the feminist movement have not recognized or acknowledged some of their own racist or elitist behaviours. Like being patronized at feminist gatherings, or being everybody's pet Indian, type of thing. Ivy Chaske told me that she stopped her involvement in feminist circles because of the failure for so many to acknowledge her position of "This is Indian land that you are living on — and you can't just make me one of you." We are not all universal sisters, we have a different history, and white women of this country are complicit in the oppression of Native women.

BL: You told me that many women talked about identity solely in terms of race and culture, even when you asked them about womanhood. I was wondering if some of it was that thing we always find ourselves doing. We run into people who want us just to be women. And at that point, we define ourselves according to our Indigenous nation. [laughs] We are women of different nations, we are not all women. I find myself arguing anti-colonialism to feminism, and feminism to traditionalists.

KA: I think that the most immediate source of oppression has been as Native people, not as women. So that is what hits the wall first, and that is what the majority of people really have to struggle with. Being women is another dimension of that. But the identity battles that they have had to do has been as Aboriginal people, and then the definition of being comes out of who we are as Aboriginal people.

Another part of resisting feminism has been responding to people who want to claim their power by becoming a white male — you know, trying to assume the same kinds of power that men have had, which is very individual based and it doesn't really change anything. And then what about the power of motherhood?

BL: I think that a central problem with feminism has been its refusal to see motherhood as empowering. For Native women, motherhood is contributing to community. Western feminism is so heavily influenced by the notion of the individual rather than the community. The notion of personhood in the West is built on individualism, on the denial of even the existence of community, those enlightenment "values." And then western thought has also been built on the subordination of women and on the subordination of non-western peoples, even within Europe. Europe had to colonize itself before it could colonize the rest of the world.

You commented that Native women on the whole didn't do very well with the housewife-ization process that they went through. I think this housewife-ization has been imposed on women worldwide, and it is just that for elite European women, the process happened a lot longer ago. For me the most exciting thing in your making this book has been this whole concept that empowerment for women means we need to talk about empowerment for communities. Because that is another big difference I see with feminism and why it doesn't work for Native women. Because what positions are Native men really in? Some Native men have had access to economic power, just through being men. But on the other hand, large numbers of Native men have been cut out of the power structure. So the gender inequalities, the disproportionate power that white men have that fuels feminism, often doesn't apply in Native communities. We face phenomenal levels of violence in our communities, but that is a function, in fact, of histories of male powerlessness in the face of colonialist violence, as well as our own victimization, of course. In any case, we need to talk about empowering our men. We need empowered families.

The thing that I find fascinating about this whole work is your emphasis on the idea about complementarity of roles actually empowering women. I remember you talking a long time ago about how a man can't have a baby. And if the man tried to breastfeed, he was getting in the woman's space. He was taking over her space. An acknowledgment of men's roles and women's roles would acknowledge that the man's role in pregnancy and in motherhood is to support the woman. That seems the clearest example to me how complementarity actually empowers women. Because it doesn't involve the negation of your powers, the negation of your strength, the negation of your value. Which maybe ties to that whole history of negating women's power, women's value. Feminism has tried to approach female empowerment through the notion that equality equals sameness, that gendered roles are inherently oppressive to women. You are demonstrating the exact opposite, in fact.

KA: What is really central is the motherhood ideology, which taken in its truest sense is very empowering. I think that is a big thing that women are struggling with in feminism, because at one time, the family structure was seen as the oppressor. Being a mother was the oppressive part of being a woman. But you don't throw out the whole motherhood issue just because the structure that has been built up around it is totally unsupportive. That is what western patriarchy does. It takes a very powerful whole thing — motherhood — and turns it into this oppressive thing. I know that feminists have been working with motherhood, but there are many women who still have a hard time seeing this as an empowering experience.

BL: And when it comes to empowerment, they don't often support poor men. Feminism still sees even poor men as the enemy. As a competitor for power. But where does that leave our men?

# REFERENCE LIST/
# PARTICIPANT BIOGRAPHIES

JEANNETTE ARMSTRONG (Okanagan)
*Interviewed September 25, 1998, Ottawa, Ontario*

Jeannette is a writer, teacher, artist, sculptor and activist. A resident of the Penticton reserve in British Columbia, Jeannette speaks both Okanagan and English and is well-versed in the traditional education she received from her Okanagan elders. Jeannette is the director of the En'owkin International School of Writing in Penticton, a creative-writing school organized by and for Native people.

SIMONA ARNATSIAQ (Inuit)
*Interviewed by phone, January 5, 1999, Iqaluit, Nunavut*

Simona (Amarualik) has lived in Ottawa and Winnipeg, but has recently returned to Nunavut, where she works as the co-ordinator of the Women's Program, Qiqiktani Inuit Association. She was the president of the Baffin Region Aggvik Society women's shelter at the time of this writing. Simona has two daughters, Siobhan (Attagut-tuk) and Tara (Auqajaaq) and one beautiful grandchild, Aija (Tati-gat).

MICHÈLE AUDETTE (Innu)
*Interviewed April 16, 1999, Montreal, Quebec*

Of both Innu and Québecois heritage, Michèle's childhood was divided between Montreal and the Innu community of Takuaikan Uashat Mak Mani-Uteman First Nation near Sept Isles in Quebec. Michèle has worked extensively in Native organizations in the province of Quebec and is the current president of the Quebec Native Women's Association. She is the mother of two young sons.

GERTIE BEAUCAGE (Ojibway)
*Interviewed August 18, 1996, and January 17, 1997, Toronto, Ontario*

Gertie Beaucage/Zhawanobinaissi'kwe, is a member of the Bear Clan. She was raised at Nipissing First Nation near North Bay, Ontario, under the guidance of her grandparents and extended family. She is a mother and grandmother and is a member of the Three Fires Society — first degree Midewiwin. Gertie works for the Ontario Federation of Indian Friendship Centres as a trainer.

MARLENE BRANT CASTELLANO (Mohawk)
*Interviewed July 24, 1998, Tyendinaga Mohawk Territory [Ontario]*[1]

Marlene Brant Castellano is a member of the wolf clan of the Mohawk Nation, professor emeritus of Trent University, and former co-director of research with the Royal Commission on Aboriginal Peoples. From her home on Tyendinaga Mohawk Territory, Marlene continues with writing and occasional teaching in Native studies while balancing growing responsibilities as a grandmother.

MARIA CAMPBELL (Cree/Métis)
*Interviewed by phone July 27, 1998, Gabriel's Crossing, Saskatchewan*

Maria is the author of seven books, including her well-known auto-biography *Halfbreed* and her most recent book *Stories of the Road Allowance People*. A playwright and filmmaker, she is currently work-ing on a documentary about older women and is completing a master's degree at the University of Saskatchewan. She is a mother of four and has seven grandchildren.

SHAWANI CAMPBELL STAR (Métis)
*Interviewed by phone, July 26, 1996, Vancouver, BC*

Shawani is a mixed-blood person who identifies with the métis. She came to Toronto as a young woman and has been active in the Native community as an educator and a healer for over thirty years. She divides her time between Ontario and British Columbia. Although semi-retired, Shawani continues to work with women on their healing journey.

IVY CHASKE (Dakota)
*Interviewed March 25, 1998, Toronto, Ontario*

Ivy is originally from Manitoba, but has lived and worked in Toronto for many years. Ever active among women, Ivy was one of the founders of the Native Women's Resource Centre of Toronto. She is currently the executive director of Pedahbun Lodge, an Aboriginal residential drug and alcohol treatment centre in Toronto.

ANDREA CHRISJOHN (Onya:ta'ka)
*Interviewed July 28, 1996, Toronto, Ontario*

Andrea's home is the Onya:ta'ka First Nation, near London, Ontario. She has worked out of Toronto since 1966, and is an active member of the Toronto community through her work with the Council Fire Native Cultural Centre. Andrea was the executive director of the Chiefs of Ontario for twelve years. She currently works with the Centre for Indigenous Sovereignty.

MELANIE CORBIERE (Ojibway)
*Interviewed January 28, 1997, Toronto, Ontario*

Melanie Corbiere is the pseudonym for an Ojibway woman from central Ontario. She wishes to remain anonymous.

CAROL COUCHIE (Ojibway)
*Interviewed April 28, 1998, Toronto, Ontario*

Carol is from the Ojibway people of Nipissing First Nation, but was raised in Niagara Falls. She was the first registered Native midwife in Ontario and is currently practising in Toronto. Carol is often called upon to teach Native women about matters related to pregnancy and birth, which she does from a traditional perspective.

DIANE EAGLESPEAKER (Blood)
*Interviewed by telephone, June 15, 1999, Calgary, Alberta*

Diane comes from the Blackfoot Confederacy on both sides of the Canada/US border. She spent her childhood migrating between various cities in the United States and returning to the Blood reserve in southern Alberta. She currently lives in Calgary, where she works as a schoolteacher in a program designed for Aboriginal youth. Diane is a pipe holder and a Sun Dancer.

LAVERNE GERVAIS-CONTOIS (Ojibway/Cree/Sioux)
*Interviewed April 16, 1999, Montreal, Quebec*

Laverne is a member of the Peguis Band of Manitoba. She is the eldest in a family of fifteen and a mother of two. A resident of Montreal since 1984, Laverne has worked as a counsellor in the area of addictions and family violence. She recently completed a Bachelor of Arts from Concordia University and is a life-long student of Native ways.

KATHLEEN GREEN (Cree)
*Interviewed April 25, 1998, Victoria Harbour (Enahtig Healing Lodge),*
*Ontario, and by phone July 20, 1999, Iskatewizaagegan First Nation*

Kathleen is a Cree Elder who is called upon by many First Nations and Aboriginal organizations to share her traditional knowledge. She is originally from Manitoba and now lives in northwestern Ontario with her husband, Elder Robin Green.

DIANE HILL (Mohawk)
*Interviewed March 18, 1998, Six Nations of the Grand River*
*Territory [Ontario]*

Diane helps First Nations people to heal from the effects of trauma and colonization. She works as an instructor with the First Nations Technical Institute situated on the Tyendinaga First Nation. She has authored several publications related to her work in Aboriginal education and traditional healing.

MONICA ITTUSARDJUAT (Inuit)
*Interviewed by telephone April 9, 1999, Igloolik, Nunavut*

Monica was born in a winter camp between Igloolik and Arctic Bay, and was sent to Chesterfield Inlet to go to school at the age of seven. She holds a Bachelor of Education. and has spent most of her life in Iqaluit working as an educator. A mother and a grandmother, Monica has written five children's books in Inuktitut.

VALERIE KING-GREEN (Ojibwe)
*Interviewed August 12, 1996, Mississaugas of the Credit First Nation [Ontario]*

Valerie, Edebwed Ogichidaa Kwe (Speaks the Truth Warrior Leader Woman) has a background in early childhood education, social work, holistic therapies and counselling. She is active in the cultural and spiritual revival of Aboriginal peoples through her activity as a traditional singer, drummer, jingle dress dancers, storyteller and facilitator. She lives at Mississaugas of the Credit First Nation with her seven children.

### IDA LaBILLOIS-MONTOUR (Mi'kmaw)
*Interviewed December 4, 1998, Montreal, Quebec*

Ida is from Listuguj First Nation on the Quebec/New Brunswick border, but she has lived in Montreal for most of her adult life. Ida has been the executive director of the Montreal Friendship Centre for twelve years and is a well-known leader in local, provincial and national Native organizations. She lives with her husband and two children on Kahnawake First Nation.

### NENA LACAILLE-JOHNSON (Seneca)
*Interviewed April 9, 1998, Victoria Harbour (Enahtig Healing Lodge), Ontario*

Nena is originally from Seneca territory in Pennsylvania. She came up to Canada at the age of sixteen with Vietnam war draft dodgers and has lived in southern Ontario since that time. Nena operates her own farm and is the mother of six children. She is currently the executive director of the Enahtig Healing Lodge, located near Barrie, Ontario.

### MYRA LARAMEE (Cree/Métis)
*Interviewed by phone January 19, 1999, Winnipeg, Manitoba*

Myra grew up in Winnipeg, where she has been an educator for twenty-five years. A traditional teacher, she works with the Aboriginal community in the areas of healing, spirituality and cultural recovery. Myra is a mother and a grandmother and is currently employed as the principal of the Niji Mahkwa elementary school in Winnipeg.

### SANDRA LARONDE (Ojibway)
*Interviewed April 6, 1998, Toronto, Ontario*

Sandra is from the Teme-Augama-Anishnabe (People of the Deep Water) in Temagami, Ontario, and now resides in Toronto. Sandra is an actor, writer, co-artistic director of Native Earth Performing Arts and founder of Native Women in the Arts, a North American network for Native female artists. Her recent acting credits include *Snailfingers, Jumping Mouse, Warrior Poet, The Tempest* and *Chinook Winds.*

EMMA LAROCQUE (Cree/Métis)
*Interviewed by phone, March 12, 1999, Winnipeg, Manitoba*
Originally from northeastern Alberta, Emma is a writer, poet, historian, social and literary critic and a professor at the University of Manitoba. She has lectured both nationally and internationally on issues of human rights, focusing on Native history, colonization, literature, education and identity. Emma is the author of *Defeathering the Indian* (1975) and has written numerous scholarly and popular articles.

JANICE LONGBOAT (Mohawk)
*Interviewed February 19, 1997, Toronto, Ontario*
A knowledgeable herbalist, healer and Elder, Jan operates the Earth Healing Herb Gardens and Retreat Centre on the Six Nations reserve near Brantford, Ontario. She travels extensively to conduct workshops on traditional teachings, healing and lifeways at conferences in Canada and the United States. Jan is an instructor at McMaster University, the University of Toronto and Mohawk College.

EDNA MANITOWABI (Ojibway)
*Interviewed April 21, 1997, Toronto, Ontario*
Originally from Wikwemikong First Nation, Edna is a well-known spiritual leader and Elder/grandmother/traditional teacher. She has been initiated into the fourth degree of the Midewiwin Lodge. Edna is a tenured professor at Trent University, in Peterborough, Ontario.

LEE MARACLE (Sto:lo/Métis)
*Interviewed August 4, 1998, Barrie, Ontario*
Lee Maracle is of Coast Salish origin. She is an author, editor, orator and lecturer. She is an instructor at the University of Toronto and the Native Theatre School. Two reprints of previously published work and two new publications — *Daughters Are Forever* and *Bent Box* — are due in the spring of 2000.

SYLVIA MARACLE (Mohawk)
*Interviewed February 4, 1997, and April 12, 1999, Toronto, Ontario*
Sylvia is from the Mohawks of the Bay of Quinte, near Belleville,
Ontario. She has been the executive director of the Ontario Federation of Indian Friendship Centres for twenty years. Sylvia is a leader
in community work at the local level in the city of Toronto, as well
as at the provincial and national levels. She is often called upon as a
traditional teacher.

CATHERINE MARTIN (Mi'kmaw)
*Interviewed by phone, October 12, 1998, West Dover, Nova Scotia*
Catherine is a filmmaker and a singer. Her films include *Kwa'nu'te:
Micmac and Maliseet Artists* and *Mi'kmaq Family/Migmaoei Otjiosog*,
both produced out of the National Film Board. Catherine has
worked extensively with Aboriginal artists in the Atlantic provinces.
She lives in West Dover, Nova Scotia, with her husband and two
children and is currently working with the NFB on a documentary
about Annie Mae Aquash.

VERA MARTIN (Ojibway)
*Interviewed July 20, 1999, Peterborough, Ontario*
A Grandmother to the Ojibway nation, Vera has been active in the
Native healing movement and the spiritual and cultural revival of
Aboriginal peoples since the 1970s. She has worked as an Aboriginal
addictions counsellor and trainer and with women who are survivors
of abuse. Vera raised eight children and has recently become a great-
grandmother.

LILLIAN MCGREGOR (Ojibway)
*Interviewed August 25, 1996, Toronto, Ontario*
Lillian is an Ojibway from Whitefish River First Nation [Ontario].
She left her home to complete her high school education in Toronto
at the age of fifteen and has been living in the "mega-city" since the
1940s. After a career in nursing, she retired to become one of the
most active Elders in the Toronto Aboriginal community. Along with
her other responsibilities, she is the Elder for First Nations House at
the University of Toronto.

RUTH MORIN (Cree)
*Interviewed by phone, September 22, 1998, Edmonton, Alberta*

A member of Saddle Lake First Nation [Alberta], Ruth is a traditional teacher and is employed as the chief executive officer of the Nechi Training, Research and Health Promotions Institute. Working in the field of addiction for nineteen years, Ruth uses her own experiences in "wounded-ness" in a compassionate way towards others. She is a wife, a mother and a grandmother.

BARBRA NAHWEGAHBOW (Ojibway)
*Interviewed August 6, 1996, Toronto, Ontario*

Barbra Nahwegahbow, Wolf Clan, is a member of the Whitefish River Ojibway First Nation in northern Ontario. Her late father was a trapper and her mother raised eleven children. Barbra has lived in Toronto for the past twenty-eight years where she has been a political activist and community organizer. Barbra still speaks her language (Ojibway) and is a writer and a traditional singer.

MAGGIE PAUL (Passamaquody)
*Interviewed April 13, 1999, Toronto, Ontario*

Maggie is from the Passamaquody reservation near Perry, Maine, but she has lived in New Brunswick since age fourteen. A traditional singer and cultural teacher, Maggie's work has included twenty-nine years as a volunteer in prisons across Canada. She continues to work with medicine people in Canada, the United States, Mexico, Venezuela and Belize.

DORRIS PETERS (Sto:lo)
*Interviewed August 24, 1998, Mission, BC*

Born and raised on Peters Reserve, Dorris (Theltothelwit) is a healer, mother, grandmother, great-grandmother and foster parent. She still resides in the Fraser Valley of British Columbia. Dorris is semi-retired, but still works with communities across North America in the area of traditional healing.

KATIE RICH (Innu)
*Interviewed by phone, October 6, 1998, Davis Inlet, Labrador*

Katie has served several terms as the Chief of Davis Inlet [Labrador], and later as the president of the Innu Nation. In this capacity, she has been very active and successful in seeking social justice for the Innu people. Katie has six children.

LILA TABOBONDUNG (Ojibway/Pottawatomi)
*Interviewed by phone, August 10, 1996, Wasauksing First Nation [Ontario]*

Lila's spirit name is Waubenopitchakwe, which means Eastern Doorway Songbird Woman. After spending many years in Toronto, she returned to her home community of Wasauksing First Nation. She completed a Bachelor of Arts through Laurentian University and is currently employed as the band administrator for Wasauksing. Lila is a hand drummer and a traditional singer.

THERESA TAIT (Wit'suwet'en)
*Interviewed by phone, April 9, 1999, Moricetown, BC*

Theresa is a Hereditary Chief for the Wit'suwet'en people, whose traditional territory covers a large area of central BC. She spent many years in Vancouver working in Aboriginal justice and now lives in her home community of Moricetown First Nation. She carries the hereditary name and title of Wihaliy'te, which means Big Medicine.

HELEN THUNDERCLOUD (Algonquin)
*Interviewed February 18, 1997, Toronto, Ontario*

Helen is a Toronto-based educator and trainer specializing in communications and alternative dispute resolution. Originally from Kitigan Zibi First Nation in Quebec, Helen spent years in Manitoba working for the Federal Human Rights Commission and teaching at Community Colleges in northern Manitoba and northwest Ontario. She was a member of the Thunder Eagle Society, who successfully lobbied for the establishment of Aboriginal schools in Winnipeg.

WANDA WHITEBIRD (Mi'kmaw)
*Interviewed May 12, 1998, Toronto, Ontario*

Wanda grew up in Nova Scotia, but has been living and working in Ontario for fifteen years. She has worked with both Native men and women in prison and is currently working as a traditional counsellor at Anishnawbe Health Toronto.

SHIRLEY WILLIAMS (Ojibway/Odawa)
*Interviewed April 27, 1998, Peterborough, Ontario*

Shirley is originally from Wikwemikong Unceded First Nation on Manitoulin Island [Ontario]. She is the translator for the Union of Ontario Indians and often travels to Native communities to give lectures on Native language, culture and residential schools. Shirley is an associate professor at Trent University and is currently working on several Ojibway language textbooks and an Ojibway dictionary.

# NOTES

## INTRODUCTION

1. Patricia Hill Collins, *Black Feminist Thought: Knowledge, Consciousness and the Politics of Empowerment* (Boston: Unwin Hyman, 1990), 68.

2. Ibid., 95.

3. Sylvia Maracle cited in Marlene Brant Castellano and Janice Hill, "First Nations Women: Reclaiming Our Responsibilities," in Joy Parr, ed., *A Diversity of Women: Ontario, 1945–1980* (Toronto: University of Toronto Press, 1995), 46.

## SETTING OUT & CHAPTER ONE

1. Patricia Monture-Angus, *Thunder in My Soul: A Mohawk Woman Speaks* (Halifax: Fernwood Publishing, 1995), 44–45.

2. Ibid., 45

3. Ibid.

4. Margaret Laurence, *The Diviners* (Toronto: McClelland and Stewart, 1974).

5. Now, after having re-read *The Diviners* almost twenty years later, I have plenty of other things to say about the way Native people serve as a backdrop for the identity struggle of the main protagonist in the book. I don't intend to digress here, but for those who are interested in a critical Indigenous reading of Margaret Laurence's Native characters, I recommend Janice Acoose, *Iskwewak. Kah'Ki Yaw Ni Wahkomakanak: Neither Indian Princesses nor Easy Squaws* (Toronto: Women's Press, 1995).

6. Sylvia Maracle, personal communication, September 1997.

7. I will get into a more extensive discussion about the use of culture and tradition in the next chapter.

8. I have borrowed this phrase from Mary Crow Dog (now Brave Bird), *Lakota Woman* (New York: Grove Press, 1990), 23.

9. Of course, there are generous, kind and respectful men in all cultures. These men likely call on certain things from their respective traditions while they work through the many systems that encourage them to be patriarchal, individualistic, sexist, homophobic and racist. My dad has had to navigate these same systems, but our ancestors, a people who valued balance, reciprocity, relationships and respect for all creation, have walked with him on that journey.

10. It is important, however, to consider the question my friend Bonita posed after reading this section: "What about the mixed-blood people to whom the Elders don't offer any recognition?"

11. I use a capital "E" when referring to people who are recognized as teachers in our communities. The small "e" elders refers to people who are Aboriginal seniors.

12. Whereas motherhood was what really jolted my consciousness, I believe with age I would have become more cognizant about the way patriarchy structures our society. I have observed, for instance, that as my peers and I move through our years in the workforce, we are becoming more astute at picking up the ways in which patriarchy shapes that particular forum.

## CHAPTER TWO

1. Leslie Marmon Silko, *Yellow Woman and a Beauty of Spirit* (New York: Touchstone, 1996), 200.

2. Haunani-Kay Trask, *From a Native Daughter: Colonialism and Sovereignty in Hawaii* (Monroe, ME: Common Courage Press, 1993).

3. Paula Gunn Allen, *The Sacred Hoop: Recovering the Feminine in American Indian Tradition* (Boston: Beacon, 1986), 78.

4. Ibid., 44.

5. In a footnote entry, LaRocque writes, "Many early European observations as well as original Indian legends (e.g. Cree Wehsehkehcha stories I grew up with) point to pre-contact existence of male violence and sexism against women."

6. Emma LaRocque, "The Colonization of a Native Woman Scholar," in Christine Miller and Patricia Chuchryk, eds., *Women of the First Nations: Power, Wisdom and Strength* (Winnipeg: University of Manitoba Press, 1996), 14.

7. Beatrice Medicine, "Indian Women: Tribal Identity as Status Quo," in Marion Lowe and Ruth Hubbard, eds., *Women's Nature: Rationalizations of Inequality* (New York: Pergamon, 1983), 70.

## CHAPTER THREE

1. I have drawn on a lot of different resources to create this book. It began as a master's thesis that I did for the Ontario Institute for Studies in Education of the University of Toronto. Because it was a thesis, I was obliged to review and use literature about Native women. I knew that I wasn't going to get the kind of information I was looking for solely out of books, and so I decided to base the thesis on interviews with twelve local women. When I began to expand the thesis into a book, I continued to read, and went on to interview more women on the subject of Native womanhood. The resources that comprise this book are therefore both written and oral.

2. See Janice Acoose, *Iskewewak. Kah'Ki Yaw Ni Wahkomakanak: Neither Indian Princesses nor Easy Squaws* (Toronto: Women's Press, 1995), 39–68; Patricia Albers and Bea Medicine, *The Hidden Half: Studies of Plains Indian Women* (Washington: University Press of America, 1983), 1–5; Rayna Green, *Women in American Indian Society* (New York: Chelsea House, 1992), 14–16; Laura F. Klein and

Lillian Ackerman, eds., *Women and Power in Native North America* (Norman, OK: University of Oklahoma Press, 1995), 3–8.

3. Patricia Monture-Angus, *Thunder in My Soul: A Mohawk Woman Speaks* (Halifax: Fernwood Publishing, 1995), 60.

4. I apologize in advance if I have not recognized or have misnamed any of the Native authors. The spelling of nations may differ as I have tried to follow the particular spelling and definition that each author has used to describe her/himself.

5. Gretchen M. Bataille and Kathleen Sands, *American Indian Women: A Guide to Research* (New York: Garland Publishing, 1991), in preface.

6. Ruth Landes, *Ojibwa Woman* (New York: Columbia University Press, 1938).

7. Ibid., 85, 100–103, 135, 144, 158, 168.

8. Ibid., 5.

9. Ibid., 31–35, 49, 46, 131.

10. Ibid., 177.

11. Ibid., vii.

12. Steve Wall, *Wisdom's Daughters: Conversations with Women Elders of Native America* (New York: HarperCollins Publishing, 1993).

13. Greg Young-Ing, "Marginalization in Publishing," in Jeannette Armstrong, ed., *Looking at the Words of Our People: First Nations Analysis of Literature* (Penticton, BC: Theytus Books, 1993), 179–187.

14. A number of anthologies of fiction and poetry have been produced by Native women, but every collection of Native female voice/transcription that I have found has been edited by non-Native people.

15. Wall, *Wisdom's Daughters*, xii.

16. Ibid., xiii.

17. bell hooks, *Black Looks: Race and Representation* (Toronto: Between the Lines Press, 1992), 21.

18. H. Henrietta Stockel, *Women of the Apache Nation: Voices of Truth* (Reno: University of Nevada Press, 1991).

19. Ibid., xv.

20. University of Toronto, November 15–16, 1996.

21. Paula Gunn Allen, *The Sacred Hoop: Recovering the Feminine in American Indian Tradition* (Boston: Beacon, 1986), 234–240.

## LOOKING BACK & CHAPTER FOUR

1. Statistics Canada Census, 1991.

2. Anne McGillivray and Brenda Comaskey, *Black Eyes All of the Time: Intimate Violence, Aboriginal Women and the Justice System* (Toronto: University of Toronto Press, 1999), 8–17.

3. Although all Indigenous peoples in Canada now have "contact," the colonial process continues as Native people are pressured to move off traditional lands and to give up rights.

4. Kaaren Olsen, "Native Women and the Fur Industry," *Canadian Woman Studies* 10, nos. 2/3 (1989), 55.

5. Sylvia Maracle, interview by author, Toronto, Ontario, April 12, 1999.

6. Henry S. Sharp, "Asymmetric Equals: Women and Men Among the Chippewayan," in Laura F. Klein and Lillian Ackerman, eds., *Women and Power in Native North America* (Norman, OK: University of Oklahoma Press, 1995), 58.

7. Judith K. Brown, "Economic Organization and the Position of Women Among the Iroquois," in W.G. Spittal, *Iroquois Women: An Anthology* (Ohsweken, ON: Iroqrafts, 1990), 192–194.

8. Clara Sue Kidwell, "Choctaw Women and Cultural Persistence in Mississippi," in Nancy Shoemaker, ed., *Negotiators of Change: Historical Perspectives on Native American Women* (New York: Routledge, 1995), 118.

9. Carol Devens, *Countering Colonization: Native American Women and the Great Lakes Missions, 1630–1900* (Berkeley: University of California Press, 1992), 12.

10. Ibid.

11. See Priscilla K. Buffaloehead, "Farmers, Warriors, Traders: A Fresh Look at Ojibway Women," *Minnesota History* 48, no. 6 (Summer 1983), 40; and Lucy Eldersveld Murphy, "Autonomy and the Economic Roles of Indian Women of the Fox-Wisconsin River Region, 1763–1832," in Shoemaker, ed., *Negotiators of Change*, 78.

12. Alice B. Kehoe, "Blackfoot Persons," in Klein and Ackerman, eds., *Women and Power in Native North America*, 114–116.

13. Marie Annette Jaimes with Theresa Halsey, "American Indian Women: At the Center of Indigenous Resistance in Contemporary North America," in M. Annette Jaimes, ed., *The State of Native America: Genocide, Colonization, and Resistance* (Boston: South End Press, 1992), 318.

14. Diane Rothenburg, "The Mothers of the Nation: Seneca Resistance to Quaker Intervention," in Eleanor Leacock, ed., *Women and Colonization: Anthropological Perspectives* (New York: Praeger Publishers, 1980), 68.

15. Joy Bilharz, "First Among Equals? The Changing Status of Seneca Women," in Klein and Ackerman, eds., *Women and Power in Native North America*, 102.

16. See Cyndy Baskin, "Women in Iroquois Society," *Canadian Woman Studies* 4, no. 2 (1982), 43.

17. The references to "the Plateau" in this section include various peoples who traditionally lived in eastern Washington, northern Idaho, portions of eastern Oregon, parts of Montana and southern British Columbia (as identified by anthropologist Lillian Ackerman).

18. Lillian Ackerman, "Complementary But Equal: Gender Status in the Plateau," in Klein and Ackerman, eds., *Women and Power in Native North America*, 83–84.

19. The change from a land-based economy covers a lengthy historical period, and is still happening to Indigenous peoples around the world.

20. Devens, *Countering Colonization.*

21. Ibid., 16–17.

22. Alan M. Klein, "The Political Economy of Gender: A Nineteenth Century Plains Indian Case Study," in Patricia Albers and Beatrice Medicine, eds., *The Hidden Half: Studies of Plains Indian Women* (Washington: University Press of America), 156.

23. Theda Purdue, "Women, Men and American Indian Policy: The Cherokee Response to 'Civilization,'" in Shoemaker, ed., *Negotiators of Change*, 90–114.

24. Sally Roesch Wagner, "The Iroquois Confederacy: A Native American Model for Non-Sexist Men," in Spittal, ed., *Iroquois Women: An Anthology*, 221.

25. Quoted in Laura F. Klein, "Mother as Clanswoman: Rank and Gender in Tlingit Society," in Klein and Ackerman, eds., *Women and Power in Native North America*, 35.

26. Carol Douglas Sparks, "The Land Incarnate: Navajo Women and the Dialogue of Colonialism," in Shoemaker, ed., *Negotiators of Change*, 138.

27. In Jane Katz, *Messengers of the Wind: Native American Women Tell Their Life Stories* (New York: Ballantine Books, 1995), 56.

28. Jennifer Blythe and Peggy McGuire, "The Changing Employment of Cree Women in Moosonee and Moose Factory," in Christine Miller and Patricia Chuchryk, eds., *Women of the First Nations: Power, Wisdom and Strength* (Winnipeg: University of Manitoba Press, 1996), 136.

29. Rosemary Brown, "The Exploitation of the Oil and Gas Frontier: Its Impact on Lubicon Lake Cree Women," in Miller and Chuchryk, eds., *Women of the First Nations*, 151–165.

30. Ibid.,154.

31. Ibid., 157.

32. Marilou Awiakta, *Selu: Seeking the Corn Mother's Wisdom* (Golden, CO: Fulcrum Publishing, 1993), 9.

33. See Spittal, ed., *Iroquois Women: An Anthology.*

34. Sally Roesch Wagner, "The Iroquois Confederacy: A Native American Model for Non-sexist Men," in Spittal, ed., *Iroquois Women: An Anthology*, 220.

35. Of course, these traditional political systems still exist among the Iroquois, but they do not hold the same political power that they once did. Elected band councils now hold the *official* authority for community governance. I use the past tense in this section to refer to a time when the traditional Iroquois system was the only means of governance.

36. Baskin, "Women in Iroquois Society," 43.

37. See Awiakta, *Selu: Seeking the Corn Mother's Wisdom*, 38, 119; Paula Gunn Allen, *The Sacred Hoop: Recovering the Feminine in American Indian Tradition* (Boston: Beacon Press, 1986), 36; and Wilma Mankiller and Michael Wallis, *Mankiller:*

*A Chief and Her People* (New York: St. Martin's Press, 1993), 19.

38. Theresa Tait, telephone interview by author, Moricetown First Nation, April 9, 1999.

39. Ackerman, "Complementary But Equal: Gender Status in the Plateau," 88–89.

40. Robert Stephen Grumet, "Sunksquaws, Shamans and Tradeswomen: Middle Atlantic Coastal Algonkian Women During the Seventeenth and Eighteenth Centuries," in Eleanor Leacock, ed., *Women and Colonization: Anthropological Perspectives* (New York: Praeger Publishers, 1980), 49; Carolyn Reyner, *Cante Ohitika Win (Brave-hearted Women): Images of Lakota Women from the Pine Ridge Reservation, South Dakota* (Vermillion: University of South Dakota Press, 1991), 5.

41. Beverly Hungry Wolf, *The Ways of My Grandmothers* (New York: William Morrow and Company, 1980); Marla Powers, *Oglala Women: Myth, Ritual, and Reality* (Chicago: University of Chicago Press, 1986).

42. In Janet Silman, *Enough is Enough: Aboriginal Women Speak Out* (Toronto: The Women's Press, 1987), 226.

43. Lee Guemple, "Gender in Inuit Society," in Klein and Ackerman, eds., *Women and Power in Native North America* , 25.

44. Joanne Fiske, "Child of the State, Mother of the Nation: Aboriginal Women and the Ideology of Motherhood," *Culture* 12, no. 1 (1993), 17–35.

45. Kathleen Jamieson, *Indian Women and the Law in Canada: Citizens Minus* (Ottawa: Advisory Council on the Status of Women, 1978), 1.

46. Ibid.

47. Janice Acoose, *Iskwewak. Kah'Ki Yaw Ni Wahkomakanak: Neither Indian Princesses nor Easy Squaws* (Toronto: Women's Press, 1995), 47.

48. Osennontion and Skonaganleh:ra, "Our World," *Canadian Woman Studies* 10, nos. 2/3 (1989), 8.

49. Beatrice Medicine, "Indian Women and the Renaissance of Traditional Religion," in Raymond J. Demallie and Douglas R. Parks, eds., *Sioux Indian Religion: Tradition and Innovation* (Norman, OK: University of Oklahoma Press, 1987), 166.

50. Allen, *The Sacred Hoop*, 6.

51. See Ackerman, "Complementary But Equal: Gender Status in the Plateau," 91; Guemple, "Gender in Inuit Society," 26; Clara Sue Kidwell, "The Power of Women in Three American Indian Societies," *Journal of Ethnic Studies* 5, no. 3 (1975), 119; Klein, "Mother as Clanswoman: Rank and Gender in Tlingit Society," 36; Martha C. Knack, "The Dynamics of Southern Paiute Women's Roles," in Klein and Ackerman, eds., *Women and Power in Native North America* , 150; and Grumet, "Sunksquaws, Shamans and Tradeswomen," 53.

52. Sponsoring a ceremony means taking responsibility to make sure that it happens and doing the tasks that are necessary to this end, as in the example below about the Horn Society Sun Dance.

53. Alice B. Kehoe, "Blackfoot Persons," in Klein and Ackerman, eds., *Women and Power in Native North America* , 116.

54. Art Solomon, *Songs for the People: Teachings on the Natural Way* (Toronto: NC Press, 1990), 35.

55. Kehoe, "Blackfoot Persons," 116.

56. In Steve Wall, *Wisdom's Daughters: Conversations with Women Elders of Native America* (New York: HarperCollins Publishers, 1993), 109–110.

57. Shirley Williams, "Women's Role in Ojibway Spirituality," *Journal of Canadian Native Studies* 27, no. 3 (1992), 102.

58. Thomas Buckley and Alan Gottlieb, eds., *Blood Magic: The Anthropology of Menstruation* (Berkeley: University of California Press, 1988), 14.

59. Joanne Arnott, *Breasting the Waves: On Writing and Healing* (Vancouver: Press Gang Publishers, 1995), 96; Allen, *The Sacred Hoop*, 46–47; Beatrice Medicine, "Indian Women and the Renaissance of Traditional Religion," 169; and Lena Sootkis in Wall, *Wisdom's Daughters*, 57.

60. In Dianne Meili, *Those Who Know: Profiles of Alberta's Native Elders* (Edmonton: NeWest Publishers Limited, 1991), 152.

61. Victoria D. Patterson, "Evolving Gender Roles in Pomo Society," in Klein and Ackerman, eds., *Women and Power in Native North America,* 140.

62. Suzanne Fournier and Ernie Crey, *Stolen From Our Embrace: The Abduction of First Nations Children and the Restoration of Aboriginal Communities* (Vancouver: Douglas and McIntyre, 1998), 50.

63. Ibid., 61.

64. Isabelle Knockwood, *Out of the Depths: The Experience of Mi'kmaw Children at the Indian Residential School at Shubenacadie, Nova Scotia* (Lockeport, NS: Roseway Publishing, 1992), 92.

65. Ibid., 91–92.

66. Ibid., 93

67. Ibid., 123.

68. Allen, *The Sacred Hoop*, 41.

69. Karen Anderson, *Chain Her by One Foot: The Subjugation of Native Women in Seventeenth-Century New France* (NY: Routledge, 1991), 163–164.

70. Jordan Paper, "Through the Earth Darkly: The Female Spirit in Native American Religions," in Christopher Vescey, ed., *Religion in Native North America* (Moscow, ID: University of Idaho Press, 1990), 17.

71. Leacock, *Women and Colonization,*18.

72. Joanne Fiske, "Gender and the Paradox of Residential School Education in Carrier Society," in Miller and Chuchryk, eds., *Women of the First Nations: Power, Wisdom and Strength* , 179.

73. Ibid., 169.

74. Dolores T. Poelzer and Irene A. Poelzer, *In Our Own Words: Northern Saskatchewan and Métis Women Speak Out* (Saskatoon: Lindenblatt and Harmonic, 1986), 33.

CHAPTER FIVE

1. Karen Anderson, *Chain Her By One Foot: The Subjugation of Native Women in Seventeenth-Century New France* (New York: Routledge, 1991), 165.

2. Cited in Nancy Wachowich, *Saqiyuq: Stories from the Lives of Three Inuit Women* (Montreal: McGill-Queen's University Press, 1999), 36–42.

3. Clara Sue Kidwell, "Choctaw Women and Cultural Persistence in Mississippi," in Nancy Shoemaker, ed., *Negotiators of Change: Historical Perspectives on Native American Women* (New York: Routledge, 1995), 119.

4. Lillian Ackerman, "Complementary But Equal: Gender Status in the Plateau," in Laura F. Klein and Lillian Ackerman, eds., *Women and Power in Native North America* (Norman, OK: University of Oklahoma Press, 1995), 86.

5. Virginia Driving Hawk Sneve, *Completing the Circle* (Lincoln: University of Nebraska Press, 1995), 11.

6. Ibid., 24.

7. Mary Shepardson, "The Gender Status of Navajo Women," in Klein and Ackerman, eds., *Women and Power in Native North America*, 169.

8. Ibid.

9. Virginia Driving Hawk Sneve, *Completing the Circle*, 11.

10. Beverly Hungry Wolf, *The Ways of My Grandmothers* (New York: Quill Press, 1982), 27.

11. See Patricia Albers, "Sioux Women in Transition: A Study of Their Changing Status in Domestic and Capitalist Sectors of Production," in Patricia Albers and Beatrice Medicine, eds., *The Hidden Half: Studies of Plains Indian Women* (Washington: University Press of America, 1983), 191; Priscilla K. Buffaloehead, "Farmers, Warriors, Traders: A Fresh Look at Ojibway Women," *Minnesota History* 48, no. 6 (Summer 1983), 242; and in Laura F. Klein and Lillian Ackerman, eds., *Women and Power in Native North America* (Norman, OK: University of Oklahoma Press, 1995) see Lee Guemple, "Gender in Inuit Society," 23; Martha C. Knack, "The Dynamics of Southern Paiute Women's Roles," 149; Richard A. Sattler, "Women's Status Among the Muskogee and Cherokee," 222; and Henry S. Sharp, "Asymmetric Equals: Women and Men Among the Chippewayan," 54.

12. Shepardson, "The Gender Status of Navajo Women," 160.

13. Ackerman, "Complementary But Equal," 86.

14. Katherine M.B. Osburn, "Dear Friend and Ex-Husband: Marriage, Divorce, and Women's Property Rights in the Southern Ute Reservation, 1887–1930," in Shoemaker, ed., *Negotiators of Change: Historical Perspectives on Native American Women*, 158–159.

15. Some nations (for example, the Sto:lo) had slavery.

16. Paula Gunn Allen, *The Sacred Hoop: Recovering the Feminine in American Indian Tradition* (Boston: Beacon Press, 1986), 7.

17. Eleanor Leacock, "Montagnais Women and the Jesuit Program for Colonization," Eleanor Leacock, ed., *Women and Colonization: Anthropological Perspectives* (New York: Praeger Publishers, 1980), 28.

18. Lisa E. Emmerich, "Right In the Midst of My Own People: Native American Women and the Field Matron Program," *American Indian Quarterly* 15, no. 2 (1991), 201–216.

19. See Joanne Fiske, "Gender and the Paradox of Residential Education in Carrier Society," in Christine Miller and Patricia Chuchryk, eds., *Women of the First Nations: Power, Wisdom and Strength* (Winnipeg: University of Manitoba Press, 1996), and Laura Waterman Wittstock, "Native American Women: Twilight of a Long Maidenhood," in Beverly Lindsay, ed., *Comparative Perspectives of Third World Women* (New York: Praeger, 1980), 214.

20. Fiske, "Gender and the Paradox of Residential Education in Carrier Society," 171.

21. Cited in Rayna Green, "Diary of a Native American Feminist," *Ms.* (July-August 1982), 172.

22. Mary Crow Dog and Richard Erdoes, *Lakota Woman* (New York: Grove Press, 1990), 13–14.

23. Elizabeth Cook-Lynn, *Why I Can't Read Wallace Stegner and Other Essays* (Madison: University of Wisconsin Press, 1996), 115–116.

24. In Anderson, *Chain Her By One Foot*, 78.

25. Marla Powers, O*glala Women: Myth, Ritual, and Reality* (Chicago: University of Chicago Press, 1986), 74, 88.

26. Marlene Brant Castellano, "Women in Ojibwa and Huron Societies," *Canadian Woman Studies* 10, nos. 2/3 (1989), 46; Somer Brodribb, "The Traditional Roles of Native Women in Canada and the Impact of Colonization," *Canadian Journal of Native Studies* 4, no. 1 (1984), 87–88; Carol Devens, *Countering Colonization: Native American Women and the Great Lakes Missions* (Berkeley: University of California Press, 1992), 125.

27. Sattler, "Women's Status Among the Muskogee and Cherokee," 218–219.

28. Walter L. Williams, *The Spirit and the Flesh: Sexual Diversity in American Indian Cultures* (Boston: Beacon Press, 1991), 91.

29. Leslie Marmon Silko, *Yellow Woman and a Beauty of Spirit* (New York: Touchstone, 1996), 67.

30. Ibid., 67–68.

31. Ernie Benedict, Keynote Address, Trent University Elders' Gathering, Peeteborough, Ontario, February 19, 1999.

32. Beverly Hungry Wolf, *Daughters of Buffalo Women: Maintaining the Tribe Faith* (Skookumchuck, BC: Canadian Caboose Press, 1996), 107.

33. Valerie L. Sherer Mathes, "A New Look at the Role of Women in Indian Society," *American Indian Quarterly* 2 (1975), 133.

34. Williams, *The Spirit and the Flesh*, 101.

35. In Allen, *The Sacred Hoop*, 197.

36. Sabine Lang, "Various Kinds of Two Spirit People: Gender Variance and Homosexuality in Native American Communities," in Sue Ellen Jacobs, Wesley Thomas and Sabine Lang, *Two-Spirit People: Native American Gender Identity,*

*Sexuality and Spirituality* (Chicago: University of Illinois Press, 1997), 103.

37. Teresa D. Laframboise and Anneliese M. Heyle, "Changing and Diverse Roles of Women in American Indian Cultures," *Sex Roles* 22, no. 7/8 (1990), 459.

38. Allen, *The Sacred Hoop*, 196–197.

39. Marmon Silko, *Yellow Woman and a Beauty of Spirit*, 67.

40. Cited in Peter Kulchyski, Don McCaskill and David Newhouse, *In the Words of Elders* (Toronto: University of Toronto Press, 1999), 149.

41. Ibid., 300.

42. See the interviews with Ernie Benedict and Mary Anne Mason, in Kulchyski, McCaskill and Newhouse, *In the Words of Elders*.

43. Marie Annette Jaimes, "American Indian Women at the Centre of Indigenous Resistance in Contemporary North America," in M. Annette Jaimes, ed., *The State of Native America: Genocide, Colonization and Resistance* (Boston: South End Press, 1992), 333.

44. Jane Willis, *Geneish, An Indian Girlhood* (Toronto: New Press, 1973).

45. Martin Cannon, "The Regulation of First Nations Sexuality," *The Canadian Journal of Native Studies* 18, no. 1 (1998), 118.

46. Barbara-Helen Hill, *Shaking the Rattle: Healing the Trauma of Colonization* (Penticton, BC: Theytus Books, 1995), 100.

47. J.R. Miller, *Shingwauk's Vision: A History of Native Residential Schools* (Toronto: University of Toronto Press, 1997), 234–235.

48. Ibid., 219.

49. Ibid., 235.

50. See Roland Chrisjohn, Sherri Young and Michael Maraun, *The Circle Game: Shadows and Subsistence in the Indian Residential School Experience in Canada* (Penticton, BC: Theytus Books, 1997); Assembly of First Nations, *Breaking the Silence: An Interpretive Study of Residential School Impact and Healing as Illustrated by the Stories of First Nations Individuals* (Ottawa: Assembly of First Nations, 1994).

51. Suzanne Fournier and Ernie Crey, S*tolen from Our Embrace: The Abduction of First Nations Children and the Restoration of Aboriginal Communities* (Vancouver: Douglas and McIntyre, 1997), 121.

52. Calvin Morrisseau, *Into the Daylight: A Wholistic Approach to Healing* (Toronto: University of Toronto Press, 1998), 40.

53. See Brodribb, "The Traditional Roles of Native Women in Canada and the Impact of Colonization," 89; Daniel Malz and Joallyn Archambault, "Gender and Power in Native North America: Concluding Remarks," in Klein and Ackerman, eds., *Women and Power in Native North America,* 47–48.

54. Sylvia Maracle, "A Historical Viewpoint," *Vis à Vis: A National Newsletter on Family Violence* (Canadian Council on Social Development) 10, no. 4 (1993), 1.

55. Patricia Monture-Angus, *Thunder in My Soul: A Mohawk Woman Speaks* (Halifax: Fernwood Publishers, 1995), 175, 186.

56. Sally Roesch Wagner, "The Root of Oppression is the Loss of Memory," in W.G. Spittal, ed., *Iroquois Women: An Anthology* (Oshweken, ON: Iroqrafts, 1990), 225.

57. Lynne Plume, cited in Carolyn Reyner, *Cante Ohitika Win (Brave-hearted Women): Images of Lakota Women from the Pine Ridge Reservation, South Dakota* (Vermillion: University of South Dakota Press, 1991), 68–69.

58. Ackerman, "Complementary But Equal," 87.

59. Plume in Reyner, *Cante Ohitika Win*, 71.

60. Fournier and Crey, *Stolen From Our Embrace*, 144.

61. Ibid.

62. Ibid.

63. Ibid.

64. Maracle, "A Historical Viewpoint," 1, 4; Alison MacDonald, "Holistic Healing," *Vis àVis: A National Newsletter on Family Violence* (Canadian Council on Social Development) 10, no. 4 (1993), 5.

65. Jaimes, "American Indian Women at the Center of Indigenous Resistance in North America," 325; Powers, *Oglala Women*, 173.

66. Anonymous Ojibway male cited in Kim Anderson, "Who? What? Healing our Men," *Beedaudjimowin* 3, no. 1 (1993), 12.

67. Fournier and Crey, *Stolen From Our Embrace*, 145.

68. Maracle, "A Historical Viewpoint," 4.

69. Morrisseau, *Into the Daylight*, 40.

## CHAPTER SIX

1. Rayna Green, "The Pocahontas Perplex: The Image of the Indian Woman in American Culture," *Sweetgrass* (July-August 1984), 19.

2. Ibid.

3. This was a typical application of Indigenous women in other colonial contexts, as explained in Ann McClintock, *Imperial Leather: Race, Gender and Sexuality in the Colonial Context* (New York: Routledge, 1995).

4. Elizabeth Cook-Lynn, *Why I Can't Read Wallace Stegner and Other Essays* (Madison: University of Wisconsin Press, 1996), 145.

5. Beth Brant, *Writing as Witness: Essay and Talk* (Toronto: Women's Press, 1984), 83–103; Clara Sue Kidwell, "Indian Women as Cultural Mediators," *Ethnohistory* 39, no. 2 (Spring 1992), 97–107.

6. Cook-Lynn, *Why I Can't Read Wallace Stegner and Other Essays*, 106.

7. Green, "The Pocahontas Perplex," 20.

8. Carol Douglas Sparks, "The Land Incarnate: Navajo Women and the Dialogue of Colonialism," in Nancy Shoemaker, ed., *Negotiators of Change: Historical Perspectives on Native American Women* (New York: Routledge), 135–156.

9. Ibid., 147.

10. Sarah Carter, *Capturing Women: The Manipulation of Cultural Imagery in Canada's Prairie West* (Montreal: McGill-Queen's University Press, 1997), 158–193.

11. Ibid., 160.

12. Ibid., 162.

13. Ibid., 183.

14. Ibid., 191.

15. Ibid., 205.

16. Rita Joe, *Song of Rita Joe: Autobiography of a Mi'kmaq Poet* (Charlottetown, PEI: Ragweed Press, 1996), 62; Anna Lee Walters, *Talking Indian: Reflections on Survival and Writing* (Ithaca, NY: Firebrand Books, 1992), 211.

17. Janice Acoose, *Iskwewak. Kah'Ki Yaw NiWahkomakanak: Neither Indian Princesses nor Easy Squaws* (Toronto: Women's Press, 1995), 29.

18. Joanne Arnott, *Breasting the Waves: On Writing and Healing* (Vancouver: Press Gang, 1995), 76; Brant, *Writing as Witness*, 13, 119–120; Maria Campbell, *Halfbreed* (Toronto: McClelland and Stewart Limited, 1973), 47, 90; Janet Campbell Hale, *Bloodlines: Odyssey of a Native Daughter* (New York: Harper-Perennial, 1993), 139–140; Beatrice Culleton, *In Search of April Raintree* (Winnipeg: Pemmican Publications, 1983); Paula Gunn Allen, *The Sacred Hoop: Recovering the Feminine in American Indian Tradition* (Boston: Beacon Press, 1986), 48–49; Lee Maracle, *I Am Woman* (Vancouver: Press Gang Publishers, 1996), 14–19; Anna Lee Walters, *Talking Indian: Reflections on Survival and Writing* (Ithaca, NY: Firebrand Books, 1992), 52.

19. Barbara Helen-Hill, *Shaking the Rattle: Healing the Trauma of Colonization* (Penticton, BC: Theytus Books, 1995).

20. bell hooks, *Black Looks: Race and Representation* (Toronto: Between the Lines Press, 1992), 21–39.

21. Ibid., 25.

22. Quoted in Bonita Lawrence, "'Real' Indians and Others: Mixed-Race Urban Native People, *The Indian Act*, and the Rebuilding of Indigenous Nations" (PhD thesis, Ontario Institute for Studies in Education of the University of Toronto, 1999), 261–262.

23. Ibid.

24. Maracle, *I Am Woman*, 56.

25. Emma LaRocque, "The Colonization of a Native Woman Scholar," in Patricia Chuchryk and Christine Miller, eds., *Women of the First Nations: Power, Wisdom, and Strength* (Winnipeg: The University of Manitoba Press, 1996), 12.

26. See Acoose, *Iskwewak*.

27. Emma LaRocque, "Tides, Towns and Trains," in Joan Turner, ed., *Living the Changes* (Winnipeg: University of Manitoba Press, 1990), 87.

28. Sherene Razack, *Looking White People in the Eye: Gender, Race and Culture in Courtrooms and Classrooms* (Toronto: University of Toronto Press, 1998), 68–72.

29. Anne McGillivary and Brenda Comaskey, *Black Eyes All of the Time: Intimate Violence, Aboriginal Women, and the Justice System* (Toronto: University of Toronto Press, 1999), 100.

30. Rick Arnold, Bev Burke, Carl James, D'Arcy Martin and Barb Thomas, *Educating for a Change* (Toronto: Between the Lines and the Doris Marshall Institute for Education and Action, 1991), 91–92.

## CHAPTER SEVEN

1. Maria Campbell, *Halfbreed* (Toronto: McClelland and Stewart Ltd., 1973).

2. Anna Lee Walters, *Talking Indian: Reflections on Survival and Writing* (Ithaca, NY: Firebrand Books, 1992), 49.

3. Leslie Marmon Silko, *Yellow Woman and a Beauty of Spirit* (New York: Touchstone, 1996), 17.

4. Ibid., 66.

5. Wilma Mankiller and Michael Wallis, *Mankiller: A Chief and Her People* (New York: St. Michael's Press, 1993), 186–205.

6. For more information, see Lilianne Ernestine Krosenbrink-Gelissen, "The Native Women's Association of Canada," in James Frideres, ed., *Aboriginal Peoples in Canada: Contemporary Conflicts,* 5th ed. (Scarborough, ON: Prentice Hall Allyn and Bacon Canada, 1998), 299–325.

7. Many people refer to Vera as an Elder, but she prefers the descriptive "Grandmother" which complies with her role as a grandmother to the Ojibway nation.

8. See Janet Silman, *Enough is Enough: Aboriginal Women Speak Out* (Toronto: The Women's Press, 1987).

9. Jeannette Armstrong, "Sharing One Skin," *New Internationalist* (Jan-Feb 1997), 287.

10. I have chosen to keep these comments anonymous.

11. I discuss this more fully in Section IV, "Reclaim."

12. Interview with anonymous participant.

13. Paula Gunn Allen, *The Sacred Hoop: Recovering the Feminine in American Indian Tradition* (Boston: Beacon Press, 1986), 45.

14. Silko, *Yellow Woman and a Beauty of Spirit,* 152.

15. Ibid., 71–72.

## CHAPTER EIGHT

1. Marlene Brant Castellano cited in Secretary of State, Canada, *Speaking Together: Canada's Native Women* (Ottawa: Secretary of State, Canada, 1975), 82.

2. Janice Acoose, *Iskwewak. Kah'Ki Yaw NiWahkomakanak: Neither Indian Princesses nor Easy Squaws* (Toronto: Women's Press, 1995), 30–31.

3. Rita Joe, cited in *Kelusultiek: Original Women's Voices of Atlantic Canada* (Halifax: Institute for the Study of Women, 1994), 51.

4. Theresa Johnson Ortiz, "Mirror Image," in Osaka Hlodan, ed., *The Sweet Grass Road: Stories and Poems for Survival Written by Native Women* (Toronto: Native Women's Resource Centre of Toronto, 1993).

5. Ibid.

6. In Joy Harjo and Gloria Bird, eds., *Reinventing the Enemy's Language: Contemporary Native Women's Writings of North America* (New York: W.W. Norton and Company, 1997), 498–499.

7. Gloria Bird, "Introduction," in Harjo and Bird, eds., *Reinventing the Enemy's Language*, 39.

8. In Harmut Lutz, *Contemporary Challenges: Conversations with Native Canadian Authors* (Saskatoon: Fifth House, 1991), 181.

9. Rita Joe, *Song of Rita Joe: Autobiography of a Mi'kmaq Poet* (Charlottetown, PEI: Ragweed Press, 1996), 129.

10. Anna Lee Walters, *Talking Indian: Reflections on Survival and Writing* (Ithaca, NY: Firebrand Books, 1992), 53.

11. Beth Brant, *Writing as Witness: Essay and Talk* (Toronto: Women's Press, 1994), 13.

12. For more information, call NWIA at (416) 598-4078.

13. Richard Wagamese, *Keeper 'N Me* (Toronto: Doubleday, 1994).

14. Joe, *Song of Rita Joe*, 62.

15. Joanne Arnott, *Breasting the Waves: On Writing and Healing* (Vancouver: Press Gang Publishers, 1995), 64.

16. Ibid., 59.

17. Rhonda Johnson, Winona Stevenson and Donna Greschener, "Peekiskwetan," *Canadian Journal of Women and the Law* 6 (1993), 156.

18. Maria Campbell, *Halfbreed* (Toronto: McClelland and Stewart, 1973), 29–30.

19. Ibid.

20. Joe, *Song of Rita Joe*, 56.

21. Ibid., 64.

22. Ibid., 65.

## Chapter Ten

1. Ursuline de l'Incarnation, quoted in Suzanne Fournier and Ernie Crey, *Stolen From Our Embrace: The Abduction of First Nations Children and the Restoration of Aboriginal Communities* (Vancouver: Douglas and McIntyre, 1997), 52.

2. J. R. Miller, *Shingwauk's Vision: A History of Residential Schools* (Toronto: University of Toronto Press, 1997), 55–56.

3. Fournier and Crey, *Stolen From Our Embrace*, 52–53.

4. Miller, *Shingwauk's Vision*, 46.

5. Tom Porter, Trent University Elders' Gathering, Peterborough, Ontario, February 19, 1999.

6. The "White Paper" was issued by the Trudeau government in 1969, under the direction of Jean Chrétien, the Minister of Indian Affairs at the time. It proposed to do away with the *Indian Act*, dismantle Indian Affairs, shift all responsibility for Aboriginal peoples to the provinces and eventually eliminate treaty rights. Native leaders protested that the proposed policy was another strategy for assimilation and a denial of their rights. The "White Paper" was withdrawn in 1970.

7. For an excellent history of "the abduction of First Nations children" and the impact on our communities, please see Fournier and Crey, *Stolen From Our Embrace*.

8. Shirley Bear, "Equality Among Women," *Canadian Literature* (Spring-Summer 1990), 133–137.

9. Ivy Chaske tells me that this is a misinterpretation — that going into a sweat is not about going back to the womb, rather it is about honouring the life force of Mother Earth and the life force within the women who give our nations life. Women, therefore, do not need to sweat, as they have other ways of cleansing and connecting with this life force.

10. For more information about berry fasting, please see my article "Honouring the Blood of the People: Berry Fasting in the Twenty-First Century," which will be published in a forthcoming textbook tentatively titled *Introduction to Native Studies*, edited by J. Waldram, R. Liberte, P. Settee and F.L. Barron (Saskatoon: University of Saskatchewan Extension Press, 2000).

11. Some Aboriginal women resist being told they "have to wear a skirt" for ceremonies. This practice can be seen as part of the regulating of women through tradition, as explored by Bonita and me in the Concluding Dialogue. It has also been pointed out to me that Natives did not always have pants!

12. Marilou Awiakta, "Amazons in Appalachia," in Gloria Bird and Joy Harjo, eds., *Reinventing the Enemy's Language: Contemporary Native Women's Writings of North America* (New York: W.W. Norton and Co., 1997), 472.

13. Art Solomon, *Eating Bitterness: A Vision Beyond the Prison Walls* (Toronto: NC Press, 1994), 130–131.

## CHAPTER ELEVEN

1. In Ronnie Farley, *Women of the Native Struggle: Portraits and Testimonials of Native American Women* (New York: Orion Books, 1993), 79.

2. Haunani-Kay Trask, *From a Native Daughter: Colonialism and Sovereignty in Hawaii* (Monroe, ME: Common Courage Press, 1993), 154.

3. In Osennontion and Skonaganleh:rà, "Our World," *Canadian Woman Studies* 10, nos. 2/3 (1989), 18.

4. Janice Acoose, *Iskwewak. Kah'Ki Yaw Ni Wahkomakanak: Neither Indian Princesses nor Easy Squaws* (Toronto: Women's Press, 1995), 19.

5. Janet Campbell Hale, *Bloodlines: Odyssey of a Native Daughter* (New York: HarperPerennial, 1993), 171.

6. Cited in Marlene Brant Castellano and Janice Hill, "First Nations Women: Reclaiming our Responsibilities," in Joy Parr, ed., *A Diversity of Women: Ontario, 1945–1980* (Toronto: University of Toronto Press, 1995), 245.

## CHAPTER TWELVE

1. Marilou Awiakta, *Selu: Seeking the Corn Mother's Wisdom* (Golden, CO: Fulcrum Publishing, 1993), 252.

2. See Calvin Morrisseau, *Into the Daylight: A Wholistic Approach to Healing* (Toronto: University of Toronto Press, 1998), 38–40.

3. Rita Joe, *Song of Rita Joe: Autobiography of a Mi'kmaq Poet* (Charlottetown, PEI: Ragweed Press, 1996), 62.

4. Morrisseau, *Into the Daylight*, 39.

## CHAPTER THIRTEEN

1. Betty Bastien, "Voices Through Time," in Christine Miller and Patricia Chuchryk, eds., *Women of the First Nations: Power, Wisdom, and Strength* (Winnipeg: University of Manitoba Press, 1996), 127.

2. Tom Porter, "Pregnancies and Mohawk Tradition," *Canadian Woman Studies* 10, nos. 2/3 (1989), 115.

3. Ibid.

## CHAPTER FOURTEEN

1. In Canada, Royal Commission on Aboriginal Peoples, *Report of the Royal Commission on Aboriginal Peoples*. Volume 4: *Perspectives and Realities* (Ottawa, ON: Ministry of Supply and Services Canada, 1996), 7.

2. Ibid.

3. "The Life of a Chief: An Interview with Nora Bothwell," *Canadian Woman Studies* 10, nos.2/3 (1989), 35.

4. E-mail correspondence with Indian and Northern Affairs Canada, Department Library, Publications and Public Inquiries, August 26, 1999.

5. Joanne Fiske, "Child of the State, Mother of the Nation: Aboriginal Women and the Ideology of Motherhood," *Culture* 13, no. 1 (1993), 17–35.

## CHAPTER FIFTEEN

1. Many creation stories speak about the instructions we received when we were created as peoples. These instructions include taking responsibility for the care of everything in creation.

2. Beverly Hungry Wolf, "Life in Harmony with Nature," in Christine Miller and Patricia Chuchryk, eds., *Women of the First Nations: Power, Wisdom, and Strength* (Winnipeg: University of Manitoba Press, 1996), 80–81.

## CHAPTER SEVENTEEN

1. In Marlene Brant Castellano and Janice Hill, "First Nations Women: Reclaiming Our Responsibilities," in Joy Parr, ed., *A Diversity of Women: Ontario, 1945–1980* (Toronto: University of Toronto Press, 1995), 246.

2. Joanne Fiske, "Carrier Women and the Politics of Mothering," in Gillian Creese and Veronica Strong-Boag, eds., *British Columbia Reconsidered: Essays on Women* (Vancouver: Press Gang Publishers, 1992), 210.

3. Ibid.

4. Quoted from Jane Katz, *Messengers of the Wind: Native American Women Tell Their Life Stories* (New York: Ballantine Books, 1995), 159.

5. Emma LaRocque, "Re-examining Culturally Appropriate Models in Criminal Justice Applications," in Michael Ash, ed., *Aboriginal and Treaty Rights in Canada: Essays on Law, Equity, and Respect for Difference* (Vancouver: UBC Press, 1997).

## PAUSE/REFLECT

1. I am sure that every Native woman who reads this book will come to her own conclusions about how it applies to her life and her identity, and I hope that they will discuss their insights with others.

## CONCLUDING DIALOGUE

1. Mary Ellen Turpel, "Patriarchy and Paternalism: The Legacy of Canadian State for First Nations Women," *Canadian Journal of Women and the Law* 6 (1993), 179.

2. Joanne Fiske, "Child of the State, Mother of the Nation: Aboriginal Women and the Ideology of Motherhood," *Culture* 13, no. 1 (1993), 17–35.

## REFERENCE LIST/BIOGRAPHIES

1. I use square brackets to help the reader situate the First Nation and to be mindful that the First Nation may not consider itself to be a part of that province or of Canada.

# BIBLIOGRAPHY

Acoose, Janice (Nehiowe-Métis/Nahkawe). *Iskwewak. Kah'Ki Yaw Ni Wahko-makanak: Neither Indian Princesses nor Easy Squaws.* Toronto: Women's Press, 1995.

Albers, Patricia, and Beatrice Medicine (Lakota Sioux), eds. *The Hidden Half: Studies of Plains Indian Women.* Washington, DC: University Press of America, 1983.

Allen, Paula Gunn (Laguna Pueblo/Lakota Sioux). *The Sacred Hoop: Recovering the Feminine in American Indian Tradition.* Boston: Beacon Press, 1986.

Anderson, Karen. *Chain Her by One Foot: The Subjugation of Native Women in Seventeenth-Century New France.* New York: Routledge, 1991.

Anderson, Kim (Cree/Métis). "Who? What? Healing Or Men." *Beedaudji-mowin* 3, no. 1 (1993): 12–13, 15.

_____ "Honouring the Blood of the People: Berry Fasting in the Twenty-First Century," *Introduction to Native Studies,* edited by J. Waldram, R. Liberte, P. Settee and F.L. Barron (Saskatoon: University of Saskatchewan Extension Press, forthcoming 2000).

Armstrong, Jeannette (Okanagan). "Sharing One Skin." *New Internationalist* (Jan-Feb 1997).

Arnott, Joanne (Métis). *Breasting the Waves: On Writing and Healing.* Vancouver: Press Gang Publishers, 1995.

Assembly of First Nations. *Breaking the Silence: An Interpretive Study of Residential School Impact and Healing as Illustrated by the Stories of First Nations Individuals.* Ottawa: Assembly of First Nations, 1994.

Awiakta, Marilou (Cherokee/Appalachian). *Selu: Seeking the Corn Mother's Wisdom.* Golden, CO: Fulcrum Publishing, 1993.

Baskin, Cyndy (Métis). "Women in Iroquois Society," *Canadian Woman Studies* 4, no. 2 (1982): 42–46.

Bataille, Gretchen M. and Kathleen Sands. *American Indian Women: A Guide to Research.* New York: Garland Publishing, 1991.

Bear, Shirley (Mingwon/Maliseet). "Equality Among Women." *Canadian Literature* 124–125 (1990): 133–137.

Brant, Beth (Mohawk). *Writing as Witness: Essay and Talk.* Toronto: Women's Press, 1994.

Brant Castellano, Marlene (Mohawk) and Janice Hill (Mohawk). "First Nations Women: Reclaiming our Responsibilities." *In A Diversity of Women: Ontario, 1945-1980,* edited by Joy Parr, 233–249. Toronto: University of Toronto Press, 1995.

Buckley, Thomas, and Alan Gottlieb, eds. *Blood Magic: The Anthropology of Menstruation.* Berkeley: University of California Press, 1988.

Buffaloehead, Priscilla K. "Farmers, Warriors, Traders: A Fresh Look at Ojibway Women." *Minnesota History* 48, no. 6 (1983).

Brodribb, Somer. "The Traditional Roles of Native Women in Canada and the Impact of Colonization." *Canadian Journal of Native Studies* 4, no. 1 (1984): 85–103.

Campbell, Maria (Cree/Métis). *Halfbreed.* Toronto: McClelland and Stewart, 1973.

Campbell Hale, Janet (Coeur d'Alene). *Bloodlines: Odyssey of a Native Daughter.* New York: Harper Perennial, 1993.

Canada. Royal Commission on Aboriginal Peoples. *Report on the Royal Commission on Aboriginal Peoples.* Volume 4: *Perspectives and Realities.* Ottawa, ON: Ministry of Supply and Services, Canada, 1996.

Canada. Secretary of State. *Speaking Together: Canada's Native Women.* Ottawa, ON: Secretary of State, Canada, 1975.

Cannon, Martin. "The Regulation of First Nations Sexuality." *The Canadian Journal of Native Studies* 18, no. 1 (1998): 1–18.

Carter, Sarah. *Capturing Women: The Manipulation of Cultural Imagery in Canada's Prairie West.* Montreal: McGill-Queen's University Press, 1997.

Chrisjohn, Roland (Onyota'a:ka), Sherri Young and Michael Maraun. *The Circle Game: Shadows and Substance in the Indian Residential School Experience in Canada.* Penticton, BC: Theytus Books, 1997.

Collins, Patricia Hill. *Black Feminist Thought: Knowledge, Consciousness and the Politics of Empowerment.* Boston: Unwin Hyman, 1990.

Cook-Lynn, Elizabeth (Sioux). *Why I Can't Read Wallace Stegner and Other Essays.* Madison: University of Wisconsin Press, 1996.

Crow Dog, Mary (Lakota Sioux), and Richard Erdoes. *Lakota Woman.* New York: Grove Press, 1990.

Culleton, Beatrice (Métis). *In Search of April Raintree.* Winnipeg: Pemmican Publications, 1983.

Devens, Carol. *Countering Colonization: Native American Women and the Great Lakes Missions, 1630-1900.* Berkeley: University of California Press, 1992.

Driving Hawk Sneve, Virginia (Sioux). *Completing the Circle.* Lincoln: University of Nebraska Press, 1995.

Emmerich, Lisa. "Right in the Midst of My Own People: Native American Women and the Field Matron Program." *American Indian Quarterly* 15, no. 2 (1991): 201–216.

Farley, Ronnie. *Women of the Native Struggle: Portraits and Testimonials of Native American Women.* New York: Orion Books, 1993.

Fiske, Joanne. "Child of the State, Mother of the Nation: Aboriginal Women and the Ideology of Motherhood," *Culture* 12, no. 1 (1993): 17–35.

_____ "Carrier Women and the Politics of Mothering." In *British Columbia Reconsidered: Essays on Women,* edited by Gillian Creese and Veronica Strong-Boag. Vancouver: Press Gang, 1992.

Fournier, Suzanne, and Ernie Crey (Sto:lo). *Stolen From Our Embrace: The Abduction of First Nations Children and the Restoration of Aboriginal Communities.* Vancouver: Douglas and McIntyre, 1997.

Green, Rayna (Cherokee). *Women in American Indian Society.* New York: Chelsea House, 1992.

_____ "The Pocahontas Perplex: The Image of the Indian Woman in American Culture." *Sweetgrass* (July-August 1984): 17–23.

_____ "Diary of a Native American Feminist." *Ms.* Magazine (July-August 1982): 170–172, 211–213.

Harjo, Joy (Creek), and Gloria Bird (Spokane), eds. *Reinventing the Enemy's Language: Contemporary Native Women's Writings of North America.* New York: W.W. Norton and Company, 1997.

Hill, Barbara-Helen (Mohawk/Cayuga). *Shaking the Rattle: Healing the Trauma of Colonization.* Penticton, BC: Theytus Books, 1995.

Hlodan, Oksana, ed. *The Sweet Grass Road: Stories and Poems of Survival Written by Native Women.* Toronto: Native Women's Resource Centre of Toronto, 1993.

hooks, bell. *Black Looks: Race and Representation.* Toronto: Between the Lines Press, 1992.

Hungry Wolf, Beverly (Siksika). *The Ways of My Grandmothers*. New York: William and Morrow Company, 1980.

_____ *Daughters of Buffalo Woman: Maintaining the Tribal Faith*. Skookumchuck, BC: Canadian Caboose Press, 1996.

Jacobs, Sue Ellen, Wesley Thomas (Navajo), and Sabine Lang. *Two Spirit People: Native American Gender Identity, Sexuality and Spirituality*. Chicago: University of Illinois Press, 1997.

Jaimes, Marie Annette, (Juaneno/Yaqui), ed. *The State of Native America: Genocide, Colonization and Resistance*. Boston: South End Press, 1992.

Jamieson, Kathleen. *Indian Women and the Law in Canada: Citizens Minus*. Ottawa: Advisory Council on the Status of Women, 1978.

Joe, Rita (Mi'kmaw). *Song of Rita Joe: Autobiography of a Mi'kmaq Poet*. Charlottetown, PEI: Ragweed Press, 1996.

Johnson, Rhonda (Métis), Winona Stevenson (Cree/Assiniboin/Saulteaux/Anglo), and Donna Greschener. "Peekiskwetan." *Canadian Journal of Women and the Law* 6 (1993): 153–173.

Katz, Jane. *Messengers of the Wind: Native American Women Tell Their Life Stories*. New York: Ballantine Books, 1995.

*Kelusultiek: Original Women's Voices of Atlantic Canada*. Halifax: Institute for the Study of Women, Mount St. Vincent University, 1994.

Kidwell, Clara Sue (Chippewa/Choctaw). "The Power of Women in Three American Indian Societies." *Journal of Ethnic Studies* 5, no. 3 (1975): 113–121.

_____ "Indian Women as Cultural Mediators." *Ethnohistory* 39, no. 2 (1992): 97–107.

Klein, Laura F., and Lillian A. Ackerman, eds. *Women and Power in Native North America*. Norman, OK: University of Oklahoma Press, 1995.

Knockwood, Isabelle (Mi'kmaw). *Out of the Depths: The Experience of Mi'kmaw Children at the Indian Residential School at Shubenacadie, Nova Scotia*. Lockeport, NS: Roseway Publishing, 1992.

Kulchyski, Peter, Don McCaskill, and David Newhouse (Onondaga). *In the Words of Elders*. Toronto: University of Toronto Press, 1999.

Krosenbrick-Gelissen, Lilianne. "The Native Women's Association of Canada." In *Aboriginal Peoples in Canada: Contemporary Conflicts, Fifth Edition*, edited by James S. Frideres, 297–325. Scarborough, ON: Prentice Hall Allyn and Bacon Canada, 1998.

Laframboise, Teresa D. and Anneliese M. Heyle. "Changing and Diverse Roles of Women in American Indian Cultures." *Sex Roles* 22, nos. 7/8 (1990): 455–476.

Landes, Ruth. *The Ojibwa Woman.* New York: Columbia University Press, 1938.

LaRocque, Emma (Plains Cree/Métis). "Tides, Towns and Trains." In *Living the Changes,* edited by Joan Turner. Winnipeg: University of Manitoba Press, 1990.

_____ "Re-examining Culturally Appropriate Models in Criminal Justice Applications." In *Aboriginal and Treaty Rights in Canada: Essays on Law, Equity and Respect for Difference,* edited by Michael Asch. Vancouver: UBC Press, 1997.

Laurence, Margaret. *The Diviners.* Toronto: McClelland and Stewart, 1974.

Lawrence, Bonita (Mi'kmaw). "'Real' Indians and Others: Mixed-Race Urban Native People, the *Indian Act,* and the Rebuilding of Indigenous Nations." PhD thesis, Ontario Institute for Studies in Education of the University of Toronto, 1999.

Leacock, Eleanor, ed. *Women and Colonization: Anthropological Perspectives.* New York: Praeger Publishers, 1980.

Lutz, Harmut. *Contemporary Challenges: Conversations with Native Canadian Authors.* Saskatoon: Fifth House, 1991.

Mankiller, Wilma (Cherokee), and Michael Wallis. *Mankiller: A Chief and Her People.* New York: St. Martin's Press, 1993.

Maracle, Lee (Sto:lo/Métis). *I Am Woman.* Vancouver: Press Gang Publishers, 1996.

Mathes, Valerie Sherer. "A New Look at the Role of Women in Indian Society." *American Indian Quarterly* 2 (1975): 131–139.

McClintock, Ann. *Imperial Leather: Race, Gender and Sexuality in the Colonial Context.* New York: Routledge, 1995.

McGillivary, Anne, and Brenda Comaskey. *Black Eyes all of the Time: Intimate Violence, Aboriginal Women, and the Justice System.* Toronto: University of Toronto Press, 1999.

Medicine, Beatrice. (Lakota Sioux). "Indian Women: Tribal Identity as Status Quo." In *Women's Nature: Rationalizations of Inequality,* edited by Marion Lowe and Ruth Hubbard, 63–73. New York: Pergamon, 1983.

_____ "Indian Women and the Renaissance of Traditional Religions." In *Sioux Religion: Tradition and Innovation,* edited by Raymond J. Demallie and Douglas R. Parks, 159–171. Norman: University of Oklahoma Press, 1987.

Meili, Diane (Cree/Métis). *Those Who Know: Profiles of Alberta's Native Elders.* Edmonton: NeWest Publishers Ltd., 1991.

Miller, Christine, and Patricia Chuchryk, eds. *Women of the First Nations: Power, Wisdom and Strength.* Winnipeg: University of Manitoba Press, 1996.

Miller, J.R. *Shingwauk's Vision: A History of Native Residential Schools.* Toronto: University of Toronto Press, 1997.

Monture-Angus, Patricia (Mohawk). *Thunder in My Soul: A Mohawk Woman Speaks.* Halifax: Fernwood Publishers, 1995.

_____. *Journeying Forward: Dreaming First Nations' Independence.* Halifax: Fernwood Publishers, 1999.

Morrisseau, Calvin (Ojibway). *Into the Daylight: A Wholistic Approach to Healing.* Toronto: University of Toronto Press, 1998.

Olsen, Kaaren. "Native Women and the Fur Industry." *Canadian Woman Studies* 10, nos. 2/3 (1989).

Paper, Jordan. "Through the Earth Darkly: The Female Spirit in Native American Religions." In *Religion in Native North America*, edited by Christopher Vescey, 3–19. Moscow, ID: University of Idaho Press, 1990.

Poelzer, Dolores T., and Irene A. Poelzer. *In Our Own Words: Northern Saskatchewan and Métis Women Speak Out.* Saskatoon: Lindenblatt and Harmonic, 1986.

Powers, Marla. *Oglala Women: Myth, Ritual and Reality.* Chicago: University of Chicago Press, 1986.

Razack, Sherene. *Looking White People in the Eye: Gender, Race and Culture in Courtrooms and Classrooms.* Toronto: University of Toronto Press, 1998.

Reyner, Carolyn. *Cante Ohitika Win (Brave Hearted Women): Images of Lakota Women from the Pine Ridge Reservation, South Dakota.* Vermillion: University of South Dakota Press, 1991.

Shoemaker, Nancy, ed. *Negotiators of Change: Historical Perspectives on Native American Women.* New York: Routledge, 1995.

Silko, Leslie Marmon (Laguna Pueblo). *Yellow Woman and a Beauty of Spirit.* New York: Touchstone, 1996.

Silman, Janet. *Enough is Enough: Aboriginal Women Speak Out.* Toronto: The Women's Press, 1987.

Solomon, Art (Ojibway). *Songs for the People: Teachings the Natural Way.* Toronto: NC Press, 1990.

_____ *Eating Bitterness: A Vision Beyond the Prison Walls.* Toronto: NC Press, 1994.

Spittal, W.G. *Iroquois Women: An Anthology.* Ohsweken, ON: Iroqrafts, 1990.

Stockel, H. Henrietta. *Woman of the Appache Nation: Voices of Truth.* Reno: University of Nevada Press, 1991.

Trask, Haunani-Kay (Hawaiian). *From a Native Daughter: Colonialism and Sovereignty in Hawaii.* Monroe, ME: Common Courage Press, 1993.

Turpel, Mary-Ellen (Cree). "Patriarchy and Paternalism: The Legacy of Canadian State for First Nations Women." *Canadian Journal of Women and the Law* 6, (1993): 174–192.

Wachowich, Nancy. *Saqiyuq: Stories from the Lives of Three Inuit Women.* Montreal: McGill-Queen's University Press, 1996.

Wagamese, Richard (Ojibway). *Keeper 'N Me.* Toronto: Doubleday, 1994.

Wall, Steve. *Wisdom's Daughters: Conversations with Women Elders of Native America.* New York: HarperCollins Publishers, 1993.

Walters, Anna Lee (Pawnee/Otoe). *Talking Indian: Reflections on Survival and Writing.* Ithaca, NY: Firebrand Books, 1992.

Waterman Witstock, Laura. "Native American Women: Twilight of a Long Maidenhood." In *Comparative Perspectives of Third World Women,* edited by Beverly Lindsay, 207–228. New York: Praeger, 1980.

Williams, Shirley (Ojibway/Odawa). "Women's Role in Ojibway Spirituality." *Journal of Canadian Native Studies* 27, no. 3 (1992): 100–104.

Williams, Walter. *The Spirit and the Flesh: Sexual Diversity in American Indian Cultures.* Boston: Beacon Press, 1991.

Willis, Jane (Cree). *Geneish: An Indian Girlhood.* Toronto: New Press, 1973.

Young-Ing, Greg (Cree). "Marginalization in Publishing." In *Looking at the Words of Our People: First Nations Analysis of Literature,* edited by Jeannette Armstrong, 179–187. Penticton, BC: Theytus Books, 1993.

# INDEX

Aboriginal, 14
   teachings, 21-22
Acoose, Janice (Nehiowe-Métis/Nahkawe),
   70, 106, 138, 181, 182
act, 225, 229
activism, 124-27, 213-14, 235-38
Addiction, and social breakdown, 97-98
"adoption breakdown" syndrome, 24
age, and authority, 67-68, 238
Ah'-Dunn (Margaret Hind-Man), 87-88
alcohol. See addiction
Allen, Paula Gunn (Laguna Pueblo/Sioux),
   35, 36, 71, 83, 106, 131
American Indian Movement (AIM), 125,
   271
Anderson, Kim (Cree/Métis)
   and cultural practices, 262, 264-68, 269
   Euro-Canadian ancestry, 23, 29-31
   and feminism, 274-75
   Native heritage and identity formation,
      24-33
Armstrong, Jeannette (Okanagan)
   biography, 278
   economic authority of women, 63, 64-65,
      68, 80
   gender-divided responsibilities, 217
   grandmother, influence of, 120
   healing and land, 127
   homosexuality among land-based
      peoples, 91
   Indigenous language, 130
   self-determination, 245-46
   sense of purpose in life, 203-4
   sexual mores of land-based societies, 86
Arnatsiaq, Simona (Inuit)
   biography, 278
   gender fluidity among the Inuit, 89
   healing process of men, 241
   Native arts, 144
Assembly of First Nations, 220-21
assimilation, 24, 301n6
   resisting, 144-46
Audette, Michèle (Innu), 47
   biography, 278
   childrearing practices, 161
   connection to land, 224
   flexible gender roles, 59

and gender equality, 220-21
   raising sons, 224, 243-44
aunties, 121, 172-73, 196
Awa, Apphia Agalakti (Inuit), 80
Awiakta, Marilou (Cherokee/Appalachian),
   65, 170, 198

balance, 13, 173-79, 262
   in community work, 216-18
   in parenting, 206, 207-9
   in politics, 65-71
   in spirituality, 71-79
Bear, Shirley (Mingwon/Maliseet), 164
Beaucage, Gertie (Ojibway), 57, 231
   biography, 279
   challenging stereotypes, 139
   church, resistance to, 147
   grandmother, influence of, 119-20
   healing and land, 128
   political consciousness, 122, 125
   racism and violence against women, 109
   self-determination, 244-45, 246
   female role models, 121
Benedict, Ernie (Mohawk), 87
Bennett, Ramona (Puyallup), 239
berry fast, 166, 186, 197-98
big drum, 177, 178
Bilharz, Joy, 61
Bird, Gloria (Spokane), 140
birth control, 87-88, 197
blood memory, 24-25
Blue Quills Residential School, 92-93
Blythe, Jennifer, 63-64
body, sacredness of, 194-201
Bothwell, Nora (Ojibway), 214
Brant, Beth (Mohawk), 106, 141
Brant Castellano, Marlene (Mohawk)
   age and authority of women, 238
   biography, 279
   challenging stereotypes, 137-38
   self-determination, 248
   mothering and workplace , 214-15
   female role models, 118, 150
   supportive family, 117

Campbell Hale, Janet (Coeur d'Alene),
   106, 182

Campbell, Maria (Cree/Métis), 106, 267
  age and authority of women, 68, 238
  biography, 279
  children and Native social organization, 158-59, 161-62
  economic roles of women, 59
  grandmother, influence of, 118-19
  Indigenous language, loss of, 131
  land and feminine identity, 184
  moon and feminine identity, 186
  priests, childhood memories of, 146
  supportive family, 121
  traditional sanctions against sexual abuse of children, 96
  traditional stories, 132-33
Campbell Star, Shawani (métis)
  biography, 279
  self-determination, 246
  land and feminine identity, 183
  lifegiving power of women, 223
  standing up for justice, 236
Carrier, 77-78, 237
Carter, Sarah, 102
ceremonies
  berry fast, 166, 186, 197-98
  Blackfoot, 72-73
  exclusion of menstruating women, 265-67
  Full Moon, 179, 186
  gender roles in, 175, 177-78
  menstrual taboos and, 165-67
  puberty rites, 165-66, 198
  Sun Dance, 37, 38, 72, 165, 178
  sweat lodge, 73-74, 164-65, 178
  Uwipi, 37
  See also cultural traditions
Chaske, Ivy (Dakota), 27, 28
  biography, 280
  childrearing practices, 160
  community responsibility, 169
  environment, 224
  Indigenous language, 130
  lifegiving power of women, 223
  sacredness of children, 162-63
  and sweat lodge ceremony, 73-74
  teaching gender roles, 178
chieftainships, 66, 67
  Indian Act political system, 218
childbirth, and spirituality, 72

childrearing
  balance in, 205-8
  daughters, 244-49
  Native practices, 159-162
  sons, 241-44
  See also family
children
  adoption of white, 87
  born out of wedlock, 86-87, 91, 194
  community sanctions against sexual abuse of, 96-97
  forcible removal of, 161-62
  health and sexuality, 197-98
  and independent female role models, 116-22
  love and intimacy, 199-201
  in Native culture, 32-33, 159, 162-64, 172-73
  and Native social organizations, 158-59, 161-62
  and New France schools, 159-60
  puberty rites, 165-66, 198
  racism and violence against, 108-9, 110
  residential school experience, 92-94, 139-40, 143, 145, 147-48, 199
  self-determination, 242-49
  sex education for girls, 166
  sexual abuse of, 96-97, 200
Chrisjohn, Andrea (Onya:ta'ka)
  biography, 280
  lifegiving power of women, 169
  female role models, 120-21
church
  and abusive marriages, 148-49
  and children born out of wedlock, 91
  and homosexuality, 91
  and Native marriage practices, 83
  resistance against, 146-49
  role of Eve and Native women, 77
  role of the Virgin Mary and Native women, 77
  sexual abuse of children, 93
  and sexual mores of Native peoples, 91-94
  shame-based views on menstruation, 75-78
clan responsibilities, 217-18
colonialism
  family violence, 97-98

marginalization of Native men, 97, 239-40

marginalization of Native women, 58, 62-65, 68-71, 75-78

Native marriage practices, 83-85

sexual condemnation, 91-94

community, 123-27, 213-17, 235-38

Cook, Katsi (Mohawk), 84, 180

Cook-Lynn, Elizabeth (Lakota), 84, 101

Cooper, Manny (Tsartlip), 96

Corbiere, Melanie (Ojibway)

biography, 280

land and healing, 129

positive attitude, 151-52

cosmology, 173-75, 176-79

Couchie, Carol (Ojibway), 22, 148-49

biography, 280

female-male balance, 175

female mentors, 127

health, 195

sweat lodge ceremony, 164-65

creation, 180-82

duality of, 173-75

stories, 71-72, 132

women's relation to, 223-25

See also land

creativity, 142-44

Cree, 63, 64

Crow Dog, Mary (Lakota), 84

cultural traditions

adaptation of, 36-37

alienation of women, 38-39, 263-66

critical approach to, 263-64

debates around changing, 177-78, 269

Euro-Christian patriarchal influences on, 36, 268

gender-balanced explanations and practices, 166-67, 176-77

non-sexist approach to, 38, 142-53, 266-67

rigid adherence to, 264

womanhood in, 57

See also ceremonies; land-based societies

culture, Native, 35

and change, 27, 34-35

children in, 32-33, 158-59, 162-64

gendered nature of, 37

See also land-based societies

Devens, Carol, 60, 61

divorce, 81-83, 84

Driving Hawk Sneve, Virginia (Sioux), 81

drugs. See addiction

Eaglespeaker, Diane (Blood)

biography, 280

community tie, 123

home life, respect for, 232

inclusion of women in ceremonies, 166-67

practice of birth control, 88

sexual mores, 86

Sun Dance ceremony, 48

womanhood and feminine identity, 166

"eating the Other" syndrome, 44-45, 107

economic authority, 61, 62-64, 120-21

Elders, 288 n11

exalted status of, 267-68

sexist attitudes, 268

environmental protection, 224-25

Equal Rights for Indian Women, 126

family

balance in, 205-9

extended, 209-12

of girls, 126

patriarchal, 83-84, 205

as source of strength, 116-27

fathers, 117-18, 121-22, 207-8

feminine identity

land and, 180-84, 187

moon and, 185-87

water and, 184-85, 187

feminism

critique of, 272-77

third world, 269

Fiske, Joanne, 220, 270

Full Moon ceremony, 179, 186

gender

complementarity of roles, 64, 276

fluidity of, 89-90

in Indigenous languages, 130-31

and parenting roles, 205-9

shifting roles in ceremonies, 177-79

symbols of duality, 174-75

unbalanced female-male relationships, 188

and work, 59, 121-22

gender equity, 36
    and division of labour, 59-65
    *See also* balance
Gervais-Contois, Laverne (Ojibway/Cree/
    Sioux), 38
    biography, 281
    community ties, 124
    denial of Native identity, 144
    racism and degradation of women, 105
    sacredness of man, 240
    self-determination, 248
    skirt, as symbol of womanhood, 168
    supportive family, 122
*Gradual Enfranchisement Act*, 68
grandmothers
    authority of, 120, 210-11
    as mentors, 128, 211
    as strong female role models, 118-21
Great Law of the Iroquois, 61-62
Green, Kathleen (Cree), 38
    biography, 281
    moon and feminine identity, 187
    puberty rites, 166
    residential school experience, 75
    supportive family, 121

healing circle, 241
health, 194-95, 197-201
Hill, Barbara-Helen (Mohawk/Cayuga), 92
Hill, Diane (Mohawk)
    biography, 281
    motherhood, 211-12
    sense of purpose, 202
    spirituality, 135
Hind-Man, Margaret. *See* Ah'-Dunn
homosexuality, 90-91
hooks, bell, 107
Hungry Wolf, Beverly (Siksika), 81, 87
Hurons, 60
    of New France, 77, 159

identity, Native
    "adoption breakdown," 24
    and cultural traditions, 157
    denial of, 144, 145-46
    gender and, 32-33, 173-79
    and inherited values, 27-28
    land and, 180-82
    land-based culture and, 27

and persons of mixed-blood, 29-31, 265
    problems of loss of, 13, 27
    and standards of Indianness, 25-27, 265
    western construction of, 99-112
*Indian Act*, 68-70, 91, 122, 126
Indian name, 203, 232
"Indian princess" image of, 100-2, 105,
    106-7
Innu, 59, 67-68, 80
Inuit, 89
Iroquois, 60, 61-62, 65, 80, 95, 159, 292n35
Ittusardjuat, Monica (Inuit)
    biography, 281
    Indigenous language, loss of, 130
    political authority of women, 67
    political representation, 219-20
    sewing and feminine identity, 143

Jaimes, Marie Annette (Juaneño/Yaqui),
    61, 90
Jamieson, Kathleen, 69
Joe, Rita (Mi'kmaw), 105, 138, 141,
    144-45, 147-48, 199-200
Johnson Ortiz, Theresa (Ojibway), 138, 145

Kehewin, George, 74
Kehoe, Alice, 73
Kidwell, Clara Sue (Chippewa/Choctaw), 60
King-Green, Valerie (Ojibwe)
    biography, 281-82
    healing and land, 128
    healing men, 240, 241
    self-love, 231
    sense of purpose, 201, 203
Knockwood, Isabelle (Mi'kmaw), 75, 76
knowledge, 21, 22, 261
    oral, 45-46, 45-48, 131-33
Kuper Island Residential School, 93

LaBillois-Montour, Ida (Mi'kmaw)
    biography, 282
    childrearing practices, 160-61
    community ties, 123
    leadership and management skill, 215-16
    parenting, 244
labour, division of, 59-65
Lacaille-Johnson, Nena (Seneca)
    biography, 282
    extended family and childrearing, 209

healing and land, 128
land and feminine identity, 183-84
spirituality, 135
Lakota, 71, 80, 95
land
dispossession of, 181-82
and feminine identity, 180-84
healing and, 127-29, 254
ownership, 61-62
as private property, 188-89
land-based societies
attitudes towards women, 36
chieftainships, 66, 67
divorce, 81-83
family violence, 94-97
food production and distribution, 60-62
gendered division of labour, 59-62
gender equity, 42, 57
household economy, 63
male violence, 36, 94-97
marriage practices, 79-85
mother-centred cultures, 271
motherhood in, 83
political authority of women, 65-71
property rights of women, 61-62
sexism, 36, 57
sex and sexuality, 85-92
traditional Iroquois systems of governance, 66
women's role in politics, 65-68
Landes, Ruth, 41-43
language
Indigenous, 129-31
and resistance, 140
Laramee, Myra (Cree/Métis), 87, 266
biography, 282
ceremonies, 167
female-male balance, 174, 179
learning from ancestors, 30
menstruation, 74
menstruation taboo, 38
raising sons, 243
sexuality and sex education, 199
spiritual power of women, 71
supportive father, 117
teaching gender roles, 177
water and female identity, 185
LaRocque, Emma (Plains Cree/Métis), 36,
268, 271

biography, 283
challenging stereotypes, 140-41
healing process of men, 241
ideology of motherhood, 172
"Indian princess" stereotype, 101, 108
interpretation of cultural traditions,
152-53
Laronde, Sandra (Ojibway)
biography, 282-83
Native writings, publication of, 142
oral tradition, 132
traditional dances, 176
tradition and change, 178
Laurence, Margaret, 24, 288n5
Laverdure, Betty (Seneca), 73
Lawrence, Bonita (Mi'kmaw)
critical approach to cultural practices,
263-64
critique of feminism, 272-77
Indian identity and womanhood, 264-65
reverence for Elders, 268
role of women, 261-62
leadership, female
administrative, 216-18
mothering role and, 214-15
in politics, 218-22
LeJune, Paul, 61, 83
lifegiving power, 164-65
and feminine identity, 164-69
skirt, as hoop of life, 168
literary resources, 40-45
Longboat, Janice (Mohawk)
biography, 283
sacredness of the body, 195
self-love and well-being, 230
supportive father, 207
women and decision making, 171

McGregor, Lillian (Ojibway)
biography, 283
sense of purpose, 203
supportive families, 116
ties to urban organizations, 123-24
McGuire, Peggy, 63
McKay, Eva (Dakota Sioux), 90

Manitowabi, Edna (Ojibway)
biography, 283
land and feminine identity, 183

relationship to drum, 142-43
self-love, 230
sense of purpose, 203
teachings, 194-95
unbalanced relationships, 188
Mankiller, Wilma (Cherokee), 124-25
Maracle, Lee (Sto:lo/Métis), 106
    balanced family structure, 232-33
    biography, 283
    dehumanizing stereotypes, 108
    gender-divided responsibilities, 216-17
    grandmother, role of, 209-10
    racism and violence, 95, 110
    traditional female economic activity, 61
    urban organizations, 124
    women's political authority, 66
Maracle, Sylvia (Mohawk), 24
    biography, 284
    clan responsibilities, 218
    community development, 235
    drugs, alcohol, and violence, 94, 97-98
    environmental protection, 225
    Indigenous language, 131
    Native men, 239
    pregnancy, 196-97, 206
    sex education, 200-1
    standing up for justice, 235-36
    ties to urban organizations, 124
    water and feminine identity, 184
Marmon Silko, Leslie (Laguna), 34, 86,
        87, 89, 119, 132
marriage
    abusive, 148-49
    arranged, 80
    fidelity in, 86
    heterosexual, 91
    Indian-white monogamous, 81
    in matrilocal societies, 80, 82
    polygamous, 80-81
    principle of non-interference, 79, 82-83
    as symbol of female-male balance, 174-75
Martin, Catherine (Mi'kmaw)
    biography, 284
    female-male balance, 176
    Indigenous languages, 131
    marginalization of Native women, 69-70
    mothering role of women, 171
    racism and violence, 110
    relationship to drum, 143

spirituality, 134
status of Native women, 13
Martin, Vera (Ojibway), 37, 39, 152
    age and authority of women, 238
    biography, 284
    female mentors, 127
    political consciousness, 126
    self-determination, 245
    sex education, 197-98
    symbols of womanhood, 168
Mathes, Valerie, 88
Medicine, Bea (Lakota), 37
men, Native
    healing, 239-41
    loss of autonomy and dignity, 97
    marginalization of, 97, 239-40
    parenting role, 207-9
    role during pregnancy, 206-7
menopause, 186-87
menstruation
    approaches to taboo, 269
    shame-based interpretations of, 75-78
    spiritual significance, 74
    taboos, 37-38, 88, 166, 264-67
    traditional understandings of, 74-75
mentoring role
    of aunties, 121, 172-73
    of grandmothers, 128
    of mothers, 121, 169-71
    of women, 127, 172-73
Miller, J.R., 92, 159, 160
monogamy, 81
Monture-Angus, Patricia (Mohawk), 21,
        40, 94-95
moon, and feminine identity, 185-87
moon lodges, 166
Morin, Ruth (Cree)
    biography, 285
    health and sex education, 198, 201
    skirt, as symbol of womanhood, 168
    spirit name, 232
Morrisseau, Calvin (Ojibway), 94
Mosher, Liz (Odawa), 90
Mother Earth. See land
"mother of the nation" ideology, 270-72
motherhood, 33
    centrality of children, 162-64
    "discourse," 220
    and empowerment, 272-74, 275

ideology of, 168-73, 237, 275-77
mentoring role, 169-72
and responsibility for community, 168-71
status in land-based societies, 83
*See also* womanhood, Native
mothers, 118, 121, 122, 127
music
big drum, 177, 178
Native drumming, 142-43
songs, 176

Nahwegahbow, Barbara (Ojibway)
alienation of women, 37
biography, 285
lifegiving power of women, 164
sense of purpose, 202
supportive families, 117
Native peoples, 24
"Authentic Indian" stereotype, 26-27
of mixed-blood, 29, 31
of Native peoples, 21-22
"Vanishing Indian" stereotype, 25-26
Native urban organizations, 123-24
Native Women in the Arts, 132, 142
Native Women's Association of Canada,
(NWAC), 20, 271
Navajo, 63, 71, 80, 82, 86

objectification, of Native peoples, 21-22
Olsen, Kaaren, 59
oppression, triangle of, 111
oral resources, 45-48
Osbourne, Helen Betty, 109

patriarchal family, and social breakdown,
36-37, 83-84, 97-98
patriarchy, 42-43, 58-78
Paul, Maggie (Passamaquody)
biography, 285
mothering role of women, 171
Native spirituality, 135-36
Peters, Dorris (Sto:lo)
biography, 285
church, resistance to, 146-47
mothering and workplace, 214
self-worth, 150-51
supportive father, 118
women's political authority, 66
Plateau, 67, 80, 82, 95

Pocohontas (Disney), 101, 107
politics, women in, 65-68, 170-71,
218-22
polygamy, 80-81
Porter, Tom (Mohawk), 160, 206
poverty, 55, 163-64
Power, Jordan, 77
pregnancy, 86-88
and commitment, 196
role of men during, 206-7
support mechanisms, 196-97
teen, 87, 195-96
princess-squaw, 40-41
property, 62
in divorce, 82-83
land, 188-89
rights of Native women, 61-62
Pueblo, 34-35, 71, 89, 132

Qiqiktani Inuit Association, 66, 241
Quebec Native Women's Association,
(QNWA) 61, 220

racism, 104, 105-6, 107-12, 137-40
Razack, Sherene, 111
reader response-ability, 49-51
reclaim, 31-32, 34, 157
relationships, 180-82, 193
residential schools, 75-76, 83, 92-94, 97,
139-40, 143, 145, 147-48, 199
resist, reclaim, construct and act, 15-17,
253
resistance
against assimilation, 144-46
against church, 146-49
against stereotypes, 137-42
community ties and, 123-27
and connection to land, 127-29
creative expression, identity and, 142-44
humour and, 152
Indigenous language and, 129-31
oral tradition and, 131-33
political consciousness and, 122-23,
124-27
self-worth and, 150-52
spirituality and, 133-36
strong female role models and, 118-22
supportive families and, 116-23
writing as, 140-42

responsibilities, Native female. *See*
  womanhood, Native
Rich, Katie (Innu)
  biography, 285-86
  father, 117-18
  social activism, 213-14
  standing up for justice, 236
  welfare of children, 163-64

Sacajewea, 101
St. Joseph's Residential School, 92
self-definition, 15
self-determination, 242, 244-49
self-hate, 231
self-love, 230-33
sense of purpose, 201-4
separation. *See* divorce
sex education, 197-201
sexism
  in cultural traditions, 268
  in land-based societies, 36
  in Native communities, 33, 36
sexuality, 199-201
  fluidity of, 88-89
  gender roles, 89-90
  homosexuality, 89, 90-91
  of land-based societies, 85-91
  premarital sex, 85, 87
  repression of, 91-94, 103-4
Shepardson, Mary, 81
Shubenacadie Indian Residential School,
  75-76, 147-48
skirt, as symbol of womanhood, 167-68
Solomon, Art (Ojibway), 72, 174, 202, 206
Sparks, Douglas Carol, 102
spirituality
  dreams and visions, 134-35
  persistence of Native practices, 135-36
  and resistance, 133-36
  and women's power, 71-75
squaw, images of, 99-100, 102-12
state
  and cycle of domestic violence, 97
  destruction of traditional values, 83-84
  forcible removal of Native children,
    161-62
  and heterosexual marriage, 91
  promotion of "dirty squaw" stereotype,
    102-5

stereotypes
  challenging, 137-42
  context of exploitation, 101-3
  and degradation of women, 105-12
  as gauge for white femininity, 104-5
  "Indian princess", 100-2
  and self-destructive behaviour, 106
  sexualized Native femininity, 106-7
  squaw, 102-12
  in textbooks, 137-38
  white ideal, 247-9
storytelling, 131-33
suicide, 81, 202
Sun Dance, 37, 38, 72, 165, 178
sweat lodge ceremony, 73-74, 164-65, 178,
  302n9

Tabobondung, Lila (Ojibway/
  Pottawatomi), 127
  biography, 286
  humour, 152
taboos. *See* menstruation, taboo
Tait, Theresa (Wit'suwet'en)
  biography, 286
  childrearing practices, 160
  grandmothering role, 211
  political authority of women, 237-38
  seeking justice, 110-11
  spirituality, 123, 223
  traditional Wit'suwet'en society, 222, 237
teachings, 21-22, 263-65
Thundercloud, Helen (Algonquin)
  biography, 286
  self-determination, 246-47
  homosexuality in land-based societies, 91
  independent female role models, 116-17
  land and identity, 180-81
tipi, as symbol of womanhood, 168-69,
  256-57
tobacco, custom of giving, 196
traditions
  defined, 35
  questioning of, 261-62, 263, 265-67,
    269-70
  selective use of, 36-37
  *See also* ceremonies; cultural traditions;
    culture, Native
Trask, Haunani-Kay (Native Hawaiian),
  35, 181

Two-Axe Early, Mary (Mohawk), 126
two-spirited people, 89

urban organizations. *See* Native urban organizations
urban traditionalism, 270

violence against women, 55
  destruction of traditional values, 83-84, 97-98
  eradication of Native sexual attitudes, 91
  in land-based societies, 36, 94-97
  racism and, 106-12

Wagamese, Richard (Ojibway), 144
Wagner, Sally Roesch, 62-63
Wall, Steve, 43-44
Walters, Anna Lee (Pawnee/Otoe), 105, 106, 119, 141
water, and feminine identity, 184-85, 187
western culture
  depiction of Native women, 100-5
  and family life, 94-98
  and women, 30, 57-58, 60, 83, 275-76
Whitebird, Wanda (Mi'kmaw), 148
  biography, 286
  female-male balance, 174-75
  teaching gender roles, 177
White Buffalo Woman, 71, 132
Whitehorse, Emmi (Navajo), 63
white ideal, deconstruction of, 247-48
Williams, Shirley (Ojibway/Odawa)
  biography, 287
  challenging stereotypes, 139-40
  racism and degradation of women, 105
  residential school experience, 75, 76, 92, 93, 94, 139-40, 199
  supportive father, 118
Willis, Jane (Cree), 91
womanhood, Native, 36, 57
  and and lifegiver teaching, 254-55
  and balanced lives, 255-57
  and community, responsibility for, 213-22
  and creation, responsibility for, 223-25
  and family, responsibility for, 205-12
  and female body, responsibility for, 194-201
  and healing process of men, 239-44

negative images of, 105-112
reconstructing, 193
and self-determination, 244-49
and sense of purpose, 201-4
sexualization of, 107-9
skirt, as symbol of, 167-68
standing up for justice, 235
tipi, as symbol, 168-69, 256-57
western depiction of, 100-5
*See also* motherhood
womanspirit, 71-72, 223-24
women
  age and authority, 67-68, 238
  childbearing responsibility, 273-74
  competing demands on, 264-65
  cultural practices, 36-38, 261-68
  economic authority, 61-64
  hunting and trapping skills, 59
  Indian status of white, 70
  and internalized racism, 106
  in land-based societies, 36
  mentoring role of, 269-73
  Mohawk grand council, 66
  patriarchal nuclear family and, 83-85
  political authority of, 65-68, 170-71
  provision and distribution of food, 60
  role models, 30, 118-21, 274
  and sexism in Native societies, 33
  sexual freedom, 85-88
  shamans and medicine people, 72
  spiritual power of, 71-75
  and trade, 61
  wage economy and, 64-65
  warriors, 59
  *See also* motherhood; violence against women; womanhood, Native
writing, as a form of resistance, 140-42